Dublin's Famous People
and Where They Lived

DUBLIN has long been home, inspiration and muse to many famous people. The city appears as a backdrop to the works of playwrights such as Sean O'Casey, the novels of those such as James Joyce, and the very poems such as that of Kavanagh. Dublin was also the scene of many of the most important events in the history of modern Ireland, involving revolutionaries, politicians and statesmen. In this updated edition of *Dublin's Famous People and Where They Lived* there are biographies of over two hundred of the best-known of these inhabitants together with their addresses. The result is part guidebook, part historical biography.

'A magnificent book which should be
a standard work for natives and visitors alike'
Ulick O'Connor, *Sunday Independent*

'The text is lovely, with a nice quirky touch.'
The Irishman's Diary, *The Irish Times*

JOHN COWELL grew up in Sligo and, as a doctor, practised in wartime London. He later returned to Ireland and spent his working life with the Irish anti-tuberculosis campaign. His memoir of the Longford theatre group, *No Profit but the Name*, drew on his involvement in the celebrated productions by Hilton Edwards and Mícheál Mac Liammóir and the Longford productions at the Gate Theatre in Dublin. He has also published a novel, *The Begrudgers*, and *Sligo, Land of Yeats' Desire*, a guide and general history to his adopted County of Sligo.

DUBLIN'S FAMOUS PEOPLE
and where they lived

John Cowell

THE O'BRIEN PRESS
DUBLIN

This revised edition first published in hardback 1980
by The O'Brien Press Ltd.,
20 Victoria Road, Rathgar, Dublin 6, Ireland.
Reprinted in paperback 1996

British Library Cataloguing-in-publication Data
A catalogue reference for this title is available from the British Library

ISBN 0-86278-468-9

2   3   4   5   6   7   8   9   10
96   97   98   99   00   01   02   03   04

The O'Brien Press receives assistance from
The Arts Council/An Chomhairle Ealaíon

Typesetting, editing, layout, design: The O'Brien Press Ltd.
Cover illustration: 'The River Liffey' by Flora Mitchell
courtesy of the National Gallery of Ireland
Cover separations: Lithoset Ltd.
Printing: Hartnolls Ltd

CONTENTS

ACKNOWLEDGEMENTS

My thanks to all who assisted me with ideas or suggestions in the preparation of this book. Among them are: Mr Charles Acton; Mrs J B Dunlop; Mr Brendan J Ellis FRIAI; Mr V W Graham MA; Mrs Vera Holmes; Commandant D V Horgan; Dr Thomas Houlihan; Mr Henry Jordan; Mr Ralph Kennedy; Mr Denis Larkin; Christine, Countess of Longford; Mrs Rosemary Muldoon; Mr Peter Seward, British Film Institute, London; Father Daniel Shields SJ; Dr Brigid Lyons Thornton; Mr Martin Walton; Mr Michael Wynne, National Gallery of Ireland; the Belgian Ambassador; the Press Office, Arthur Guinness, Son and Co (Dublin) Ltd; Foreign Publicity Dept, Paramount Pictures Corporation, New York; United States Information Services, American Embassy, Dublin; the Public Relations Dept, Aer Lingus; and the librarians and the staffs of the National Library of Ireland, the Royal Dublin Society Library and Pembroke Library, Ballsbridge.
For their work in getting the book through the press,
I am indebted to Michael O'Brien and to his staff.
The publishers would like to thank and acknowledge the following for permission to reproduce photographs.
All the photographs of the buildings are by George Gmelch unless otherwise stated.
Robert Allen photography page 172; Bord Fáilte page 181; Camera Press page 56; Central Photographic Unit p60; Central Catholic Library page 137, 138; E Chandler page 47; Peter Costello page 97; Richard Dann, photographer, page 101; Hot Press page 109; Vivian Joyce (photographer Pat Tutty) page 185; Marsh's Library page 124; National Gallery of Ireland page 33, 65, 80, 81, 89, 112, 141, 147, 179, 185; National Library of Ireland pages 9, 122, 162; National Museum of Ireland page 45, 53, 100; Dublin Writers Museum page 180; Jas D O'Callaghan, photographer, page 139.
In the instances where it has been impossible to trace copyright, the publishers would be grateful if the holders would contact The O'Brien Press.

St Stephen's Green, Dublin, 1726

INTRODUCTION

I admit to a peculiar satisfaction when I learn from a wall or a
hoarding that Kilroy was here. More intriguing, and stimulating
by far, I find such knowledge as that Goldsmith scratched his name
on this pane of glass in Trinity College, or that Edmund Burke as
a boy swam in that river they call the Griese in County Kildare.
These are simple facts which humanise historic characters, bringing them down from their high pedestals and making them real
by associating them with what is still visible before us. Though
perhaps not always willing to admit it, I know there are many who
secretly share with me this peculiar inquisitiveness, which
amounts to a form of hero-worship

This book is therefore for the merely inquisitive and not for
the searching specialist. Mostly it is for the reader with limited
time, anxious to know something of Dublin, something of its
noteworthy citizens and of the houses where they lived. Leafing
these pages, I hope he may come on unexpectedly pleasant sur-
prises, like for instance, some of the great citizens of other lands
who for longer or shorter periods became Dubliners by adoption.

Once the Second City of the Empire, Dublin became a provincial city after the Act of Union in 1800. For the next 150 years
much of its glorious heritage of Georgian architecture fell into
decay. Yet at their worst, the slum houses in Dublin's meanest
streets still offered glimpses of her faded glory. Their atmosphere
was permeated by the ghosts of those who lived and loved and
died in these once elegant rooms.

Dublin escaped the blitz of World War II. But destruction of
another kind lay ahead. With the growth of Irish affluence came
the 'developer' with his bulldozer. In the name of progress large
areas were laid waste. Many houses with historic associations
disappeared without trace. Rome can also progress, yet still preserve the haunts of the Caesars. Why should these things be
ordered differently in Dublin?

However, there is hope. No longer is conservation a word for ridicule. Serious efforts have begun to save something of old-world Dublin – even if it amounts to saving some of her Georgian facades while accommodating their interiors to modern requirements. For instance, in Upper Merrion Street the birthplace of Wellington is to become a luxury hotel, and in nearby Merrion Square it is still possible to view the Dublin mountains as they rise at the end of a long straight road, every foot of it flanked by flourishing Georgian houses saved for posterity when commerce crowded into a prestigious neighbourhood.

The preparation of this book brought pleasure and pain: pleasure when one found a certain historic house where it should be, and perhaps still lived in; pain when it was discovered in dilapidation, or worse, when it was no longer to be seen. But ghosts are determined creatures. They won't be vanquished, even by bulldozing their haunts out of existence. I trust these pages may help to capture something of the lives they once lived in Dublin.

Space dictated the brevity of the biographical notes. If, however, as a sort of primer for the inquisitive the book should lead to wider reading, then something worthwhile will have been accomplished.

John Cowell 1996

Mother Mary Aikenhead
(1787-1858)
56 St Stephen's Green, 2

On the road between Dublin and Dun Laoghaire stands Elm Park, one of Ireland's great modern hospitals. In the vestibule there hangs a portrait of Mary Aikenhead, the woman whose foresight and compassion have brought hope and relief to millions of the world's distressed. Daughter of a Protestant physician practising in Cork, Mary Aikenhead became a Catholic at the age of sixteen. Motivated from childhood by a sense of caring for others, what she saw in Dublin in the early 1800s moved her to extreme pity. There were forty-five thousand destitute families plagued by repeated epidemics of typhus, with at least a hundred deaths a day.

Mary Aikenhead founded an order of nuns called the Irish Sisters of Charity. Stanhope Street convent was their original foundation, after which they set up a Magdalen home in Townsend Street. Pressed for space, for £1500 they purchased Donnybrook Castle, once the home of Henry Flood, the great orator of Grattan's Parliament.

The Irish Sisters of Charity were not enclosed, a novelty in Dublin at that time. Instead they visited the sick in their homes. The sisters frequently contracted diseases and many died prematurely. Their foundress wrote: 'We must sincerely deplore that we have not the means to erect a hospital where our care of the sick might be attended with more beneficial results.'

A postulant brought an unexpected dowry of £3000. With this Mary Aikenhead purchased the Georgian mansion of the Earl of Meath at 56 St Stephen's Green. This was opened as St Vincent's Hospital for the Sick Poor on 23 January 1834. Meanwhile, the hospital acquired some neighbouring property for expansion. It continued, however, at its official address in St Stephen's Green for the next one hundred and forty years, until it moved to Elm Park in 1974.

Mother Mary Aikenhead spent the last twelve years of her life as an invalid in the Hospice at Harold's Cross, another of her many foundations. She lies in a crypt in the convent cemetery at St Mary Magdalen's in Donnybrook.

Sara Allgood (1883-1950) and
Mollie Allgood (1885-1952)
28 Claude Road, Drumcondra, 9

Chance influenced the launching of the careers of two of the most famous Abbey Theatre actresses, the sisters Sara and Mollie Allgood (the latter adopted Máire O'Neill as her stage-name).

First attracted to politics, Sara joined *Inghinidhe na hÉireann*, or the Daughters of Erin, Maud Gonne's separatist movement. In its drama class she was spotted by William Fay, the producer, and was recruited to the National Theatre Society, the precursor of the Abbey Theatre. Shortly afterwards her sister Mollie followed her.

Sara Allgood's first big part was in Lady Gregory's *Spreading the News* on 27 December 1904, the opening night of the Abbey Theatre. With a hauntingly vibrant voice, she played every emotional part during her Abbey career. As O'Casey's Juno, her favourite part, she toured the world. Married in Melbourne in 1916, she was widowed by 1918. In 1929 she began her Hollywood career, eventually becoming a US citizen. Comparatively poor and lonely, she died at Woodland Hills in California in 1950.

Máire O'Neill's career was as distinguished as her sister's. She made her reputation by creating the part of Pegeen Mike in Synge's *The Playboy of the Western World*. She was engaged to be married to Synge when he died. He left her an annuity. Her career on stage and screen kept her mainly in London, where she died in 1952 after a tragic accident.

Arthur Edward Guinness, Lord Ardilaun (1840-1915) St Anne's, Raheny, 5

As they walk through St Stephen's Green, the citizens of Dublin have reason to remember gratefully Arthur Edward Guinness, Arthur III, the great-grandson of the founder of the brewery.

Born in Dublin, he was educated at Eton and Dublin University. He inherited his father's title and parliamentary seat and was head of the brewery for nine years. A philanthropist, he opted out of business in 1877 and completed the reconstruction of Marsh's Library, begun by his father, Sir Benjamin Lee Guinness. He also rebuilt the Coombe

Lying-in Hospital.

The thirty-acre area that is now St Stephen's Green had been levelled in 1670 when residential building was in progress. Later four tree-lined avenues traversed its perimeter, some being fashionable promenades. In 1711 Swift advised Stella to go there because 'the walks are finer-gravelled than the Mall'. Dublin's citizens were denied their Green when, in 1815, it was railed in to become the property of the residents.

In 1877, through an act of parliament, Sir Arthur Edward Guinness reopened the Green to the public. He also landscaped the area at his own expense, laying paths and creating the lake, the bridge, the cascade and the gardens at the centre. On 6 August 1880 he formally restored St Stephen's Green to the citizens of Dublin. In return he was raised to the peerage as Baron Ardilaun of Ashford, the name of the castle he had built on his three-and-a-half-thousand acre estate on Lough Corrib, now the Ashford Castle hotel. In 1889 he built All Saints Church on his land in Raheny, while in 1899 he bought Muckross Estate in Killarney to save it from commercial exploitation.

On the west side of St Stephen's Green a grateful citizenry set up a statue of their benefactor. The inscription reads: 'Lord Ardilaun by whose liberality this park was laid out and beautified for the use and enjoyment of the citizens of Dublin. Erected by public subscription 1892.'

Lord Ardilaun died at St Anne's, Raheny, the house he had converted into an Italianate country mansion. The property was donated to the City of Dublin to become St Anne's Park, Raheny, with its famous rose gardens.

Francis Bacon (1909-1992)
83 Lower Baggot Street, 2

The most famous painter since Picasso, a myth in his own lifetime, Francis Bacon was born in Dublin and grew up in the village of Kilcullen, County Kildare. He lived through the Anglo-Irish and Civil wars. His father, a retired army officer, was a race horse trainer. Bacon's hatred of his father dated from his banishment, aged sixteen, for having sex with a groom. He never afterwards denied his homosexuality. He claimed to be 'totally without belief, but totally dedicated to futility'.

Without formal education, or training in art, Bacon began to paint for his own amusement. Exempted from wartime service as an asthmatic, he worked in the London ambulance service. The sight of so much death and so many mangled bodies, together with his penchant for viewing slaughter houses, is said to have influenced his painting style.

Bacon was middle-aged when his genius first broke over the world of art. His studies of popes and crucifixions made an immediate impact. Viewers probed his imagery, coming up with interpretations probably never dreamt of by the artist. Often described as lurid and revolting, his studies of distorted human anatomy with massive single limbs and hideously split faces

became highly desirable commodities in the commercial world of art. The work of Picasso had strongly influenced Bacon ever since the 1920s, when he saw an exhibition by the Master in Paris – ever after he acknowledged his debt. Bacon's work was dearly loved or greatly hated, but always aroused strong emotions.

There was nothing of the freezing attic or near-starvation in Bacon's life. He indulged himself generously: food, drink and foreign travel whenever the humour took him. Nor did he deny his friends the help they sometimes needed. He was generous to a fault. He held no sentimentality about the land of his birth. As well as blaming his asthma on the Irish climate, he may well have sensed a rejection of his work.

Francis Bacon died in Madrid on 28 April 1992.

Michael William Balfe (1808-1870)
10 Pitt Street (now Balfe Street), 2

Balfe's birthplace in Dublin, together with its surroundings, has seen much change. No. 10 Pitt Street was demolished and the street renamed in honour of the composer. Now commercialised, it runs past the Westbury Hotel.

At the age of nine, young Balfe made his first appearance as a violinist in Dublin. At fifteen his father died and he was forced to emigrate to London where he earned a living by playing the violin at oratorio concerts. At sixteen he was acting conductor of the Drury Lane theatre orchestra. In his spare time he studied singing.

Under the patronage of a Count Mazzara, Balfe went to Italy and studied music in Milan where his ballet, *La Perouse*, was a success at La Scala. In 1827 in Paris he sang Figaro in Rossini's *Barbière*. On returning to Italy he produced his first opera, *I Rivali di se Stessi*, at Palermo, and married a singer called Lina Rosa.

Balfe's reputation as a composer and a performer was established when he returned to London in the 1830s. In 1835 his *Siege of Rochelle* was produced at Drury Lane, and three years later his *Falstaff* at Her Majesty's Theatre. Apart from composing, much of his time was spent as a performer in extended tours throughout Europe, including Ireland.

The name of Balfe is, of course, most readily associated with his famous opera *The Bohemian Girl*, composed in London and first produced there in 1843. Its melodies have retained their popularity ever since. In 1857 Balfe became conductor at Covent Garden Opera House. There he produced *The Rose of Castile* and several other operas, none of which achieved the same success as *The Bohemian Girl*. He died in 1870 at Rowney Abbey in Hertfordshire and is buried in Kensal Green Cemetery in London.

Nora Barnacle (1884-1951)
1 and 2 Leinster Street, 2

From Nassau Street, when the leaves have fallen, you can still read through the bare branches the words 'Finns' Hotel' on the gable of No.s 1 and 2 Leinster Street. One afternoon in June 1904 the hotel's young chambermaid went for a stroll. A young man spoke to her. She took their conversation lightly, but he anxiously made an appointment to meet her again. On 16 June 1904 Nora Barnacle again met James Joyce. Discovering they were both 'unfellowed, friendless and alone', they strolled by the Liffey, a stroll that changed the course of English literature, and created a date to be honoured by future generations as Bloom's Day. Without Nora Barnacle, Joyce might well have ended as another of Dublin's promising writers, telling what might have been through a drunken haze.

Born in a Galway workhouse, Nora had a disturbed homelife. At thirteen she became a convent porteress. Her first boyfriend, Michael Bodkin, died of tuberculosis aged eighteen when Nora was fifteen (he is represented by the character of Michael Furey in *The Dead*). At nineteen she was thrashed by a puritanical uncle for dating a Protestant boy. It was then that she ran away to Dublin. When she eloped with Joyce she had to board the boat at the North Wall unknown to the friends and relatives who saw him off, because they considered her 'common'. But when she returned eight years later to promote the book *Dubliners*, she had become socially acceptable. Joyce's father met her at Westland Row Station and took her to Finns' Hotel for a celebration meal.

Although unmarried until 1931, Joyce depended upon Nora to hold his life together, his inspiration for *Ulysses*

– the first copy was inscribed to her in 1922. Unimpressed, she remarked, 'I guess the man's a genius, but what a dirty mind he has, hasn't he?' When Yeats's body was returned to Ireland, Nora sought, but was refused, the same honour from the Irish government for her husband. Embittered, she refused the manuscript of *Finnegans Wake* to the National Library of Ireland, donating it instead to the British Museum.

At the funeral of Nora Barnacle in Zurich, a Roman Catholic priest called her 'a great sinner'. Her priest biographer, Father Padraic Ó Laoi, considered the remark 'harsh on the woman whose courage, loyalty and humour gave so much to world literature in that she was an essential part of Joyce and his art'.

Thomas Barnardo (1845-1905)
4 Dame Street, 2

There are countless adults throughout the world who were once destitute children but whose lives were changed by the children's charity known as Dr Barnardo's Homes. As a medical student the young Barnardo was moved to pity by the destitution he saw in Dublin and later in London. As a result he became a social reformer and an ardent evangelist, and the good he did outweighed by far his personal weakness for domination and flamboyance.

Thomas John Barnardo was born at 4 Dame Street, one of six houses which once stood between Palace Street (leading into Dublin Castle) and Exchange Court (running alongside the City Hall). The location, opposite the Olympia Theatre, is now occupied by a little park commemorating 1988, Dublin's millennium year.

John Michaelis Barnardo, a German furrier, had settled in Dame Street early in the nineteenth century. Thomas John was the youngest of his four sons. The family attended St Werburgh's Church, but at the age of eighteen, in the 1860s, Thomas was influenced by a religious revival which swept Dublin. He converted to the Plymouth Brethren and left Dublin to become a missionary in China. But he got no further than Stepney in the East End of London where the sight of destitute children arrested his attention. He was moved to action and was the first fund-raiser to use the 'before' and 'after' photographic technique. It paid off. Within five years he had established the fastest-growing mission in the East End. In ten years he was handling £25,000 per annum in his mission of rescue, supported by his evangelical movement.

Demand for his services grew. In addition to opening one Barnardo Home after another, he introduced a boarding-out scheme for children, as well as emigration to Canada for 'past-pupils'. By 1905 Barnardo had rescued some sixty thousand children from destitution, and had qualified as a doctor. His work continues today.

Barnardo left one child, a daughter, Syrie. She married Henry Wellcome, the American-born founder of the drug firm, Burroughs Wellcome. The marriage failed, after which she became the wife of Somerset

Maugham, the writer. This marriage also failed. As Syrie Maugham she launched a fashionable interior decorating business. The Barnardo furrier business begun at No. 4 Dame Street is today carried on at No. 108 Grafton Street.

Kevin Barry (1902-1920)
8 Fleet Street, 2

In the month of November 1920, the Anglo-Irish War touched its nadir. One atrocity followed another with such rapidity that the country was plunged into a sense of hopelessness: after seventy-four days of hunger-strike, Terence MacSwiney, Lord Mayor of Cork, had died in Brixton Prison; court-martialled on 20 October, Kevin Barry, an eighteen-year-old medical student, awaited sentence.

8 Fleet Street, 2

The public believed Barry's youth would save him from a death-sentence. But public opinion just then was pre-occupied with the drama in Brixton until, suddenly, it broke on 28 October that Barry was to be hanged on 1 November. Four days of strenuous efforts followed in Dublin and London to obtain a reprieve. Desperate attempts at rescue were mounted, only to be abandoned. Days dwindled to hours, while mass emotion hardened into a national frenzy of anger. Throughout this turmoil the calmest man in Ireland was young Kevin Barry, by then in the condemned cell at Mountjoy Prison. To a distressed visitor he said with amusement: 'They're not going to let me like a soldier fall. They're going to hang me like a gentleman,' a reference to *The Devil's Disciple*, the last play he had seen. To the end, Barry showed an extraordinary courage and amused indifference.

Born at 8 Fleet Street, Dublin 2, on 20 January 1902, Barry's parents also owned a farm at Tombeagh, Rathvilly, County Carlow. For a period he attended Rathvilly National School. Aged fifteen, while studying at Belvedere College, he joined the Volunteers. He played on the school junior rugby team, and later with the senior XV. To evade the British military search parties, he often slept at his uncle's house at 58 South Circular Road.

A medical student at University College, Dublin, Barry, with others, took part in a fateful ambush in Church Street in September 1920, in which three British soldiers died. Despite torture, he went to his execution without informing on his comrades. Thousands prayed in the streets of Dublin on the morning of his death. The name of Kevin Barry was afterwards to inspire many songs and ballads.

Samuel Beckett (1906-1989)
Cooldrinagh, Brighton Road,
Foxrock, 18

Beckett was born on a Good Friday at Cooldrinagh, a handsome house built by his father, a quantity surveyor. Despite an indifferent mother, he had a happy childhood, attending Miss Ida Elsner's Kindergarten in Stillorgan. His preparatory school was Earlsfort House, then standing at the corner of Earlsfort Terrace and Adelaide Road. At Portora Royal School, Enniskillen, County Fermanagh, he had good academic and sporting records. Between 1922 and 1927 he read Modern Literature at Trinity College, Dublin. His first contact with France came in 1926 when he cycle-toured the chateaux of the Loire.

Beckett went to Paris in 1928 to spend two years as an exchange lecturer at the École Normale Supérieure. It was there that he first met James Joyce, acting for a time as his secretary. Returning to Dublin in 1932, he became assistant lecturer in French at Trinity College. His first dramatic work, *Le Kid*, was produced there in 1931. In 1932 he settled in Paris, his slender income coming from an annuity left to him by his father. In 1930 he published *More Pricks Than Kicks*, a collection of short stories. *Murphy*, his first novel, followed in 1938. The reading public wasn't interested.

During World War II Beckett joined the French Resistance. Betrayed to the Gestapo, he fled south, ekeing out a living as an agricultural labourer. In 1944 he visited his family in Dublin. To get back to France he accepted a post as an interpreter and storekeeper at the Irish Red Cross Hospital at Saint-Lo in Normandy. Back in Paris, a burst of creativity followed: *Malone dies, Molloy* and *The Unnameable* were published. Still the reading public wasn't interested. But at last fame and fortune came on 5 January 1953 with the world premiere in Paris of *Waiting for Godot*,

Cooldrinagh, Brighton Road, Foxrock, 18

5 Anglesea Road, Ballsbridge, 4

the play that mystified, yet fascinated, audiences all over the world. After that everything Beckett wrote was an instant success. In 1969 he won the Nobel Prize for literature, the third such Irish winner. For his work with the French Resistance, de Gaulle awarded him La Croix de Guerre.

Like Nora Barnacle and the work of Joyce, it was Suzanne, Beckett's wife, who hawked his early writings round Parisian publishers until success came. She died in July 1989. His greatest prop gone, he outlived her only by five months, dying in Paris on 22 December 1989.

Brendan Behan (1923-1964)
5 Anglesea Road, Ballsbridge, 4

'I'm a Dubbalin man meself,' uttered as a challenge rather than a statement, implies a lineage of forebears unsul-

lied by a trace of culchie blood. For the truest Dublin blood, the northside has the edge. Although the Behans lived at 14 Russell Street (now demolished) on the northside, Brendan was born at Holles Street Hospital on the southside. Had the choice been his he would have arranged things differently. He was therefore a northsider by adoption, at least until he was fourteen when the family moved south to 70 Kildare Road, Kimmage. Outer suburbia meant fresh air and the bogs to the demoralised Brendan.

Apart from absences when he was a guest of the British or the Irish government, Behan lived in Kimmage for the next twenty years. For his part in a bombing in Britain he was sentenced to three years in Borstal. In 1942, back in Dublin and aged nineteen, he was involved in a shoot-up outside Glasnevin Cemetery. He was sentenced to fourteen years' penal servitude. The insides of Walton, Strangeways and Lewes prisons became familiar to him. 'The English are wonderful,' he said years later, 'first they put me in jail and then they made me rich.'

In 1954 his play *The Quare Fella* was produced in Dublin's Pike Theatre, where Brendan met Beatrice Salkeld. They married and at first lived at 18 Waterloo Road, later moving to 5 Herbert Street. In 1958 *The Hostage* burst like a catherine wheel, showering its light and laughter over London's theatreland. Then came *Borstal Boy*. Dublin's laughing boy had the world at his feet. There were first nights in Paris, Stockholm, Berlin and New York. The toast of every party, Brendan sang, danced, talked and drank liberally. But soon the world's press linked his name with words like 'bawdy', 'swaggering', 'ribald' and 'outrageous'. It was conceded that at least he was full of talent, even if he was always spoiling for a fight.

Those who knew the man intimately knew differently. Now settled at 5 Anglesea Road, Behan tried to resume his work, but the pressures of success had become too great. In public he continued to act out his reputation as the fighting showman, but in private he suffered remorse. Drink had become his refuge. After his death, the Dubliners he loved laid their laughing boy in Glasnevin, at peace with the sycophantic world that had destroyed him.

John Beresford (1738-1805)
Tyrone House, Marlborough St., 1

Like John Fitzgibbon, Earl of Clare, John Beresford was a notorious and hated man in Ireland. Both men had worked energetically for the Act of Union. Beresford, however, conferred some benefits on the City of Dublin. He planned the Custom House, including private apartments for himself and his family. In 1791 he brought James Gandon from London and commissioned him to build it. As a Wide Streets Commissioner, he helped to create Dublin streets comparable with any in Europe.

Beresford's family home was Tyrone House in Marlborough Street, now the headquarters of the Department of Education. It was built by Cassells, the German architect, for Beresford's father, Sir Marcus, later Earl of Tyrone, and still later Marquis of Waterford. Used as a torture and flogging house during the risings of 1798 and 1803, Tyrone House became known as Beresford's Riding House Establishment. It has since become part of a symmetrical design, a similar house being built to balance it, and to frame the Central Model School which stands between them.

Gandon also designed and built a country residence called Abbeywell at Kinsealy, County Dublin. Beresford acquired it and changed the name to Abbeyville. It was later occupied by Sir William Cusack, a surgeon at Dr Steevens's Hospital, whose descendants lived there into the twentieth century. The present occupier is the former Taoiseach, Charles Haughey.

John Beresford was born in Dublin, and educated at Trinity College. He became a member of parliament for Waterford in 1760 and held the seat until his death. He was chief adviser on Irish affairs to William Pitt (1759-1806), who effectively united Great Britain and Ireland. Beresford supervised the fiscal arrangements made under the Act of Union in 1800. He opposed Lord Fitzwilliam, the liberal Viceroy who sympathised with the political aspirations of Irish Catholics, and had him recalled to London. Riots broke out on the day of Fitzwilliam's departure from Dublin, and Beresford's house was attacked by an irate citizenry.

George Berkeley (1685-1753) Stafford Street (now Wolfe Tone Street), 1

Trinity College produced no more brilliant philosopher and educationalist than George Berkeley. He was born at Dysart Castle, in a wooded valley on the river Nore, downstream from Thomastown, County Kilkenny. Berkeley's Dublin home was in Stafford Street. Broadly, his philosophy claims that the essence of all reality lies in its being perceived; in other words, that nothing exists independently of perception.

Berkeley travelled widely, influencing all those he met. From the college he founded in Bermuda, he hoped to christianise the American continent. Berkeley, the University of California, is named after him. On his travels he corresponded faithfully with his Dublin friend, Thomas Prior, founder of the Royal Dublin Society. Once he pleaded with Prior: 'In answer to all my letters, I desire you send me one great one, close writ, and filled on all sides.' Prior kept Berkeley's letters, which proved invaluable to his biographers.

In 1734 Berkeley wrote to Prior from England: 'I have kissed their Majestys' hands for the bishopric of Cloyne.' On arrival in Dublin with his family he lodged in Gervais (Jervis) Street until his consecration in St Paul's Church, North King Street. He served for eighteen years (1734-1752) as Bishop of Cloyne.

Concerned about the economic state of Ireland, Berkeley questioned 'the flourishing of our Protestant gentry exclusive of the bulk of the natives'. He wished to see the majority of Irish men with 'shoes to their feet, clothes to their backs and beef in their bellies'. While living in Cloyne he encouraged the practical husbandry then long preached by his friend Thomas Prior and the Royal Dublin Society. He recruited 'sturdy vagabonds' to work the land.

Having witnessed famine, dysentery and pestilence in County Cork, Berkeley sought solutions. He studied dysentery and found a cure: by administering a 'heaped spoonful of a roisin [resin?] powdered fine in a little broth'. Later he advocated tar-water as a preventive, 'there being, so far as I can judge, no more powerful corrector of putrid humours'.

Berkeley resigned the bishopric of Cloyne in 1752 and moved to Oxford where he died the following year.

Willie Bermingham (1942-1990) 3 Canal Terrace, Bluebell, Inchicore, 12

Those who crew ambulances and firetenders see much that is hidden from the public eye. For seeing, and for publicising, what bureaucracy preferred to hide, a Dublin fireman became a myth in his own short lifetime. The fire brigade repeatedly found old people dead and dying, alone and forgotten, in the indescribable horror of filthy flats, damp, rat-infested and rubbish-strewn. Such neglect and injustice aroused one man's indignation and anger. Action was called for. As an ambulance man in 1977, Willie Bermingham took his own action – he founded ALONE ('A Little Offering Never Ends') to provide housing, clothing, food and comfort for hundreds of elderly Dubliners. He appealed, he badgered, he bellowed for help for his cause until an impatient bureaucracy hit back, calling him 'a cross between a saint and a bloody nuisance'. But Bermingham's exposure of injustice had to be answered.

The government established a task force, financing it to the extent of £1 million to alleviate the plight of the deserving elderly. In 1986 ALONE opened an eleven-house complex for old people at Alone Walk in Artane. On a granite boulder commemorating the event is carved in Irish: '*Níl aon tinteán mar do thinteán féin*,' in other words: 'There's no place like home.' Already under way is ALONE's twenty-two-unit complex at Kilmainham. Furniture, food, clothes and comforts are distributed on a regular basis.

Born in Inchicore, Willie Bermingham helped his bellman father to sell coal, logs and scrap. Seeing no future there, he became a gravedigger, a builder's helper and a

bouncer until in 1964 he found his true vocation as a Dublin fireman. But he did more than extinguish fires. It was his spare-time work that distinguished him. Amongst his awards were the International Fireman of the Year, The People of the Year (1979) and an Honorary LI.D from Trinity College in 1988. His early death evoked a remarkable display of emotion, not alone from Dublin's elderly: the President of Ireland led the distinguished mourners at an ecumenical funeral service at St Patrick's Cathedral.

Sir John Betjeman (1906-1984) Collinstown House, Clondalkin, 22

That most English of Englishmen, Britain's former Poet Laureate, was also an Irishman by adoption. Sometimes he was known to sign his letters Seán O'Betjeman. One of his Irish poems, 'Ireland with Emily', compresses into verse the essence of the West with its 'stony hills poured over space' and 'stones in every fertile place'. Emily was his friend, Lady Hemphill, who lived at Tulira Castle, County Galway. Old Oxford friends, Betjeman was a visitor to Edward and Christine Longford at Pakenham Hall (now Tullynally Castle) in the 1930s. In 1941 he was posted to Ireland as the United Kingdom Press Attaché, working at 30 Merrion Square, when Dublin was a particularly sensitive posting because of Ireland's neutrality in World War II. Serving under Sir John Maffey, he was an enormous success. He befriended and encouraged Irish writers. Patrick Kavanagh wrote a poem for his daughter, Candida, who was born at Collinstown House, Clondalkin.

Betjeman had no literary inheritance. Born at Highgate, near Hampstead Heath, his family manufactured household goods. He was indifferent at school and idle at Oxford, and was sent down without a degree. But he knew as soon as he could read and write that he must be a poet. He traced his love of poetry and of Ireland to his father reading him Goldsmith as a child. For the amusement of his friends, Betjeman could weave a verse on any subject on any pretext. For years he maintained a correspondence in verse with his friends John O'Dea, the cartoonist of *Dublin Opinion*, and Cathleen Delany, the actress.

With a passion for topography and architecture, Betjeman fought a lifelong battle against the growth of glass and chromium menageries. Awarded the CBE in 1960, he was knighted in 1969, and made Poet Laureate in 1972. Heaped with honours, in his old age he became a well-known television personality. He is buried at Trebetherick near Padstow, on the storm-lashed Cornwall coast he so loved from boyhood.

Charles Bianconi (1786-1875) Temple Bar, 2

Through chance, luck or divine providence, Charles Bianconi led a charmed life. Born near Como, this adventurous Italian emigrated to Ireland in 1802, aged sixteen, as a pedlar of holy pictures. Lodging in Dublin's Temple Bar, he often stood on Essex Bridge to admire the Liffey. With his three English words: 'Buy? One penee,' he walked to Thurles, County Tipperary, where an Italian nun befriended him. Tired and footsore, there were times when he sat by the roadside lamenting the absence of public transport. He had an idea – he began to save, he settled in Clonmel and in time bought a sidecar, and in July 1815 Carlo Bianconi began a regular transport service between Clonmel and Cahir. It was a success and soon other towns were linked. To meet the demand longer cars were invented: the 'Bians' as they were called. With a contract to carry the Royal Mail, Bianconi introduced the 'Long Bians' – the massive 'Finn Mac Cools' carrying twenty passengers, and drawn by four-in-hand. Painted yellow and crimson, and marked 'Day Mail' or 'Night Mail', these 'Bians' had a reputation for punctuality, and their drivers for sobriety and civility. Now a naturalised Irishman, Carlo Bianconi became Charles.

After the Napoleonic Wars Bianconi bought up surplus army horses. By 1843 he had 1000, covering 3800 miles a day and eating 4000 tons of hay and 40,000 barrels of oats per annum. Men were employed in stables, coachyards, repair shops, smithies and granaries. Bianconi's Dublin headquarters began with sixty horses, but expansion compelled a move to Clondalkin where two hundred horses, coaches and cars were housed in 'Bian's Barn'.

In creating a national transport

system, Bianconi made himself a wealthy man. He bought the six hundred-acre Longfield House estate near Cashel, where he entertained Daniel O'Connell, whose monument containing the Liberator's heart he later erected in the chapel of the Irish College in Rome. During the Famine he was generous to his tenants. In 1854 he purchased 86 St Stephen's Green to help Newman found his Catholic University. This gesture was to compensate for what Charles Bianconi called his own 'uneducation'.

Bianconi's long cars revolutionised travel in eighteenth-century Ireland. Their popularity ended only with the coming of the railways.

Leopold Bloom (Ageless)
7 Eccles Street, 7

In the late 1800s No. 7 Eccles Street was occupied by a John Edward Keane, Crier of the Court of Exchequer; in the early part of this century by a Thomas Wade. Its last occupant was Joyce's friend, JF Byrne, said to be the original of Cranley in *A Portrait of the Artist*. Empty and decrepit, the house was demolished in 1967 to make way for the Mater Private Hospital. Its front door was rescued and used to attract a respectful obeisance while displayed in the Bailey Restaurant in Duke Street until that historic hostelry was itself demolished.

Joyce housed the fictitious Leopold Bloom, the hero of *Ulysses*, and his wife Molly, in Lombard Street West, between Lower Clanbrassil Street and Curzon Street, off the South Circular Road. They grew to dislike this house because Rudy, their only son, died there. And so they moved to No. 7 Eccles Street where Bloom, the advertising agent – Poldy to his wife – and the musical Marion – Molly to her friends – settled into a dreary domesticity. The 16 June 1904 began with mutton kidneys which gave to Poldy's palate 'a fine tang of faintly scented urine'. Through that day he blazed a trail through Dublin that would be followed by generations of disciples, all in search of some vague cultural benevolence, like a holy indulgence, only obtainable on Bloom's Day.

The first event of the first Bloom's Day saw a group of conscience-stricken 'mourners' sensing a cold eternity at Paddy Dignam's graveside in Glasnevin Cemetery. Then Bloom traversed the *Freeman's Journal* office, past Trinity's 'surly front', to the National Library where the Quaker librarian purred, on to Davy Byrne's pub, Sandymount Strand, Holles Street Hospital, the Ormond Hotel and Mulligan's Pub in Poolbeg Street. The day ended in the smoky, whiskey-fumed twilight of Bella Cohen's brothel down Monto way. Nowadays there are other excitements, like meeting up-dated Nosey Flynns and Blazes Boylans decked out in drainpipes and Panama hats, making Bloom's Day a hilarious outing and a boost for Irish tourism.

Oliver Bond (1762-1798)
9 Lower Bridge Street, 8

'One of the most opulent and respectable merchants in Dublin,' Oliver

Bond was a wholesale woollen dealer. He was also an extremely devoted leader of the United Irishmen, being particularly active in recruitment and in administering their secret oath. In 1797 he swore in one Thomas Reynolds, the man who was to destroy him and all he stood for.

Bond's house at No. 9 Lower Bridge Street was the rendezvous of the United Irishmen, the place where their Leinster Provincial Committee met regularly in secret, usually at ten in the morning. Reynolds's treachery as an informer led to Bond's arrest, with fourteen of his associates, during a meeting at his house on 12 March

47 Lower Gardiner Street, 1

1798. Thus the imminent rising was doomed. Later Thomas Addis Emmet, Robert's elder brother, and other senior members were arrested in their homes and hiding places.

The prisoners were kept in Newgate Jail without trial, and here Bond died. He was buried in St Michan's across the river. The remaining prisoners were transferred to Fort George in Scotland, where they were still imprisoned when the rebellion of 1798 took place. Bond's wife, Eleanor, emigrated to America with their children. While the patriotism of Oliver Bond may be forgotten, the family name remains fresh in the minds of Dubliners, for a street and a block of flats are named after him.

No. 9 Lower Bridge Street has been rebuilt. The house bears a plaque erected by the 1798 Centenary Committee. Opposite stands the Brazen Head, a hostelry frequented by the men of 1798, and still going strong.

Dion Boucicault (1820-1890)
47 Lower Gardiner Street, 1

Born at 47 Lower Gardiner Street, Boucicault was the illegitimate son of Mrs Anne Boursiquot and her gentleman lodger, Dr Dionysus Lardner. Her husband was of French ancestry. Her name-conscious son eventually settled for Boucicault, by which name he has become theatrically immortal.

As a schoolboy at Dr Geoghegan's Academy in Dublin, Boucicault wrote his first play. At seventeen he abandoned his civil engineering studies and took up acting in England. Before he was twenty he had an immediate success at Covent Garden with his third play *London Assurance*. On the proceeds he set his mother up in London. Leaner times followed, so he turned to adapting French plays into English. As actor, producer or adapter of over a hundred and fifty plays, he made himself a master of the theatrical for over half a century. At the Queen's Theatre in Dublin his plays influenced Synge and O'Casey.

In 1853 Boucicault married Agnes Robertson who was to be his co-star for thirty-two years. They went to America, and there he staged sensational 'real-life' extravaganzas based on American history. In 1860 he turned to Irish history for inspiration. It was then he wrote the three plays on which his fame rests. *The Colleen Bawn* at the Adelphi Theatre, London, set the pattern, with its crafty peasants and cunning humour. *Arrah-na-Pogue* took Dublin by storm in 1864.

The best of Boucicault's Irish plays, *Conn the Shaughraun*, ran for a hundred and forty-three performances in New York in 1875, earning its author over half a million dollars. Then aged fifty-five, Boucicault unwisely cast himself as Conn. His smilingly innocent mid-fiftyish juvenile sloothering didn't please the critics.

Ninety-three years after its first production, Cyril Cusack played *Conn the Shaughraun* in a memorable Abbey Theatre production in 1968.

Elizabeth Bowen (1899-1973)
15 Herbert Place, 2

Parnell once said: 'Ireland is not a geographical fragment of England, she is a nation.' The proximity of the two islands, and the centuries of intercourse, have created for many a lifelong search for a national identity. Elizabeth Bowen was a victim and she found it disturbing.

Born at 15 Herbert Place on the Grand Canal, as a child she spent half of every year, the summer half, at her ancestral home, Bowen's Court in County Cork. The other half was spent at Herbert Place, creating the illusion that winter was perpetual in Dublin while the sun always shone in Cork.

The early death of her father ended her idyllic life in Dublin, with its 'streets terminated only by the horizon'. As an Irish schoolgirl in England she reacted to her first crisis of identity by boasting outrageously: Dublin spoke the best English; Sackville Street was the widest street in the world; and the Phoenix Park the vastest park. But life in England soon blurred the enchantment of Dublin.

It was different with Bowen's Court, her spiritual home, about which she has written so touchingly. As its first female inheritor, and without children, there was a sense of guilt in failing her ancestry by not passing on her inheritance. Becoming a financial embarrassment, Bowen's Court had to be sold in 1959, and was then demolished. 'It was a clean end,' Elizabeth Bowen consoled herself. 'Bowen's Court never lived to be a ruin.'

The author of twenty-seven books,

she died in London in 1973. At her wish she was buried in Kildorrery, near the place where once stood her beloved Bowen's Court.

Brendan Bracken, Viscount Bracken of Christchurch (1901-1958) Charleville Terrace, North Circular Road, 7

A 'chancer' in Ireland means an unreliable, self-seeking opportunist. Brendan Bracken, otherwise Viscount Bracken of Christchurch, born in Templemore, County Tipperary, was as adept a liar as Ireland ever produced. He built a fantasy world in which the kid called 'Snotty' at St Patrick's National School in Drumcondra soared from his mother's lodging house in Iona Drive, Glasnevin, to the highest social and political heights of Mayfair and Westminster. Cute and quick-witted, even the merciless grind of the Christian Brothers at O'Connell Schools failed to concentrate the mind of the irreligious Bracken. Emmet Dalton and Sean Lemass were contemporaries. Dalton remembered the irrepressible, assertive gurrier with his Dublin accent and with the reddest of Irish red hair. When his mother moved to Charleville Terrace, Bracken conscripted the Bracken gang which fought the Manor Street gang, the resulting mayhem forcing her to lock him up in a boarding school. Then with £14 she packed him off to Australia where he began his life of fantasy, firstly by generating a hatred of Ireland and a denial of any association

with his native country.

Later, reaching England, he posed as a tragic young Australian whose parents had been lost in a bushfire. Based on lies, he spent five months in a public school, enabling him to wear its tie. He lived briefly in digs in Oxford, enabling him to say 'When I was in Oxford.' He took to journalism and by chance met the self-centred Winston Churchill who fell for his sloothering blarney. The friendship was rapid and intense. A rumour circulated that Bracken was Churchill's illegitimate son. Basking in the situation, Bracken never denied it. Through the relationship he became an MP, and in 1940, aged thirty-nine, a member of His Majesty's Privy Council, even moving into Downing Street. Distrusted by everybody, Randolph Churchill called him 'God's greatest liar because he does not mind being found out.'

Brendan Bracken rose to become Minister for Information in Churchill's wartime government. Elevated to the peerage in 1952, he became Viscount Bracken of Christchurch. The fantasy world created by the snotty kid from Drumcondra had worked miracles for him. He still took every opportunity to denigrate Ireland, and when he died in 1958, a mourning Churchill, tears in his eyes, was heard to murmur, 'Poor dear Brendan'.

Christy Brown (1932-1981) 54 Stannaway Road, Crumlin, 12

Born with useless hands as a result of cerebral palsy, nature struck her hardest blow against a potential writer, yet she failed to stifle the self-expression of Christy Brown. Of all Anna Livia's literary sons his was probably the most phenomenal manifestation of genius, beginning as it did with the grit and determination of a supportive family. Twenty-two children were born to the Browns, thirteen surviving to grow up at Stannaway Road 'to hold the family fort', as Christy said.

When he was five and was labelled mentally defective his mother denied that diagnosis, refusing to have him institutionalised. And on the day he reached out and took a stick of chalk between the toes of his left foot, it was his mother who drew the letter 'A' on the floor and said, 'Copy that, Christy'. He did, and years later in his autobiography, *My Left Foot,* he wrote: 'That one letter ... was my road to a new world, my key to mental freedom.'

The story of Christy Brown is now well-known, thanks to the international hype given to the Hollywood version of *My Left Foot*, together with its Oscar-winning actors, Daniel Day-Lewis as Christy and Brenda Fricker as his mother. There were other books, including two collections of poetry (*Of Snails and Skylarks* and *Background Music*), but his literary *tour de force* was his best-selling autobiographical novel, *Down All the Days*, published in 1970 and translated into fourteen languages. Exhilarating, bawdy, sometimes brutal, it sets down in riveting prose the essence of a Dublin childhood as seen through the uniquely observant eyes of a sensitive

boy, suffering outwardly because of his incapacitation, and inwardly because he didn't want to be 'different'.

For all his literary success, Christy Brown yearned for the capacity to have 'an hour's fierce argument with a pal or a few moments of soft chatter with a girl rather than write the greatest book on earth'. Happiness came in 1972 when he married Mary Carr, his 'Rose of Tralee'. They divided their time between their homes in Rathcoole, County Dublin; Ballyheigue, County Kerry; and the village of Parbrook in Somerset where he died in 1981.

Cerebral palsy was a neglected condition in Ireland until 1948 when the late Dr Robert Collis noticed Christy Brown being carried on the shoulders of his brother. Encouraging Christy's writing, Collis also treated his disease, later setting up the first remedial clinic in Ireland.

Edward Bunting (1773-1843)
18 Lower Leeson Street, 2

Much of the folk music now so popular in Ireland might have been lost but for the interest shown by the United Irishmen in the eighteenth century. They considered it part of the cultural aspect of nationalism. A musical prodigy, born in Armagh, Edward Bunting became the first systematic collector and recorder of this music, thus saving a large part of Ireland's cultural treasure from oblivion. 'It is a debt which every man owes to his country,' he said, 'to render permanent the fleeting products of every species of genius.'

Bunting trained as an organist, but failed to find an appointment in Belfast because religious fanaticism discouraged music in places of worship. He turned to the harp festivals then being organised by the United Irishmen. In 1792 he wrote down all the airs from the performing harpers who played in the traditional manner. In 1796 he published Volume I of his *General Collection of Ancient Music of Ireland.* Volume II followed in 1809 and Volume III in 1840.

On his marriage in 1819, Bunting moved to Dublin where he was appointed organist at the recently-built (1802-1813) St George's Church, Temple Street. He lived at 18 Lower Leeson Street (now demolished). An accomplished pianist, his concerts were popular in Dublin. An English visitor remarked: 'Bunting's concerts are never mere musical evenings – they are always followed by a good supper and a store of wine and punch.'

Edmund Burke (1729-1797)
12 Arran Quay, 7

Burke's father was a Protestant barrister, his mother a Roman Catholic from Cork. His birthplace, 12 Arran Quay, was demolished in 1950. He was schooled by Abraham Shackleton (1697-1771), at Ballitore, County Kildare. Shackleton, a Yorkshire Quaker, and an antecedent of the Antarctic explorer, influenced Burke in the tolerance he showed later on religious questions.

Shackleton maintained a lifelong friendship with his most illustrious pupil. As an undergraduate at Trinity College in 1747, Burke wrote to his old schoolmaster about an ode he had composed, and expressed his despair at having it published in Dublin: 'There are so many discouragements in this town to a man turning author.'

A barrister, Burke entered politics in 1765 and settled in London. He was acknowledged as Westminster's most eloquent orator of the time. He lived extravagantly, his friends including Johnson, Reynolds and Garrick. Although contemporaries at Trinity, Burke and Goldsmith didn't meet until they lived in London. As a student, Burke was everything Goldsmith was not. He read widely, won scholarships, and even founded a debating club, to aid 'the formation of our minds and manner for the functions of civil society'. From this club came the College Historical Society, 'The Hist', which still flourishes.

As a politician Burke supported Catholic Emancipation, the foundation of Maynooth College, and the trade claims made by the Irish Volunteers in 1782. He was frightened by the excesses of the French Revolution. His reputation soared when he published his *Reflections on the Revolution in France,* in which he foresaw a threat to 'the ordered liberty of England'.

When he retired in 1795, his surviving son, Richard, succeeded him in the House of Commons. Richard however died suddenly and, heartbroken, Edmund Burke moved to his house in Beaconsfield where he died two years later.

Margaret Burke-Sheridan
(1889-1958)
6 Lower Fitzwilliam Street, 2

Born in Castlebar and orphaned as an infant, it was the local Sisters of Mercy who first recognised the unique voice of the five-year-old Margaret Burke-Sheridan. Aged nine, assisted by the parish priest, she moved to the Dominican College in Eccles Street, where she spent the next ten years under the musical tutelage of Mother Clement. Once again money was raised, this time to send the prodigy to the Royal Academy of Music in London. Margaret sang at a party at Lord Howard de Walden's house in Belgrave Square where she was heard by Guglielmo Marconi. 'This is the voice I have been waiting all my life to hear,' he said. With the Irish MP and journalist TP O'Connor, Margaret's godfather, they organised another fund, and in 1911 'Maggie from Mayo' went to Rome.

In an operatic emergency at San Carlo she stepped in, singing Mimi in *La Bohème*. Her brave and flawless performance made her name. At La Scala, Milan, she became the friend of Puccini, who said of her talent: 'It is instinctive, the ancestral memory of a great people.' He called her Mimi Sheridan, and thought her the ideal 'Butterfly'. For twenty years La Sheridan had the European world of opera at her feet. She was never heard in America, sadly nor did she ever receive an invitation to sing in Ireland, where her operatic achievements were little known.

Yet it was to Ireland she returned in 1936 while apparently still at her peak. In fact, she was in retreat from a lost love and a lost voice. She never sang again, knowing she would fail her own standards. Living a Mimi-like life in a shabby top flat at 6 Lower Fitzwilliam Street, she was a flamboyant figure in the Dublin of the forties and fifties: blue eyes and golden hair, a vivid hat and ropes of pearls. A true prima donna, La Sheridan helped to launch many a young Irish singer. Later on, ailing and lonely, hotels – principally the Shelbourne – substituted for a settled home until she moved to St Vincent's Nursing Home, 96 Lower Leeson Street. After her death the Sisters of Charity made her room a shrine in tribute, her mementos displayed there as she had placed them in the last days of her life.

Isaac Butt (1813-1879)
64 Eccles Street, 7

Francis Johnston, the architect, built No. 64 Eccles Street and rented it to the colourful barrister, Isaac Butt. Forgetful of the bailiffs and the threatening letters, the genial, generous, improvident Butt stuffed five-pound notes in the windows to keep the draughts out while he gave hilarious parties, and performed parlour tricks for his guests.

A son of the manse, Butt was born at Glenfin in County Donegal. In 1833, as a twenty-year-old student at Trinity College, he founded the *Dublin University Magazine*. As its editor he 'discovered' both Charles Lever and Joseph le Fanu.

Butt became a barrister in 1838 and later a Queen's Counsel. In 1852 he was elected MP for Harwich. Politics kept him in London where he indulged his weakness for dissipation and debt. 'He borrowed largely and he lent largely,' wrote TP O'Connor, and once he spent several friendless months in a debtors' prison.

From time to time Butt returned to Ireland where he defended the downtrodden in various historic trials. In 1864 he entertained all of Dublin when he defended Mary Josephine Travers in her libel action against Lady Wilde, mother of Oscar. He defended William Smith O'Brien and the Young Irelanders after the 'rebellion' of 1848, and the Fenians after 1866. He clamoured for their amnesty, and thus became leader of the Cause. Although he had begun his political life as an Orangeman and a Unionist, he ended it as founder of the Irish Home Rule Party in 1870. Lacking dynamic leadership, he was hampered by obstructionists, including Parnell, who supplanted him in 1877.

Married at twenty-four, Butt was allowed to live in the house of his in-laws in Hardwicke Street. He moved to 48 Eccles Street, where his first child (he had eight) was born, and later to 64 Eccles Street. It was at his last home, in North Great George's Street, that his terminal illness began. He was moved to The Cottage, Clonskeagh, the home of his married daughter, where he died. Opposite Roebuck House, The Cottage bears a plaque.

William Carleton (1794-1869)
2 Woodville, Sandford Road, 6

A bright young Paddy-go-easy, born at Prillick, County Tyrone, Carleton spent his early years enjoying country life: athletics, dancing and loving the girls. Parental ambition saw him as a priest, but religion had no place in Carleton's youth. His gaiety was a reaction to the poverty and militarism which kept Ireland in perpetual prostration. At twenty-four, and penniless, he set out on foot for Dublin. On the way he came face-to-face with the rotting bodies of young men hanging from

2 Woodville, Sandford Road, 6

gibbets, a warning to others in their fight against Orangeism.

He suffered the seamy side of life in Dublin lodgings in Bridgefoot Street, Mary's Lane, Moore and Francis streets until he met the Reverend Caesar Otway of the New Reformation Movement, dedicated to fighting Catholic Emancipation. In Carleton, Otway recognised a writing talent for his paper, the *Christian Examiner*. Carleton responded with his first article which ridiculed the Catholic practices at Lough Derg. He was reviled by his people. He reacted by becoming a Protestant. Otway redeemed himself by encouraging Carleton to write about the people he knew. Accordingly, Carleton's novels record eyewitness accounts of landlordism, evictions, famine and the dirt and drunkenness of the dispirited people of the 1830s and forties. His Famine stories, *The Black Prophet* and *The Black Spectre* are unequalled.

Much of Carleton's early writing was done at No. 3 (some say No. 2) Marino Crescent, Clontarf. Later the prolific novelist moved to 1 Rathgar Avenue. Admired by Thackeray for the genuine 'Irishness' of his writing, Carleton's large family never allowed him affluence. His last move was to 2 Woodville, Sandford Road, 6.

Edward Carson,
Lord Carson of Duncairn
(1854-1935)
4 Harcourt Street, 2

A quirk of fate decreed that the founder of Northern Ireland was born, bred and educated in Southern Ireland. Edward Henry Carson was born at 4 Harcourt Street. His architect father's increasing affluence dictated a move to No. 25, at the more fashionable end of the street. Edward was educated at Portarlington School and Trinity College. 'I was put to the Bar,' he said, because, wisely, his father gave him no choice. A mediocre student, he compared badly with a clever classmate whom he hated, a long-haired oddity called Oscar Wilde. The nearest Carson could approach Wilde, his intellectual superior, was in debate.

Called to the Bar in 1877, Carson married and set up at 9 Herbert Place. With an expanding practice he moved to 80 Merrion Square and also acquired a seaside house in Dalkey. Dublin soon became too small to contain the talents of Edward Carson. In

Edward Carson

1892 he was elected MP for Trinity College, and so began the political career that was to shape the future of Ireland. A year later he moved to London and became the first-ever Irish QC to take silk in England. From 1895 he figured in the most historic legal actions of his time, most notably the trial of his old classmate, Oscar Wilde.

Carson was briefed to defend the Marquis of Queensberry in the action taken by Wilde for criminal libel. Wilde remembered Carson from their Dublin days. 'No doubt he will perform his task,' Wilde said, 'with all the added bitterness of an old friend.' The cleverest of cross-examiners, Carson began at the Old Bailey by being hopelessly outclassed by Wilde whose intellectualism and wit were in full flight. Their legal debate on love and literature was to find its place in history. A student rivalry begun in the debating halls of Trinity College in Dublin, ended in tragedy at the Old Bailey in London.

Elected leader of the Unionist Party, Carson founded, and armed, the Ulster Volunteers. In 1914 he took full responsibility for smuggling thirty thousand rifles and three million rounds of ammunition into Larne to arm his Volunteers.

Defiance of the British government never afterwards impeded the progress of his career. He sat continuously in the House of Commons for some thirty years before going to the Upper House as Lord Carson of Duncairn.

Sir Roger Casement (1864-1916)
29 Lawson Terrace, Sandycove Road

Roger Casement's loathing of injustice was inherited from his father who died when Roger was an infant. He was born at Doyle's Cottage, 29 Lawson Terrace, Sandycove Road, though the house has since been divided, the two halves sharing a plaque erected in 1941. Roger was nine when his mother died. The family became

4 Harcourt Street, 2

Wards in Chancery and went to live with their uncle, John Casement, at Maherintemple House, Ballycastle, County Antrim. In the Diocesan School at Ballymena the name of Ireland was never mentioned. What Casement knew of his country he had to learn for himself.

His closest family tie was his mother's sister, Mrs Bannister of Liverpool. Her husband got Roger his first job, at seventeen, in the office of the Elder Dempster Shipping Line. Three years later he sailed to west Africa as a ship's purser. He joined the British Consular Service, and spent the next twenty years in Africa, during which time he made his famous report exposing the appalling conditions in the rubber trade in the Congo Free State.

On his transfer to Brazil Casement reported on the torture and brutality in the rubber industry in Peru. His reaction to his knighthood in 1911 was contradictory. Officially he accepted with fulsome words to the King, but privately he was embarrassed. 'There are many in Ireland', he said, 'will think of me as a traitor, and when I think of that country and of them – I feel I am.'

Casement returned to Ireland in 1913. He despised Carson and his anti-Home Rule campaign. He prayed for the coming of the Germans, a Protestant power, to teach the Protestants of Ulster their place in Irish life. Electing for the complete independence of Ireland, Casement sought the help of Germany. Failing in this, he tried to postpone the Easter Rising of 1916. Knowing that by then 'in England they

Sir Roger Casement

have a hangman's noose ready for me', Casement landed by German U-boat in Tralee Bay on Good Friday, 21 April 1916. He was arrested, thrust into the Tower of London, and condemned to death for high treason. He was hanged at Pentonville Prison on 3 August 1916, the sixteenth of those immortalised by Yeats in his poem 'Sixteen Dead Men'.

Following years of public lobbying, a decision was made to return Casement's body to Ireland in 1965 and was buried in a plot long reserved in Glasnevin Cemetery.

Robert Stewart,
Lord Castlereagh (1769-1822)
28 Henry Street, 1

Robert Stewart, successively Baron Stewart, Viscount Castlereagh, Earl and Marquis of Londonderry, an anti-

Irish despotic statesman, was born at his grandfather's house, 28 Henry Street. In later life he succeeded the Duke of Wellington and Lord Cloncurry as the occupier of Mornington House, 24 Upper Merrion Street.

As Captain Stewart, he once stayed in a country house in Ireland and slept in the haunted room. A beautiful naked boy appeared, his body radiating a blinding light. Those who saw this vision, it was said, were destined for power and for a violent death.

Castlereagh sat in the Irish parliament. He suppressed the 1798 rebellion with harshness, violence and cruelty. Henceforward, through bribery and corruption he worked tirelessly for his great achievement, the Act of Union of 1800. He had promised Catholic Emancipation to the

Irish, but George III reneged. In the imperial parliament power became the plaything of Castlereagh. It was while he was Foreign Secretary that the Duke of Wellington won his brilliant victories. Eventually he became as hated in England as he had been in Ireland. Harassed, haunted and depressed, he cut his throat with a penknife at Foots Cray, his home in Kent. Crowds jeered as his coffin was carried into Westminster Abbey.

Two English poets immortalised the ill-fated Castlereagh. Byron wrote:

So he has cut his throat at last! He? Who?
The man who cut his country's long ago.

while Shelley joined in with:

I met murder on the way –
He had a mask like Castlereagh –
Very smooth he looked, yet grim;
Seven bloodhounds followed him!

Eamon Ceannt (1881-1916)
2 Dolphin's Terrace,
South Circular Road, 8

The son of an RIC sergeant, Eamon Ceannt was born in Galway and as an infant came to Dublin with his family. He was educated at the Christian Brothers' School, North Richmond Street, and became a clerk in the City Treasurer's Office of the Dublin Corporation.

As a young man Ceannt experienced the sense of national resurgence of the early 1900s. He joined the Gaelic League and was elected a member of its governing body. He was interested in traditional music and played the Irish pipes. In 1913 he was a founder member of the Irish Volunteers.

Of the seven men who signed the

Eamon Ceannt

1916 Proclamation of the Easter Rising, Ceannt was one of the less well known. Yet he was one of the very few men, members of the Military Council, to whom the planning of the Rising had been entrusted.

The first members of the Council had been Pearse, Plunkett and Ceannt. His home had been their meeting place, and the confidence thus shown in him was a measure of his character.

The 4th Battalion of the Volunteers, engaged in the South Dublin Union (now St James's Hospital), saw some of the bitterest fighting of Easter Week. As Commandant, Ceannt showed himself to be a man of iron resolution, 'more naturally a physical force man than any other of the leaders'.

He was executed on 8 May 1916.

James Caulfield,
1st Earl of Charlemont (1728-1799)
Charlemont House,
Rutland Square (now Parnell Sq), 1

Macaulay said of Lord Charlemont: 'He gave the tone to the society of the age.' On a nine-year Grand Tour, Charlemont collected art treasures which he brought back to his home at 14 Jervis Street, afterwards the site of Jervis Street Hospital. In 1762 when Dr Bartholomew Mosse was laying out the surroundings of the Rotunda Hospital, Charlemont took a double site at the centre of Palace Row, otherwise Rutland Square North. Here, in 1770, to his own design, he erected one of the best of Dublin's many mansions. He transferred his treasures there from his previous residence,

Drumcondra House, now All-Hallows College.

In 1775 England was at war with America and with France. British forces in Ireland were withdrawn, creating alarm amongst Irish Protestants. A volunteer force was formed, led by the nobility and gentry and Charlemont was its supreme commander. Incensed at parliamentary corruption, the volunteers staged a show of military force in College Green. Respected by all, it was Charlemont who persuaded them to disperse.

Charlemont also built himself 'a small pleasure house' in the Palladian style at Marino, then in the country. No expense was spared in the creation of this miniature masterpiece of eighteenth-century architecture which cunningly conceals a three-storey dwelling house perfectly adapted for solitude and retirement. It is now a national monument.

A friend of James Gandon, it was Lord Charlemont who introduced him to John Beresford, and was therefore indirectly responsible for Gandon's coming to Dublin. In 1785 Charlemont was also responsible for the foundation of the Royal Irish Academy to promote the study of 'science, polite literature and antiquities'. He remained its president until his death in 1799.

Charlemont House was sold by the 3rd Earl to the government, and it was converted for use as the office of the Registrar General from 1870. Thanks to the persuasion of Sarah Purser, and the response of President WT Cosgrave, in 1930 Charlemont House became the Municipal Art Gallery, intended to house the controversial Lane pictures. It is now the Sir Hugh Lane Gallery of Modern Art.

Sir Alfred Chester Beatty (1875-1968)
10 Ailesbury Road, 4

Few of Dublin's citizens know that on Shrewsbury Road, Ballsbridge, is situated the Chester Beatty Library and Gallery of Oriental Art, a repository of treasures so rare they are beyond valuation. This precious hoard was bequeathed to the Irish nation by the late Sir Alfred Chester Beatty. Born in New York, he studied engineering at Columbia University, specialising in mining engineering. His speculations took him through the United States and beyond. Living conditions were primitive, and though his exertions gained him great wealth, they lost him his health. In addition to asthma, he developed silicosis.

Industrialisation had begun on the African continent, and Beatty saw his opportunity. Accumulating still more wealth, it was during a trip to Egypt that he bought some papyri – ancient Egyptian manuscripts written on papyrus, a rush-like plant. They proved artistically important. This was the spark that lit his interest in gathering, over the next half-century, the finest collection of its kind in the world.

Chester Beatty kept his expanding collections at Baroda House in London. In 1939 his special skills were at the service of the British wartime government. When the war was over, his reward was a knighthood, but little else. Even his attempts to travel south

10 Ailesbury Road, 4

for health reasons were met by a barrage of bureaucratic restrictions. Annoyed, Chester Beatty moved to Ireland in 1950, bringing his priceless collection with him. He built his Library and Gallery of Oriental Art on Shrewsbury Road, making it the permanent home for his vast collections – though it now moves to the city centre in 1997.

12 Bushy Park Road, Terenure, 6

They include items from 2500 BC to the present century. Geographically, they range from Ireland to the Far East. There are Egyptian and Greek papyri from the twelfth century BC, and illuminated Korans and books written in gold on slabs of jade. Some of the Far Eastern collections are unequalled, even in China or Japan. Small wonder that scholars come from all over the world to Shrewsbury Road.

In recognition of the bequest of his vast and priceless collection to the Irish nation, Sir Chester Beatty was made the first honorary Irish citizen under the Citizenship Act of 1956. He is buried in Glasnevin Cemetery.

Erskine Childers (1870-1922)
12 Bushy Park Road, Terenure, 6

As a result of his yachting trips along the German coast, Erskine Childers made his name with a novel, *The Riddle of the Sands*. Propounding a plan for a German invasion of England, it caused a sensation, influencing British naval policies. Born in London, Childers spent holidays at Glendalough House, Annamoe, County Wicklow, with the Bartons, his mother's relatives. In 1903 he visited Boston where he married Molly Osgood. Her father's wedding present was a yacht called the *Asgard*. When the British government bowed to Edward Carson's gun-running and threats against Home Rule, Childers, the man of action, responded. After a perilous twenty-one-day voyage through the British fleet assembled at Spithead, he arrived from Germany at Howth aboard the *Asgard*. There he unloaded 1500 Mauser rifles and 49,000 rounds of ammunition.

Childers later served in World War I in the Royal Naval Air Service.

His unquenchable desire for justice focused on the post-war plight of Ireland. Representing the country at the Paris Peace Conference he made no impact, thanks to an arrogant British delegation. He then decided to throw in his lot with Irish republicanism. In Dublin he was at first a guest of Alice Stopford Green at 90 St Stephen's Green. Later he moved to 20 Wellington Road, finally settling at 12 Bushy Park Road, Terenure. As Sinn Féin Director of Propaganda he worked at 6 Harcourt Street. He served as secretary to the Treaty delegation in 1921 and took the republican side in the Civil War.

In November 1922 this gentle, romantic idealist faced a firing-party in the bleak, flag-stoned yard at Beggar's Bush Barracks in Ballsbridge. Having shaken the hand of each gunner, Childers told his executioners: 'Come closer, boys, it will be easier for you.' On the verge of death, nothing could have been more characteristic of this incomprehensible man. Indeed, no man has earned so many contradictory epithets as Erskine Childers. After the Treaty negotiations, Churchill said he was 'actuated by a deadly malignant hatred for the land of his birth. Such as he is may all who hate us be.' To the mild-mannered Arthur Griffith he was 'that damned Englishman'. It was de Valera perhaps who got nearest to the gentle soul-searching personality of Erskine Childers. He was, he said, 'the model of all I'd wish to have been myself.'

Sir Winston Churchill (1874-1965)
Ratra, Phoenix Park, 8

Because of romantic intrigue in the highest of London's high society,

Ratra, Phoenix Park, 8

Winston Churchill spent three years of his young life in the Phoenix Park in the 1870s. It began with the beautiful Lady Edith Aylesford, whose sporting husband went travelling with the Prince of Wales in India. The Marquis of Blandford, elder son of the Duke of Marlborough, and uncle of Winston Churchill, fell for her, leaving his wife and family. Lord Aylesford sued for divorce. Lord Randolph Churchill, Blandford's younger brother and passionate admirer, intervened on his behalf. He asked the Princess of Wales to get the Prince to stop Aylesford's divorce plans. He indicated that he possessed certain letters written by the Prince to Lady Aylesford. After the interview he concluded: 'I have the crown of England in my pocket.'

His well-meant brotherly love misfired. The Prince of Wales was furious, and the question of a duel arose. The Queen was so greatly disturbed she caused a message to be sent to dear Mr Disraeli: 'The Queen says you are so kind – so full of tact and judgment, Her Majesty feels you will manage this perfectly.' Disraeli had in the meantime become an Earl, so it was as Lord Beaconsfield he turned his attention to the thorny problem that was by now the gossip of London.

'There's but one way,' he told the Duchess of Marlborough. 'Make your husband take the Lord Lieutenancy of Ireland and take Lord Randolph with him. It will put an end to it all.' Thus were the Churchills – three generations of them – packed off to the Phoenix Park in Dublin. Lord Randolph with his wife and young son, Winston,

lived at the Little Lodge (now Ratra) close by the Viceregal Lodge (now Áras an Uachtaráin). *The Times*, with its tongue in its cheek, reported the arrival of the large retinue: 'Few noblemen have come into the Irish capital to assume the high and responsible office of Viceroy in more auspicious circumstances.'

Austin Clarke (1896-1974)
Bridge House, Templeogue, 14

Past the house where was got
In darkness, terrace, provision shop
Wing-hidden convent opposite ...

In his thirty-first book, in a poem called 'Mnemosyne Lay in Dust' (1966), Austin Clarke invokes his birthplace in Manor Street, opposite the Stanhope Street Convent. The family moved to Mountjoy Street where he spent his childhood. In surplice and soutane, at Berkeley Road Church, he was a saintling in the May processions.

The future poet left Dorset Street National School after two days. He remained one week at the Christian Brothers' School, St Mary's Place. At seven he went to Belvedere College, having satisfied the Rector that the world was round like an orange. He was introduced to the pandebat, the leather strap, the Jesuits' instrument of torture for wicked boys. In a spell at Mungret College in Limerick he was subjected to the cold and malnutrition thought suitable for boys' boarding schools of the time. As the lesser of two evils he returned to Belvedere.

Clarke lived at St Alban's Terrace,

North Circular Road when he entered University College, Dublin. There he studied Irish under Douglas Hyde and English under Thomas MacDonagh. After MacDonagh's execution in 1916, Clarke succeeded him and lectured in English until 1921 when he left for London. 'Determined not to become an exile,' he returned to Dublin in 1937. Bridge House, his home for many years, has been demolished.

In 1948 I shared the pleasure of Austin Clarke's company at Yeats's funeral at Drumcliff, County Sligo. I have never since travelled that road without remembering our pause at Drumsna while Austin pointed out the site of Anthony Trollope's house and the countryside that inspired his first novel, *The MacDermotts of Ballycloran*. In any other country, he said, that house would have been preciously preserved. So indeed would Clarke's house by the bridge at Templeogue.

Through broadcasting some thousand poetry programmes over thirteen years, the gentle voice of Austin Clarke became well-known throughout the land.

Harry Clarke (1889-1931)
33 North Frederick Street, 1

Harry Clarke left Belvedere College at fourteen to work in his father's stained glass business. He attended night classes at the Metropolitan School of Art, and also studied briefly in London. Returning to Dublin, he continued his study under the stained glass artist, AE Child. In 1910 he won a series of awards enabling him to visit

the French cathedrals. He determined to return to Ireland to destroy his earlier work.

In 1910 Clarke received his first commission: eleven windows for the Honan Chapel in Cork, then being built in the Hiberno-Romanesque style. Clarke's windows were received ecstatically. His reputation was made and commissions poured in. Despite the aggravation of pulmonary tuberculosis, he worked feverishly for his brief life, leaving gems of his characteristic art in churches throughout Ireland.

The fate of his Geneva Window must humble those of the Irish establishment with a pretence of concern for the arts. Made originally for presentation by the Irish Free State government to the League of Nations in Geneva, it is a symbolic celebration of the genius of the Irish Literary Revival. It was turned down by that government because one panel shows a near-naked nymph dancing before Liam O'Flaherty's fictional character, the fat-bellied 'Mr Gilhooley'.

On loan to the then Municipal Gallery in Parnell Square, and exhibited in a blacked-out room, the Geneva Window was sheer magic as characters came alive from the works of Yeats, Synge, Shaw, O'Casey, O'Flaherty, Joyce and others. Although available for sale for many years, Ireland stood aloof while this national treasure was lost for ever to the Miami Museum.

Clarke's 'The Eve of St Agnes', illustrating Keats's poem, was commissioned in 1924 by Harold Jacob for

May. She continued to live at their home at Richmond Avenue, and eventually made history by moving to the Mansion House as the first woman Lord Mayor of Dublin. Like many of her generation, she wished always to be identified with her late husband, so, to the end, she was Mrs Tom Clarke – something misunderstood by latter-day feminists.

Abraham Colles (1773-1843)
21 St Stephen's Green, 2

A surgeon of immense industry, Abraham Colles gave his name to a fracture of the radius (one of the two long bones of the forearm), caused by a fall on the palm of the hand. It is the commonest fracture seen in hospital casualty departments on frosty mornings.

Born at Millmount on the river Nore in County Kilkenny, Colles came of an Anglo-Irish family made wealthy by quarrying the local black marble. He entered Trinity College in 1790. Five years later he took the qualification of the Royal College of Surgeons in Ireland. In 1797 he took the Edinburgh MD, and then worked with the great surgeon, Sir Astley Cooper (1768-1841) at Guys' Hospital in London.

Impecunious when he returned to Dublin, he took a house in Chatham Street where he opened a practice, including GP. He also rented a stable at the rear of South King Street where he taught anatomy. In his first year he managed to earn £8.16.7½. By the age of twenty-six he was appointed surgeon to Dr Steevens's Hospital, and he

moved to 10 Pitt Street (where Balfe, the composer, was born at a later date). On his marriage he moved from 71 Dame Street to 11 St Stephen's Green.

Growing affluence, and a family of ten, led to Colles setting up a permanent home at 21 St Stephen's Green. Fond of outdoor life, he had his country house at Donnybrook Cottage, about a mile beyond the village, his neighbours being the Jamesons of Montrose, the Roes of Nutley and the Wrights of Beechill. Large grounds enabled the Colles family to enjoy ponies, gardeners, grooms and gigs.

As professor of anatomy at the Royal College of Surgeons, his attraction for students compelled an extension of the premises in 1825. In 1832 William Wilde (the father of Oscar) became his apprentice. Elected twice to the Presidency of the Royal College, he first achieved that honour at the uniquely early age of twenty-nine.

A bronchitic, Colles in his old age moved to Kingstown (now Dun Laoghaire) to benefit from the air. As a last service to humanity he gave his body to medical science. He was given a public funeral at Mount Jerome Cemetery.

Michael Collins (1890-1922)
1 Brendan Road, Donnybrook, 4

Home life for Michael Collins ceased at the age of fifteen when he left Clonakilty, County Cork, to become a post-office clerk in London. Henceforth life was to be a matter of moving on, always with no fixed abode. With a price of £10,000 on his head, and his house in Ailesbury Road. Now in the Hugh Lane Gallery, this window, with Clarke's ascetic figures, their rich costumes studded as if with precious gems, won him the Art Workers' Trophy and gold medal at the Aonach Tailteann exhibition in 1924. Later that year he died in a sanatorium at Davos. His widow had to reimburse the £400 paid to her husband by the government for the Geneva Window which had so injured their sensibilities. They reminded her they *could* have charged her interest.

Thomas J Clarke (1858-1916)
10 Richmond Avenue, Fairview, 3

In the first decade of the twentieth century, Thomas Clarke represented for the new generation a living link with the Fenian tradition of resistance against British rule in Ireland. Born in England of Irish parents (his father was a British soldier), Clarke lived in South Africa until the age of ten. He then lived in Dungannon, County Tyrone, until at twenty-one he went to America and joined Clan na nGael, an off-shoot of the Fenian movement. In 1883 he arrived in England as a dynamiteer, was arrested and received fifteen years' penal servitude,

spent under the harshest conditions.

Released in 1898, broken in health, this quiet, unassuming man still radiated belief in the separatist ideal. In 1901 he married Kathleen Daly, daughter of John Daly, the Limerick Fenian leader. Through his tobacconist's shop at 75A Parnell Street, Clarke, the unrepentant revolutionary, quietly organised and guided his disciples. He revived the Irish Republican Brotherhood, and made preparations for a rising.

When the opportunity came in April 1916, Clarke, in his fifties, took his place in the General Post Office. He was a signatory of the 1916 Proclamation. With Padraic Pearse and Thomas MacDonagh he was executed on 3 May 1916. That night Kathleen Clarke, the new widow, went back to Kilmainham Jail – twice in twenty-four hours – to bid farewell to her brother, Edward Daly, executed on 4

10 Richmond Avenue, Fairview, 3

with pockets full of latchkeys to 'safe-houses', no man in Irish history had so many addresses in Dublin. Before he became a wanted man he stayed at the Munster Hotel in Mountjoy Street. When he went 'on the run' its proprietor, Myra McCarthy, a Kerrywoman, still saw to his laundry which he collected on his bicycle on Sunday mornings. Through the War of Independence he claimed No. 1 Brendan Road was his home. Owned by Batt O'Connor, it had secret hiding places and means of quick escape.

To shelter Collins took nerve. He never imposed unless the woman of the house felt she had the necessary self-control and sense of secrecy. Thanks to the patriotism of many such stoic women, Collins was never once discovered. At the end of hostilities his collection of latchkeys included those of Oliver Gogarty in Ely Place; Linda Kearns's Nurses' Home, Gardiner Place; Mrs Andrew Woods, Morehampton Road; Mrs Maurice Collins, Parnell Street; Mrs Paddy O'Keeffe, Camden Street; Walter Coles, 1 Mountjoy Square; Mrs O'Donovan, Airfield Road, Rathgar; Miss Hoey, Mespil Road; and many more.

For his offices Collins chose busy streets: 6 and 76 Harcourt Street; 3 St Andrew Street; 22 and 29 Mary Street; 21-22 Harry Street; with others in North Earl Street, Crow Street, O'Connell Street, Bachelor's Walk, North Frederick Street, and so on. All were camouflaged with fictitious name-plates. His escapes from his offices became legendary, the most hair-raising usually occurring in daylight.

Michael Collins

Often he joined the crowd in the street as they watched the British soldiers raiding for their notorious 'Scarlet Pimpernel'.

With the Civil War, Collins became a hunted man again, often being holed up with his ministers in Government Buildings. Impatience sometimes drove him to break out, resuming the use of Gogarty's latchkey in nearby Ely Place. As Commander-in-Chief from 12 July 1922, his last weeks were spent at his headquarters in Portobello Barracks. On a mission of peace, he was shot dead near his native Clonakilty. At the news even his enemies knelt to pray.

Padraic Colum (1882-1972)
11 Edenvale Road, Ranelagh, 6

Born in the workhouse in Longford where his father was the Master, Padraic Colum was the eldest of seven children. Life was relatively luxurious until, through drink, his father lost his job. He went to America, while his wife and children went to her family in County Cavan. There Padraic went to school, listened to the locals talk, and retained a feeling for the place which brought him back periodically in later life.

On returning to Ireland his father became stationmaster at Sandycove and the family moved to the railway cottage at Eden Road, Glasthule. Padraic attended the local school and, at seventeen, got a clerkship in the Railway Clearing House in Kildare Street. After his mother's death he began to write while living in many different southside lodgings: Longwood Avenue, Bushfield Avenue, Frankfort Place, Rugby Road and Chelmsford Road, amongst others. Meanwhile he had met AE (George Russell), Lady Gregory, Joyce and Yeats, and his first play, *The Fiddler's House*, was accepted by the Abbey Theatre. His second, *The Saxon Shilling*, was refused for political reasons. In protest, Arthur Griffith and Maud Gonne withdrew from the National Theatre Society.

Thomas Muskerry, probably Colum's best play, was produced in May 1910, coinciding with another Abbey Theatre crisis. King Edward VII had died, and the theatre failed to show due respect. It remained open. Miss Annie Horniman, the English philanthropist from Manchester, and the Abbey's fairy godmother, resigned. With her went her valuable subsidy of £400 per annum.

Colum married Mary Maguire of Collooney, County Sligo, herself a writer, and once the sweetheart of Thomas MacDonagh. They lived in Donnybrook in a house which she described as 'dampish, largish, and uncomfortable'. It was there, on New Year's Eve 1913, they toasted the new year in strong tea. Shortly afterwards they moved to Howth and later, in 1914, they went to America for six months and stayed for life. Like so many emigrants, they became American citizens, but Ireland remained their spiritual home.

After Mary's death in 1957, Padraic Colum lived with his sister at 11 Edenvale Road, Ranelagh. For the next twelve years he lectured regularly throughout the United States. Aged ninety, he died at Enfield, Connecticut, in 1972. Padraic and Mary Colum are buried in St Fintan's Cemetery in Sutton.

William Congreve (1670-1729)
Trinity College, 2

Born at Bardsey near Leeds, Congreve came to Ireland as an infant when his father took command of the British army garrison at Youghal, County Cork. He was a contemporary of Swift's at Kilkenny College, and later at Trinity College, Dublin. Having tutored Swift for five years, theirs became a lifelong friendship.

Incognita, Congreve's first novel,

was said to have been written at the age of seventeen while he was still at Trinity. Intended for the Bar, he left Dublin for the Middle Temple where he resumed his writing, now more seriously. In 1693 *The Old Bachelor*, his first play, was a huge success. In the next six years he became the leading dramatist of his day, and the greatest exponent of Restoration Comedy. His plays included *The Double Dealer, Love for Love* and *The Mourning Bride*, the latter attracting all the great tragediennes of the day. In 1700 came *The Way of the World*, Congreve's most famous play.

His comedies were criticised by the puritans for their indelicacy. *The Way of the World* was received so coldly that Congreve assured his critics of his indifference to their car-

pings, for it would be the last play he would ever write. He kept his word, and retired to live the life of a gentleman.

As a result of injuries received in a carriage accident, he died in 1729 and was buried in Westminster Abbey.

James Connolly (1868-1916)
Liberty Hall, Beresford Place, 1

Born in Edinburgh, James Connolly began work at eleven years of age. He joined the Royal Scots' Regiment, serving at Spike Island detention centre in Cork Harbour, where he was detailed to guard an Irishman on the night before his execution. The experience awoke an anti-British wrath in the young British soldier, something that was to last his lifetime. After his

Head office of The Irish Transport and General Workers' Union

marriage he began his social activities. 'The great appear great,' he told the Edinburgh unemployed, 'because we are on our knees. Let us rise.'

In 1896 Connolly came to Dublin to organise socialism. His family's first home was in a tenement in Queen Street. They moved to tenements at 76 Charlemont Street and 54 Pimlico in the Liberties. Then, as Connolly's daughter Nora records, they moved to a cottage in Weaver Square 'that we did not have to share with anyone'.

James Connolly fasted that his children might eat. Such poverty forced them to emigrate to America in 1903 where, in relative opulence, the family lived at 76 Ingalls Avenue, Troy, a hundred and fifty miles up the Hudson River. Later they moved to Elton Avenue in the Bronx, where Connolly wrote his *Labour in Irish History*. He yearned for Ireland, but dreaded its poverty. In 1910 he returned to Dublin as an organiser for the Irish Transport and General Workers' Union and lived at South Lotts Road, Ringsend. He was then sent to organise for the union in Belfast. There the family lived at 5 Rosemary Street, moving later to Glenalina Terrace at the top of the Falls Road. The family remained in Belfast after Connolly returned to Dublin. During the stirring years between 1913 and 1916 he lived at Surrey House, Leinster Road, Rathmines, the home of Countess Markievicz. Before the 1916 Rising he moved into Liberty Hall where, in his bedroom, the IRB Military Council met on Easter Sunday and decided, despite all the setbacks, to proceed with the Rising on Easter Monday.

When Connolly, the Commander in the General Post Office, was under sentence of death, his family moved from Belfast to Countess Markievicz's cottage at the foot of Three Rock Mountain. It was there they learned how their wounded father was carried to the execution yard in Kilmainham Jail where he was propped in a chair to be executed on 12 May 1916.

Sir Dominic Corrigan (1802-1880) 4 Merrion Square, 2

Corrigan's Pulse is the name given to the throbbing pulse seen in the arteries of the head and neck in cases of incompetence of the aortic valve of the heart. Credit for the first description of this peculiar pulse went to Sir Dominic John Corrigan, a popular and highly-paid Honorary Physician to Queen Victoria in Ireland.

Born in Thomas Street, his father farmed in Kilmainham. It was the example of a kindly family doctor that inspired young Corrigan to pursue a career in medicine. With William Stokes of Dublin he qualified in Edinburgh in 1825. He returned to Dublin at a favourable time, for Corrigan was a Roman Catholic. Hitherto, the medical profession in Dublin had been predominantly Protestant. Following Catholic Emancipation in 1829 Corrigan set up at 11 Ormond Quay. In 1832 he moved to 13 Bachelor's Walk.

Appointed Honorary Physician to

the Charitable Infirmary in Jervis Street, the first voluntary hospital in these islands, Corrigan found himself in a company of surgeons, for Jervis Street was then primarily an accident hospital. Knighted in 1866, increasing affluence brought Sir Dominic to No. 4 Merrion Square. He built a seaside residence called Inniscorrig on Coliemore Road in Dalkey, and represented Dublin at Westminster from 1870 to 1874.

Founded in 1654, and given its Royal Charter in 1667, the Royal College of Physicians in Ireland was the first medical college in this country. In the middle of the nineteenth century it was still without a permanent home, its meetings taking place in the homes of its presidents, or at Sir Patrick Dun's Hospital after its completion in 1809. It was through the energy of Sir Dominic Corrigan that the present college was built in Kildare Street on the site of what was Portarlington House, and later the old Kildare Street Club. Sir Dominic was President of the College from 1859 for five successive years. His statue by John Henry Foley stands in the Great Hall.

Sir Dominic Corrigan died at Inniscorrig and is buried in the crypt of St Andrew's Church, Westland Row.

William T Cosgrave (1880-1965)
Beechpark, Templeogue, 6

In effect prime minister of southern Ireland, but officially designated President of the Executive Council of the new Irish Free State from 1922 to 1932, William Cosgrave was the un-known and self-effacing man suddenly thrust into political prominence at the hour of Ireland's direst need. 'The void left by the deaths of Griffith and Collins was not unfilled,' said Winston Churchill. 'A quiet, potent figure stood in the background ... To the courage of Collins he added the matter-of-fact fidelity of Griffith and a knowledge of practical administration and State policy all his own.'

William Cosgrave was born in 174 James's Street. A publican and a politician, his father encouraged him to follow both vocations, but from 1905 when young Cosgrave attended the first Sinn Féin convention, it was politics alone which captured him. A founding figure of the Irish Volunteers in 1913, he took part in Childers's landing of arms at Howth. He decided, however, to join the oath-bound and secret Irish Republican Brotherhood. In 1916 he fought alongside Cathal Brugha in the South Dublin Union (now St James's Hospital). He was sentenced to death, but this was commuted to penal servitude for life. He was released in the general amnesty of 1917.

When Cosgrave assumed the presidency of the Irish Free State, he inherited a formidable responsibility. Never lacking moral courage, and ignoring the charges of pro-Britishry, he set himself to bring order out of civil chaos, and to impose a respect for the rule of law. Himself without flamboyance, he led a cabinet of steely characters. With quiet determination he presided over the transition of Ireland from a British possession to a modern democracy. His far-seeing vision created the Shannon Scheme, the subsidisation of the National Theatre, the foundation of the Municipal Art Gallery in Charlemont House, and much else besides.

William Cosgrave retired from politics in 1944 at a comparatively early age. Always interested in horses, he turned to stud-farming at Beechpark, his home in Templeogue. There he lived quietly until his death in 1965. He was given a state funeral to Golden Bridge Cemetery in Inchicore.

Richard 'Boss' Croker (1843-1922)
Glencairn, Sandyford

Tammany Hall and the Tammany Benevolent Society were established in New York in 1789 by illiterate immigrants for social and charitable purposes. In time Tammany acquired overwhelming political influence, becoming notorious for its corruption and jobbery. Richard Wellstead Croker, proprietor of a liquor saloon, and a real estate business, became the boss of Tammany in 1886. And 'Boss' Croker also became a very rich man.

Croker was born in 1843 in Castletownroche, County Cork. His father emigrated during the Famine, living on a New York wasteland, now Central Park. As a street-urchin, sometimes attending a one-roomed school in Madison Square Gardens, young Croker learned life the hard way.

When his first wife died, he married an Indian princess. He had a book published about himself called *Pearls before Swine*. In 1905 he decided to retire to Ireland to enjoy his wealth. He spent £75,000 in refurbishing Glencairn, formerly the home of Justice John Murphy, and now the residence of the British ambassador. He set up racing stables, a horse called 'Orby' winning him the Derby in 1907.

Near the graves of Orby and his clan in the grounds of Glencairn, Croker built an elaborate mausoleum for his wife and himself. On his death he was duly entombed there. But eventually the princess had to mortgage the estate. Seventeen years later the 'Boss' was removed and given a second funeral, when he was buried in nearby Kilgobbin Cemetery. Orby and his clan still occupy their original resting places.

John Philpot Curran (1750-1817)
4 Ely Place (formerly No. 12), 2

'A street angel and a house divil,' is probably as good a summary as any of Curran, the great advocate. His wife left him. He insisted that his favourite daughter, killed in an accident, be buried on the lawn before The Priory, his country home in Rathfarnham. Built over by new housing, her grave has since disappeared, probably under somebody's semi-detached. Curran behaved abominably to his daughter Sarah because her love affair with Robert Emmet might have imperilled his promotion to the Bench. Although he defended all the United Irishmen tried in Dublin, he refused to respond to Emmet's appeal for legal assistance.

Outside his home and family,

however, John Philpot Curran was admired, honoured and loved. An enigmatic man, yes, but he possessed eloquence and wit which helped his tremendous legal reputation.

In October 1817 he became ill while in London. 'I fear you cough with more difficulty this morning,' said his English doctor. 'That is strange,' replied Curran, 'for I have been practising all night.' A few days later he was dead.

Buried in Glasnevin Cemetery, Curran lies under a sarcophagus modelled on the tomb of Scipio Barbatus which stands opposite the Caracalla Baths in Rome.

Cyril Cusack (1910-1993)
Pembroke Street, 2

Cyril Cusack was born in Durban, South Africa, the son of an Irish officer in the Natal Mounted Police and a London chorus girl. When their marriage failed, mother and son came to Ireland in 1916. A theatrical partnership was formed with Irish actor, Brefnie O'Rourke. As a fit-up company they regularly toured Ireland, playing in barns, parish halls and pubs. As a child actor, Cyril played anything from Ali Baba to Dick Whittington's cat. In old age he called the era 'a glorious adventure'.

After schooling at Newbridge Dominican College and the Christian Brothers' school in Synge Street, Cusack entered University College, Dublin. After graduation he joined the Abbey Theatre in 1932. Though he played all the great parts in Yeats,

Synge and O'Casey, his triumph was as Christy Mahon in *The Playboy of the Western World.*

He turned to films in 1946. *Odd Man Out*, his first, marked him as a unique film actor. Demands for his services came from London and Hollywood. Amongst his profession he became a recognised scene-stealer with a facility for up-staging the best.

Cusack published two volumes of poetry, *Timepieces* and *Between The Acts*. It was for his writing rather than his acting he wished to be remembered. He was conferred with honorary doctorates by Trinity College and University College, Dublin, and by the University of Ulster.

Dublin was privileged on 1990 when he appeared at the Gate Theatre in Chekhov's *The Three Sisters* with his three daughters, Sinead, Niamh and Sorcha.

Cyril Cusack lived in Pembroke Street until the night-life around the corner in Leeson Street drove him out. He purchased a villa in Sandycove from Eileen, the widow of Sean O'Casey, when she left Ireland. Here he created his own theatrical museum.

On the night of his death, his daughter Niamh lived out the adage 'the show must go on'. She played Nora in Ibsen's *A Doll's House* at the Gate Theatre. At the end she announced her father's death to a standing ovation. The great actor commanded his last applause as his coffin was lowered at Mount Venus Cemetery in the foothills of the Dublin mountains he loved. Star-quality was innate in Cyril Cusack. The critic Desmond Rushe summed up succinctly: 'His mother's milk,' he said, 'had been laced with grease-paint.'

General Emmet Dalton (1898-1978)
8 Upper St Columba's Road,
Drumcondra, 9

Born in the United States, Emmet Dalton grew up in Drumcondra. At the age of sixteen he joined the Irish Volunteers. In 1914 he joined the Royal Dublin Fusiliers, and his father ordered him out, saying, 'There'll be no bloody redcoat in this house.' For bravery at Ginchy on the Somme, Dalton won the Military Cross and earned the nickname 'Ginchy Dalton'. There he witnessed the annihilation of the 9th Battalion of the 'Dubs', and the death of Tom Kettle, a family friend. At that time Dalton believed he was fighting for Ireland.

In 1919 he was demobbed, returned to Dublin, and rejoined the Irish Volunteers. He worked closely with Michael Collins and was given many special assignments. In April 1921 he took Sir James Craig, the Unionist leader, to parley with de Valera at a secret Dublin rendezvous. Posing as a British army officer (and wearing his own old uniform), he led the attempted rescue of Sean MacEoin, then under sentence of death in Mountjoy Jail. He played soccer for Bohemians. Often through the Black-and-Tan War he played against British army teams in barrack compounds wired in to keep out such as he! He organised a special squad to protect Collins during the Treaty negotiations in London in 1921.

In 1922 he helped to organise the new Irish Free State Army, becoming a major-general at twenty-four. He was with Michael Collins when he was killed at Béal-na-Bláth, County Cork, on 22 August 1922. After a period as clerk to the first Irish Senate, he left Ireland for Hollywood where, as a film producer, he worked first with Paramount and then with Metro Goldwyn Mayer. Later he went into independent film production in London. With his experience, and in partnership with Louis Elliman, he founded Ardmore Film Studios in Bray.

General Dalton died on his eightieth birthday at 25 Sydney Parade Avenue, Dublin 4. Given a military funeral, he was carried to his grave by soldiers of the army he had helped to found sixty years earlier.

Edward Daly (1891-1916)
10 Richmond Avenue, Fairview, 3

The Daly family of Limerick was exceptional in the sacrifices made for Ireland's freedom. 'Ned' Daly, an only son in a family of ten, was born six months after his father's death; his grandfather had been imprisoned in 1865 for his Fenian activities; his Fenian uncle, John Daly, served twelve years in English jails. When Ned was seven Tom Clarke was released after fifteen years in jail and married Ned's sister, Kathleen Daly.

With this background it isn't surprising that as a clerk in May Roberts, a wholesale chemists in Dublin, Ned Daly enrolled in 1913 in the Volunteers.

Edward Daly

'I am at last what I wanted to be,' he said, 'a soldier.'

Ned Daly was the commandant in charge at the Four Courts in Easter Week 1916. In matters of discipline and morale his standards were excellent. Captain Brereton, a British prisoner in the Four Courts, said afterwards: 'The Sinn Féiners observed all the rules of civilised warfare and fought clean. They proved they were men of education, incapable of acts of brutality.'

James Connolly, commander at the General Post Office, called Commandant Daly's 'a splendid exploit', and fifty years later Colonel P J Hally gave a modern professional soldier's assessment: 'Daly showed excellent military skill' in an area 'well held, well defended and well led'.

Ned Daly was one of Yeats's 'Sixteen Dead Men', executed after the rebellion of 1916.

William Dargan (1799-1867)
Mount Anville, Dundrum, 14

Fronting the National Gallery in Merrion Square there is a statue with one word on its plinth, 'Dargan'. The brevity suggests a man well known. Yet today the name of William Dargan is all but forgotten, though he was to Ireland 'the arch improver of his time'.

Trained as an engineer, Dargan assisted Thomas Telford on the construction of the Holyhead Railway. As engineer, or entrepreneur, he was to be associated with the laying of almost every railway in Ireland, the first being the Dublin to Kingstown (now Dun Laoghaire) line, which opened in 1838. Dargan then lived near Sybil Hill, Raheny, which accounts for his construction of the high road from Dublin to Howth.

In the fifteen years following 1838 his railways branched out from Dublin and Belfast into the hinterlands. Dargan gave vast and well-paid employment and amassed great personal wealth by shrewd investment. For his liberality he was known to his employees as 'the man with his hand in his pocket'. He built himself a splendid country mansion in the hills south of Dublin. Mount Anville is now a fashionable girls' school. His town house was at 2 Fitzwilliam Square. He also built himself a luxurious railway carriage, now in the Ulster Transport Museum.

In May 1853 Dargan invested £100,000 in the Dublin Industrial Exhibition held on Leinster Lawn, Merrion Square, then the property of the Royal Dublin Society. After visiting it

Queen Victoria drove to Mount Anville and took tea with Mr Dargan, but he declined her offer of a baronetcy. A feature of the exhibition was a great collection of pictures. Dargan felt the collection should be placed on permanent exhibition. A testimonial was opened for a memorial to commemorate Dargan's services to his country. He made the National Gallery his memorial, and it was built in 1859-60 on Leinster Lawn, the site of Dargan's great exhibition.

In 1866 he fell from his horse and never recovered. He sold Mount Anville and retreated to 2 Fitzwilliam Square. Never having learned to delegate his work, his business interests rapidly disintegrated. Bankrupt and broken, he died a lonely man in 1867. He is buried in Glasnevin Cemetery.

Thomas Davis (1814-1845)
67 Lower Baggot Street, 2

His mother, brothers and sister, with whom Thomas Davis lived, had reservations about their wayward relative. Yet it was his generous religious and political tolerance which were the secret of his success. An obituary in the *Dublin University Magazine* noted that 'his own family in whose bosom he lived and died in all peace and affection, entertained political opinions quite opposite to his'. It wasn't moral force, Davis held, to insult a man's tastes and prejudices with the weapons of bullying and intolerance.

The son of a Welsh father, a surgeon in the Royal Artillery, and an Irish mother, Davis was born in Mal-

low, County Cork, one month after his father's death. His mother moved to Warrington Place, near Mount Street Bridge, and in 1830 to 67 Lower Baggot Street. At Mr Mangan's 'mixed seminary' in Lower Mount Street, the boy was considered dim-witted and difficult. Afterwards he claimed it was at Mangan's he learned to 'know, and knowing, to love his Catholic fellow-countrymen'. He was also undistinguished at Trinity College where he graduated in Law in 1836. He was called to the Bar in the following year.

The unsuspected fire which smouldered in Thomas Davis suddenly flared in 1841 when he went for a walk in the Phoenix Park with John Blake Dillon, another barrister, and Charles Gavan Duffy, a journalist. They agreed to collaborate in publishing a newspaper called *The Nation*. Davis insisted their paper 'must embrace Protestant, Catholic and Dissenter – Milesian and Cromwellian – the Irish of a hundred generations and the stranger who is within our gates'. The first issue appeared in October 1842, and soon its weekly circulation reached 250,000. Thus began Young Ireland and the colourful period of Irish political intellectualism of the 1840s.

Davis worked like a literary galley-slave. He was even pressed into writing verse – fifty songs and ballads in three years. Though his prose is superior, it was his poetry (collected in *The Spirit of the Nation*) which influenced so many young Irishmen. It set John O'Leary on a lifetime of patriotism. Nor did Yeats forget his debt to Davis by way of John O'Leary.

When Davis died suddenly Ireland was paralysed by shock. His massive funeral to Mount Jerome Cemetery jammed the streets of Dublin. He was instantly elevated to the pantheon of Ireland's illustrious dead.

Michael Davitt (1846-1906)
Rose Lawn, Military Road,
Ballybrack

In Horatio Nelson England has a hero who, as a rear-admiral in battle, lost his right arm at the age of thirty-nine. In Michael Davitt Ireland has a hero who, at the age of eleven, lost his right arm working for his living in a Lancashire cotton mill. The achievements of the one are perpetuated in stone, of the other in the ownership of their lands by the one-time Irish tenant farmers. This happy outcome resulted from the final destruction of landlordism through Davitt's inspiration, the Land League, whose doctrine was 'The land for the people'.

Born at Straide, County Mayo, Davitt was six when the family was evicted. Destitute on the roadside, they watched their home being battered to rubble. They emigrated to Lancashire where Davitt was influenced by a kindly Wesleyan teacher. He loved the English people; it was the injustice of the British government towards Ireland that roused his passion.

Davitt celebrated his coming of age by taking part in a Fenian raid on Chester Castle. He ended with a sentence of fifteen years' penal servitude. On release he changed his tactics from secret conspiracy (Fenianism) to open agitation. In 1879 he launched the Land League.

A fearless man, Davitt once said: 'As long as I have tongue to speak, or head to plan, or hand to dare for Ireland, Irish landlordism and English

Rose Lawn, Military Road, Ballybrack

misgovernment in Ireland shall find in me a sleepless and incessant opponent.' He was a reluctant parliamentarian, enduring the Westminster 'parliamentary penitentiary' for four years. He considered parliamentary talk a waste of time. 'Sunburstery' he called it.

Unlike O'Connell and Parnell, Davitt refused the financial tribute pressed upon him by a grateful people. However, on his marriage in 1886, to Mary Yore of Michigan, his bride was presented with a house purchased by a public testimonial in recognition of Davitt's service to the Land League. This was Rose Lawn, a villa at Ballybrack, also known as Land League Cottage.

Self-educated, Davitt became a literary figure of stature. His greatest book, *The Fall of Feudalism in Ireland*, is his history of the Land League. All his books were written at Land League Cottage where he lived until his death. He is buried at Straide, County Mayo.

Eamon de Valera (1882-1975)
Áras an Uachtaráin, Phoenix Park, 8

Born in New York, de Valera came to Ireland aged three, and grew up at Knockmore, Bruree, County Limerick. After local schooling he entered Blackrock College. With a degree

Eamon de Valera

from the Royal University he became a professor of mathematics at Carysfort Training College, Blackrock. He lived in The Castle at the College where his subsistence cost him fifteen shillings a week. Like Joyce, but for different reasons, Eamon de Valera had many addresses in Dublin. In 1908 he moved into digs in Merrion View Avenue. He married his Irish teacher, Sinéad Flanagan, in 1910. They lived at 33 Morehampton Terrace, Donnybrook. The house bears a plaque: 'The first home of Eamon and Sinéad de Valera 1910-1916'.

De Valera became commander of the Third Battalion, Dublin Brigade of the Irish Volunteers. After the 1916 insurrection, and during his imprisonment, his family lived first at 34 Munster Street, Phibsboro, then at Greystones. Released in 1917, he was re-arrested in 1918 and lodged in Lincoln Jail, from where he escaped. He took refuge in the gate-lodge of the Archbishop's house in Drumcondra. On his return from the US in 1920 his hiding places alternated between Dr Farnan's house, No. 5 Merrion Square; Loughnavale, 165 Strand Road, Merrion (since demolished); and Glenvar, a mansion on the corner of Mount Merrion and Cross avenues, Blackrock. In June 1920 he was arrested at Glenvar on the eve of the Truce negotiations. All that followed is now history. After eight years of political struggle de Valera was released from prison in 1924, the family being reunited at 18 Claremont Road, Sandymount.

In 1924 he founded Fianna Fáil. In

1932 he brought that party into government with himself as Taoiseach. He moved house to Springvale, Cross Avenue, Blackrock. In 1933 the family moved to Bellevue, Cross Avenue, formerly the home of the Bewley family. In 1940 they moved to Herberton, Cross Avenue, which they renamed Teach Chuilinn. The bells of St Philip's Church, de Valera said, would always remind him of home life at Cross Avenue, Blackrock.

As President of Ireland, from 1959 to 1973, he occupied Áras an Uachtaráin, formerly the Vice-Regal Lodge. His retirement was spent at Talbot Lodge, Blackrock, a gracious mansion in a sylvan setting (since demolished). He died there.

Anne Devlin (1780-1851)
2 Little Elbow Lane, 8

Faced with torture, imprisonment and death, the fearlessness of Anne Devlin in keeping the secrets of Robert Emmet gained her an immortal place in Irish history. She was born at Cronebeg, between Aughrim and Rathdrum in County Wicklow. Her cousins were Michael Dwyer and Hugh O'Byrne, the 1798 outlaws whose resistance forced the British to build the Military Road through the Wicklow mountains, and its strong points, the Glencree and Drumgoff Barracks. His nephews being outlaws on the run, Anne's father was arrested by the local Yeomanry and imprisoned in Wicklow Jail. Prisoners had to support themselves, their rations becoming a perquisite of the head jailer. Anne rode

a horse twice weekly to the jail with food for her father. Insurrection, jails and outlawry therefore had always been part of Anne Devlin's life.

After years of such persecution her family moved to a farm in Rathfarnham. Robert Emmet had taken the nearby Butterfield House as an ammunition dump from which supplies were ferried to depots in Dublin. Anne Devlin became his housekeeper and his faithful accomplice in the preparations for his ill-fated insurrection of July 1803. When its failure forced him to escape to Ballinascorney in the Dublin hills, Anne drove out in a jingle with letters and messages. For better or worse, Emmet returned with her, parting from her outside Rathfarnham. We know now he was trying to meet his betrothed, Sarah Curran.

After his arrest, Anne Devlin was interrogated and tortured, without result. Finally she was suspended from the shaft of an upturned cart. 'No, villains, I will tell you nothing about him,' remained her defiant reply. In another effort to force her confession she was taken in a cab past the gibbet outside St Catherine's Church in Thomas Street where Emmet was about to be executed. Impervious to mental and physical torture, she was then charged with high treason and imprisoned in Kilmainham Jail for three years.

She became a servant to a Mrs Elizabeth Hammond at 84 Sir John Rogerson's Quay. Later she lived in a garret in John's Lane, beside the Augustinian Church, before moving to 2 Little Elbow Lane (now

McClean's Lane) in the Coombe. Although she ended her life in poverty and obscurity, history has elevated Anne Devlin to a place alongside Emmet whose cause she served so faithfully.

John Dillon (1851-1927)
2 North Great George's Street, 1

John Blake Dillon (1814-1866) was one of the intellectual trio of Young Irelanders, along with Thomas Davis and Gavan Duffy, who founded *The Nation* newspaper. Dillon engaged in the 1848 Rising. He opposed Fenianism, and became an MP for Tipperary. With this distinguished inheritance, his son, John Dillon, joined a group of politically gifted young men who entered the Westminster Parliament under Parnell, and for forty years found themselves in perpetual opposition, borne along on the interminable promise of Home Rule.

In 1918 Dillon succeeded John Redmond as leader of the Irish Parliamentary Party. But in the general election of 1918, when Sinn Féin gained a landslide victory, the Irish Parliamentary Party was swept away forever, Dillon losing his seat to de Valera.

Noted for his eloquence in advocating constitutional change, Dillon always condemned physical force. At Easter 1916 he was at the family town house, 2 North Great George's Street, when the Rising broke out. Like others of the Parliamentary Party, he was out of touch, and had misread the situation. On the third day he wrote to Redmond in London: 'The situation here is terrible. We are in absolute ignorance of what has been going on, beyond the fact that fierce fighting has been in progress in many parts of the city.'

Although detesting those responsible, and thoroughly disapproving of the Rising, John Dillon rushed back to the House of Commons to make the speech of his life. Amidst daily executions in Dublin, he gave vent to a patriotic pride and a passionate indignation in demanding leniency for the men of 1916. 'It is not murderers who are being executed,' he pleaded, 'it is insurgents who fought a clean fight, a brave fight.' As always, Dillon responded to bravery however misguided the cause. An indignant House of Commons, assuming that he who pleads for rebels must himself be one, misunderstood his speech. Nevertheless, he displayed an extraordinary flair for political calculation and analysis.

A lonely and disillusioned widower, John Dillon lived to see his country in the hands of those he considered its wreckers. His years of patriotic duty, it seemed, had counted for nothing. He was father of James Dillon of the Fine Gael party, the last of a line of Irish political orators.

Dan Donnelly (1788-1820)
Townsend Street, 2

In 1815 an Irishman called Wellington thrashed a Frenchman called Napoleon on the plain of Waterloo. In the same year an Irishman called Donnelly thrashed an Englishman called Cooper on the plain of the Curragh in

County Kildare. Of the two fighting Irishmen it was of course Donnelly who became the greater hero, for Dan Donnelly was the unassailable boxing champion of Ireland.

Born in Townsend Street, Donnelly's boxing career began accidentally, more in self-defence than aggression. His first real fight was with a hulking sailor who had insulted his father. Donnelly's performance on the occasion inspired his supporters to plan promotions.

His epic fight on 13 December 1815 with George Cooper, the champion of England, took place in a natural amphitheatre three-quarters of a mile east of the Curragh Camp at the foot of Racehorse Hill. The place is still known as Donnelly's Hollow. The crowds came in thousands. The hullabaloo was deafening as the champions fought for their respective countries. In the eleventh round Donnelly put Cooper down for good, and the Irish countryside reverberated with rejoicing.

Donnelly liked porter and always drank his winnings. For convenience, he acquired his own pub in Chancery Place behind the Four Courts. At thirty-two he died. River House, the Motor Taxation Office, bears a plaque: 'This was once the site of Donnelly's public house where the legendary Irish boxing champion, Dan Donnelly, died 18 February 1820.' At Donnelly's funeral, his supporters unyoked the horses and drew the hearse themselves all the way from Chancery Place to the grave in the Hospital Fields at Kilmainham.

Sir Patrick Dun (1642-1713)
Inn's Quay, 7

Sir Patrick Dun has a high place in heaven if his canonisation by generations of Dublin patients counts for anything. Long ago he became Saint Patrick Dun, and of course his hospital was given similar sanctification. A Scot, Dun was a good man, but not in the saintly sense. Born in Aberdeen, he studied medicine on the continent, eventually setting up in practice in Dublin. He developed a special relationship with the Royal College of Physicians of which he was elected President on five occasions between 1681 and 1706, serving some twelve years in all. He fought for, and gained, the independence of the college in controlling the teaching and practice of medicine in Ireland. In 1696 he was knighted.

In making his will, the college was still his greatest concern. To it he bequeathed his wealth, but legal difficulties led to prolonged disputation as to how the money should be used. Eventually a committee of the House of Lords decided on the foundation of a hospital to be known as Sir Patrick Dun's Hospital. With thirty beds, it was opened in 1809 on Artichoke Road, a locality no longer to be found on Dublin street maps. The purpose-built hospital on Grand Canal Street was probably the first Dublin hospital to possess an efficient water-carried drainage system. During the epidemics of 1826-28 and 1846-48 over ten thousand cases of fever were treated. It remained one of Dublin's principal hospitals until 'rationalisation' closed it in the mid-1980s.

Sir Patrick Dun died in 1713 and is buried in St Michan's Church in Church Street.

John Boyd Dunlop (1840-1921)
Leighton, 46 Ailesbury Road, 4

As a boy in Ayreshire John Boyd Dunlop wanted to be an inventor. Instead, he became a veterinary surgeon, setting up practice in Belfast. On his rounds in his dog-cart, the rough roads and cobblestones aroused his sympathy for those forced to give up cycling because of the jolting from their solid-tyred bicycles. It occurred to him to fill a rubber tube with compressed air. This, he theorised, might not alone reduce vibration, but might travel faster than a solid tyre. To a disc of wood he attached an air tyre made by himself. He tested this against the solid-tyred wheel from a bicycle. When rolled along the surface of a yard, the air tyre ran the entire length and, striking a gate with considerable force, bounded backwards. In the same way Dunlop rolled the solid-tyred wheel. It never even reached the gate.

He applied for a patent. When he revealed his invention, cycle dealers showed immense interest. A year later the original company, The Pneumatic Tyre Co., was founded at 67 Upper Stephen Street, Dublin. The building bears a plaque: 'The first pneumatic tyre factory in the world was started here in 1889 to make tyres under John Boyd Dunlop's patent of 7 December 1888.' To help to develop the tyre business, Dunlop came to live in Dublin. Lacking the business instinct to foresee the commercial possibilities of his invention, he sold his interest in the company, thereby sacrificing the wealth which might have been his. He lived at Leighton, 46 Ailesbury Road, Donnybrook, while his son John lived next door at Olney, 44 Ailesbury Road. The two houses now comprise the Belgian Embassy.

Dunlop didn't usually ride a bicycle. In 1888 he bought one for demonstration purposes and restored the public's enthusiasm for cycling: a Belfast cyclist was cautioned for exceeding the speed limit; an Irish rider won a London marathon. The demand became so great, the Pneumatic Tyre

John Boyd Dunlop

Co., found difficulty in meeting orders.

During thirty years of residence in Dublin, Dunlop became a familiar figure. Chairman of Messrs Todd Burns of Henry Street, he was still a handsome man in his eighties: tall, erect, with luxurious white hair and a flowing white beard. The tragedy of his life was the early death of his son, John. They are buried in Deansgrange Cemetery.

Hilton Edwards (1903-1982)
4 Harcourt Terrace, 2

A Londoner by birth, and an implacable Englishman to the end of his life, Hilton Edwards came of Irish stock. Though he didn't shout it loudly, his maternal grandfather was an Irishman named Murphy. His education gave him no insight into Ireland or her history. He trained both as an actor and a singer and toured England, principally in Shakespearian drama, and played at the Old Vic. In 1927, at short notice, he was engaged by Anew McMaster to fill a sudden vacancy in his Irish touring company. Thus it was that in Enniscorthy, County Wexford, Hilton Edwards and Mícheál MacLiammóir, the founders of the Dublin Gate Theatre, first met. As Edwards put it: 'MacLiammóir and I, with the assistance of Madame Bannard Cogley and Gearóid Ó Lochainn, and with Michael Scott as architect, converted an ancient and beautiful Georgian concert hall into the Gate Theatre.'

A director, an actor, and a master of light and shadow, Hilton Edwards was possessed by a passion for perfect theatrical presentation. He despised slovenliness and insincerity in those who professed to be actors. Making a comparison, he once said: 'The English stage is a well-trimmed velvet lawn, the Irish an exuberant heather-clad hillside.' A frayed temper was often a feature of his rehearsals, when his players might become 'a lazy lot of undisciplined, inaudible, ineffective, heavy-handed, wooden-legged, self-satisfied so-and-so's. Look at you all,' he would bellow, 'no wonder you let yourselves be oppressed for seven hundred years!' But he got results!

In his criticisms of Ireland and the Irish he could coin a memorable aphorism, as for instance: 'It is impossible to live in Ireland without some inner compensation for a climate best suited to fish in summer, and polar bears in winter, yet fit on a few unpredictable days of the year for the gods,' or 'No Irishman can believe that if he is not Pope or Emperor or movie star, it is because of any lack of ability in himself.'

A Freeman of the City of Dublin, Edwards lived at the same Dublin address as his partner, MacLiammóir One of his most telling remarks was, 'It is dedication that gives to certain artists the quality of greatness.' His own dedication was never in doubt, nor was Hilton Edwards's greatness.

Robert Emmet (1778-1803)
124 St Stephen's Green, 2

Of all the heroic martyrs in Irish history none can compare with the romantic martyrdom of the 'bould

4 Haymarket, 7

Robert Emmet, the darlin' of Erin'. Between the Sacred Heart and the Blessed Virgin, his oleograph held its honoured place on the walls of countless Irish homes. But to the British military authorities, he was another Irish traitor, a misguided young man of respectable background who had challenged Dublin Castle by appearing on a Saturday night in Patrick Street dressed up in a general's uniform, making himself the centre of a swirling rabble of drunken louts. The full significance of Emmet's effort at rebellion was only afterwards properly assessed when the authorities admitted that it was 'as formidable in its preparation and means of doing mischief as any in history'.

He was the seventeenth and youngest child of Dr and Mrs Robert Emmet of 124 St Stephen's Green (since demolished). After schooling at Samuel Whyte's Academy in Grafton Street, Emmet entered Trinity College. There he made two friends: Thomas Moore who was to immortalise him in poetry, and Richard Curran to whose sister, Sarah, he became betrothed. Influenced by the United Irishmen, Emmet's contributions to the Historical Society were so advanced, they made him a marked man. He had to leave Trinity without a degree. Often he took refuge in a dug-out under his father's country house, Casino, on the Dundrum Road, now Mount St Mary's Monastery.

Wholesale arrests followed the aborted rebellion in 1803. Emmet could have escaped to France. Instead, he sheltered in Mount Drummond Avenue, Harold's Cross, to keep in contact with Sarah Curran at the Priory, Rathfarnham. Here he was arrested by the notorious Major Sirr. Sarah's letters identified him. They also led to a public denunciation of his daughter by the famous lawyer, John Philpot Curran, who also refused Emmet's request to defend him. In the greatest speech ever made from the dock by a condemned prisoner, Emmet concluded thus:

'Let my memory be left in oblivion and my tomb remain uninscribed until other times and other men can do justice to my character. When my country takes her place among the nations of the earth, then and not till then, let my epitaph be written.'

Presented to the people of Ireland in 1966 by Irish-American admirers, a statue of Emmet by Jerome Connor stands opposite the site of the demolished house on St Stephen's Green.

Sir Thomas Farrell RHA (1827-1900)
Redesdale, Stillorgan

Terence Farrell RHA (1798-1876), the father of Sir Thomas, belonged to a dynasty of Farrell sculptors. Born in County Longford where his grandfather owned stone quarries, Terence trained as a sculptor in Dublin. He lived at 11 Warrington Place, and in 1828 he set up at 106 Lower Gloucester Street. His memorial to the Reverend Charles Wolfe, the author of *The Burial of Sir John Moore*, is in St Patrick's Cathedral.

Reared in an atmosphere of carving and chiselling, Terence Farrell trained three of his sons to follow him as sculptors: James RHA (1821-1891); Thomas RHA (1827-1900) and Michael (1834-1855). Of the three it was the shy and diffident Thomas who was to distinguish himself in the adornment of his native city with some of its most beautiful sculpture, monuments which will stand as much to the genius of the man who carved them as to the famous people they represent. He lived at 30 Mountjoy Square before moving to Redesdale, Stillorgan.

Assisted by his brother Michael, until his early death, Thomas Farrell's work soon made him the obvious successor to Dublin's famous sculptors,

John Foley and John Hogan. After public competition his design was accepted for the bas-relief on the Wellington Monument in the Phoenix Park. Representing the last charge at Waterloo, the action of both horses and men make them appear to spring from the bronze panels. Thomas Farrell is here seen to magnificent advantage.

In 1893 he was elected president of the Royal Hibernian Academy, and in 1894 he was knighted by Queen Victoria. Always a retiring man, on one occasion he fled in terror from the unveiling of a piece of his work lest it might prove unacceptable. The full-length statues of William Smith O'Brien and Sir John Gray in O'Connell Street are by Farrell. There are also several notable examples of his work in Glasnevin Cemetery: a recumbent figure of Cardinal McCabe over his grave to the left of the main entrance, and a bust of Sir John Gray over his vault near the O'Connell round tower. Appropriately, the most dramatic is his full-length statue of Barry Sullivan, the Irish actor, as Hamlet with the skull of Yorick in his hand.

Sir Thomas Farrell is buried in Glasnevin Cemetery.

John Field (1782-1837)
Golden Lane, 8

Because the Fields had music in their blood, young John had greatness thrust upon him. His grandfather was a church organist. His father was a violinist at the Theatre Royal, Crow Street. At the age of seven John began piano lessons under his grandfather. Early virtuosity resulted from strict, even unhappy supervision, for his grandfather lived in the same house. The boy soon produced his first musical compositions. In 1792 he was billed for an appearance at the Rotunda Concert Rooms: 'The young Master Field, a youth of eight years of age, will perform on the pianoforte a new concerto composed by Signor Giordani.' They had cheated. The boy was nearly ten!

When Field's father joined an orchestra in Bath, the family left Dublin, later moving to London. Here John became a pupil of Clementi who exploited his genius for personal gain. At the age of fifteen Field played his own first concerto at the Haymarket Theatre, and afterwards at Covent Garden. Clementi used him as a piano salesman, demonstrating instruments by performing on them. His playing was so sensational that people were more attracted to the player than the instrument. Clementi became jealous.

An awkward, overgrown boy, Field was taken by Clementi to Paris. When he began to play he became an artist of high technical perfection. Paris found him a sensation. Still selling pianos, Clementi took him to St Petersburg, and thence to Moscow where he abandoned him. Field's virtuosity soon won the patronage of the Russian nobility. In 1814 he published his first nocturnes, or 'night-pieces'. They were an immediate success. Though Chopin later immortalised the form, he was aged four when Field invented the nocturne. Seven concer-

tos for piano and orchestra followed, in addition to sonatas and nocturnes.

Settling in Moscow, Field toured Europe. He was acclaimed everywhere. Success had made him a Bohemian. His marriage failed after which drunkenness, debauchery and indolence took over. Aged forty-five 'the first poet of the piano' died unexpectedly. He is buried in Moscow under a tombstone erected by 'his grateful friends and scholars'. He is also remembered in Dublin. At its junction with Bride Street, near John Field Road, his portrait in bronze set in a granite pillar looks down the lane where once his music reverberated.

'Barry Fitzgerald' (1888-1961) and Arthur Shields (1896-1970) 1 Walworth Road, Portobello, 8

Brothers, William Joseph (known as Barry Fitzgerald) and Arthur Shields were born at 1 Walworth Road. The family moved to 12 Vernon Avenue, Clontarf, where the boys attended Green Lane National School and the Merchant Tailors' School. Arthur gained the nickname 'Boss' which he retained for the rest of his life. He joined the Abbey Theatre in 1914 where he played 132 parts before leaving for Hollywood in 1939.

Following Arthur Shields, his brother Will became a part-time actor at the Abbey. He worked by day as a civil servant while living at Seafield Road, Clontarf. Later he shared a flat in St Stephen's Green with his friend Gabriel Fallon, another civil servant and part-time actor. Fallon called it 'the nearest resting place we could find in comfort and decency to the back gate of Dublin Castle'. To preserve his anonymity from his civil servant chiefs, Will Shields adopted the name Barry Fitzpatrick, but a printer's error rendered it Barry Fitzgerald, the name he retained and made world-famous.

Barry Fitzgerald made his mark in 1919 in Lady Gregory's *The Dragon*. While still a part-timer he created Captain Jackie Boyle in O'Casey's *Juno and the Paycock* in 1924, one of the greatest firsts ever seen at the Abbey, until his matchless Dublin bowsie, Fluther Good, in *The Plough and the Stars* in 1926, a part written specially for him by O'Casey. During theatre riots caused by *The Plough* armed men went to his home to kidnap him – or worse. Sensing trouble, he hadn't gone home the previous night.

Fitzgerald wasn't an actor in the accepted sense. He was a great clown in the Chaplin mode. Yet he envied his brother Arthur for his ability to play straight parts. After the death of his great admirer, Lady Gregory, Fitzgerald left for Hollywood where he made forty-five films. For *Going My Way*, Bing Crosby won an Oscar for the best acting role and Barry Fitzgerald for his supporting role.

Then living at 50 Sandymount Avenue, Arthur Shield's greatest parts at the Abbey were Christy Mahon in Synge's *The Playboy of the Western World* and Canon Skerrit in *Shadow and Substance* by Paul Vincent Carroll. In Hollywood he appeared in countless films in feature roles until his death in Santa Barbara, California.

The brothers are buried side-by-side in Deansgrange Cemetery.

Lord Edward Fitzgerald (1763-1798) Leinster House, 2

There are many Dublin houses associated with Lord Edward Fitzgerald, the most colourful and tragic of Ireland's aristocratic revolutionaries. Born at Leinster House, now the seat of the Irish Government, he was the fifth son of the Duke of Leinster, head of the Fitzgeralds, Ireland's premier family. Lord Edward found Leinster House a melancholy place. 'It does not inspire the brightest ideas,' he said, a point worthy of note by our latterday legislators. Carton, near Maynooth, was the family's country seat. But their

Lord Edward Fitzgerald

favourite house was Frescati Lodge at Blackrock, County Dublin (since demolished).

Fighting with the British in America, Lord Edward was wounded in 1781. He was rescued and nursed by a negro, the 'faithful Tony', who remained Lord Edward's loyal servant for the rest of his life. The new French republic fascinated the Irish aristocrat. He renounced his title and was cashiered from the army. Henceforward he was a marked man. In 1792 he married Pamela, daughter of the Duke of Orleans, who was brother of the late King of France. The couple set up home at Frescati Lodge where, as Lord Edward wrote to his mother, they were enjoying 'the little bookroom, with its windows open, hearing the birds sing, and the place looking beautiful'.

Lord Edward's involvement with the United Irishmen forced him into hiding. With a reward of £1000 promised for his capture, his friend Lawless, a surgeon, organised many 'safe houses': Mrs Dillon's at the rear of Portobello Harbour; Cormick's, 119 Thomas Street; the Yellow Lion public house; the Brazen Head Inn, Lower Bridge Street (still in business); 20 Usher's Quay, the home of Francis Magan, who informed on Lord Edward, and finally the attic of Murphy's, the feather-sellers, 151-152 Thomas Street, where he was wounded and arrested by Major Sirr. A plaque marks the site of Murphy's house.

With his military training, and his knowledge of the methods used in the French Revolution, had Lord Edward

lived to lead the rising of 1798, things might have resulted differently. Instead, he was thrown into Newgate Jail where he died of his wound. Pamela, who had not been allowed to see him, had already been deported with her children never to return.

Lord Edward Fitzgerald is buried in the vaults of St Werburgh's Church near Dublin Castle. In the churchyard outside lies his implacable enemy, the infamous Major Sirr.

John Fitzgibbon, Earl of Clare (1746-1802)
6 Ely Place (formerly No. 10), 2

The grandfather of 'Black Jack' Fitzgibbon, otherwise the hated first Earl of Clare and Lord Chancellor of Ireland, was a Catholic peasant farmer in County Clare. His father was 'Wily John' Fitzgibbon of Ballinguile, Donnybrook, a period house which has since been demolished. 'Wily John' turned Protestant to become rich at the Bar. 'Black Jack' was educated at Trinity College and Oxford and rose rapidly as a barrister. Politically he opposed Grattan. He detested Roman Catholicism and bitterly opposed relief of any kind for that sect. 'Catholic Emancipation,' he said, 'as it is most stupidly and wickedly called, would only encourage them to proceed in their projects of treason.'

In 1793 the vote was given to the Catholics. Grattan favoured further relief. So did Lord Fitzwilliam who became Viceroy in 1795. Clare saw to it that Fitzwilliam was immediately recalled. An enraged mob attacked his house in Ely Place. Even the women were armed, their aprons full of paving stones. Ropes were fixed to his lamp-irons to hang him, but in his £7000 coach he managed to elude his attackers, suffering only minor injuries.

Following 1798, almost like another Cromwell, he advocated pitch-capping, floggings, hangings and even perpetual martial law. As a 'Visitor' (he was already Vice-Chancellor), he sat in Trinity College like a grand inquisitor to eliminate United Irishmen and sympathisers from staff and students. Those who failed to answer satisfactorily were automatically expelled. Thomas Moore satisfied 'Black Jack', but his friend Robert Emmet dared not face the ordeal, thus ending his university career.

Dr Richard Twiss, an English observer, came to Dublin and having viewed its society people, published his criticisms. In retaliation, an earthenware manufacturer printed Twiss's portrait on the bottom of his chamberpots. A daughter of 'Burn Chapel' Whaley, and a sister of 'Buck' Whaley of 86 St Stephen's Green, the Lord Chancellor's wife, Lady Clare, composed a ditty to accompany the portrait:

Here you may behold a liar,
Well deserving of hell-fire:
Everyone who likes may p –
Upon the learned Doctor T –.

In Irish history and folklore, Clare stands as *the* protagonist and chief architect of the Union of Ireland with Britain in 1800. Public hatred of the man didn't end with his death. On the day of his funeral another mob gath-

6 Ely Place, 2

ered in Ely Place to cheer and jeer and pelt his coffin with dead cats.

George Fitzmaurice (1878-1963)
3 Harcourt Street, 2

Son of a North Kerry manse, and of a mixed marriage, George Fitzmaurice was reared a Protestant, while his sisters grew up as Catholics. With this background, the future dramatist inherited a unique insight into the religious and social cultures of the Kerry peasantry. As a boy he was fascinated with the richly colourful dialect of the locality.

In 1907 when Fitzmaurice's first play, *The Country Dressmaker*, was scheduled for production at the Abbey Theatre, Yeats, likening him to Synge, said they would require two hundred police at the theatre for the first night.

In fact the comedy, with the magic of its Kerry idiom, was rapturously received, proving Yeats a false prophet. It heralded a new and exciting playwright.

The Pie-Dish, a tragedy, followed in 1908. Hungry for comedy, the Abbey audience wasn't enthusiastic. W J Lawrence, a critic of the time, dismissed this powerful morality play as 'A studied insult to playgoers ... a lot of gabble strung together.' In 1913 Fitzmaurice's *The Magic Glasses* received a too-glowing reception, proving its author's undoing. Through jealousy, it was said, Yeats and Lady Gregory were not amused, and for the future kept the Kerryman's plays out of the theatre repertoire.

Like so many young Irishmen of his time, Fitzmaurice joined the British army and fought in World War I. Afterwards he became a civil servant, working for many years in the Land Commission. In 1923 he submitted his fantasy, *The Dandy Dolls*, to the Abbey. The grudge held good, and the play was turned down, a bitter blow to a sensitive writer. Thus, Fitzmaurice lost interest in the theatre. Worse, he became a recluse, indulging himself in writing plays for his own amusement.

In 1963 the eighty-six-year-old playwright was found dead. Beside him in his threadbare room an old suitcase held his life's work – the manuscripts of his plays. A plaque marks No. 3 Harcourt Street, next door to Edward Carson's birthplace.

**Colonel James Fitzmaurice
(1898-1965)
35 Mountjoy Cottages
(now Cowley Place),
North Circular Road, 7**

A pioneer to whom adventure was part of living, James Fitzmaurice became a world hero in April 1928, when he acted as co-pilot of the 300 hp Junkers monoplane, *Bremen*. Its thirty-seven-hour epic flight from Baldonnel, County Dublin, to Greenly Island, Newfoundland, was the first successful east-west Atlantic flight. With his German colleagues, Captain Hermann Köhl, co-pilot, and Baron Gunther von Hünefeld, owner of the *Bremen*, Fitzmaurice thus carved his name in the history of aviation.

James Fitzmaurice was the son of a Mountjoy prison officer. Aged eighteen, he joined the British army and served at the Somme and at Arras. On his transfer to the new Royal Air Force, he made his first historic flight in 1919 – the first night-mail cross-channel flight from Folkstone to Boulogne. In 1922 he left the RAF to join the newly-formed Flying Corps of the Irish Free State Army.

Though all attempts had failed, Fitzmaurice still dreamed of flying the Atlantic. The opportunity came in March 1928 when the *Bremen* arrived at Baldonnell from Berlin piloted by Köhl, now all set for an attempt on the Atlantic. A wealthy German aristocrat, von Hünefeld was intent on winning prestige for the Fatherland. They invited Fitzmaurice to join them as co-pilot and consequently the *Bremen*

Left to right: *Major Fitzmaurice, Floyd Bennett, "Duke" Schiller and Bernt Balchen*

news. Then a wireless message from Labrador announced: 'German plane at Greenly Island ... Crew safe.' After battling against cold, hunger, sleeplessness, blizzards, fog, ice formation, even an oil leak, the Atlantic had been conquered.

Dublin made Freemen of the *Bremen*'s crew. Fitzmaurice left the Army for the United States. In 1939 he opened a club for servicemen in London. He returned to Dublin in 1951 and lived in retirement in the Hatch Hotel.

carried the Irish tricolour alongside the German flag. Fitzmaurice forecast with accuracy: 'This country will be at the centre of trans-Atlantic aviation in the future.'

Early on 12 April, helped by the headlights of motor cars, the heavily-laden monoplane trundled down Baldonnel's grass runway, barely topping the trees at the end of the airfield. At ninety mph the *Bremen* passed over Galway. After that there was silence, for she carried no wireless. For over two days the world's telephone lines hummed in search of

John Henry Foley (1818-1874)
6 Montgomery Street
(now Foley Street), 1

The greatest sculptor of his time, the work of Foley is to be seen from Cork to Calcutta. Amongst his London pieces the best known is the figure of the Prince Consort, the centre-piece of the Albert Memorial in Kensington Gardens. While he worked on this figure Queen Victoria visited his studio to see its progress. This commission was the culminating achievement of Foley's career.

Born at 6 Montgomery Street (the Monto district of *Ulysses*), young Foley was introduced to sculpture by his grandfather, himself a sculptor. He attended the Royal Dublin Society of Sculpture, then in Leinster House, where he was trained by John Smyth, son of Edward Smyth, Gandon's sculptor for the Custom House and the Four Courts. Foley won so many prizes some jealous students broke a model of his. He stayed in school all night to re-make the model. Aged fifteen, the Royal Academy in London accepted him as a pupil. By the age of twenty-two he was in the first rank of living artists.

Foley married and settled in London, giving every hour to his work. 'I've got to create,' he said. But in fact he took too many commissions and, reluctantly, he had to employ assistants. Dublin is fortunate in its wealth of Foley statuary. Grattan, Burke and Goldsmith are familiar pieces in College Green. Lord Ardilaun sits comfortably in St Stephen's Green, as does Sir Benjamin Lee Guinness near the south porch of St Patrick's Cathedral. There are three pieces in the Royal College of Physicians in Kildare Street: Sir Henry Marsh (1790-1860); Sir Dominic Corrigan (1802-1880); and William Stokes (1804-1878). Dublin's Albert Memorial stands in the shadow of the Natural History Museum in Upper Merrion Street, a handsome, though hidden, monument. Birr, Tuam and Lisburn also

possess pieces, and of course 'The Statue' in Cork is Foley's tribute to Father Theobald Mathew, the apostle of temperance.

Foley became wealthy by pandering to the requirements of the British Empire. For instance, there are three of his equestrian statues in Calcutta. Though ill, he insisted on continuing his work on the O'Connell monument, now in O'Connell Street. He had completed the figure of O'Connell when he died. Eight years later Thomas Brock completed the monument. Foley is buried in St Paul's Cathedral.

Percy French (1854-1920)
35 Mespil Road, 4

'I was born a boy and have remained one ever since.' Percy French's self-assessment applied as aptly to Samuel Lover. Both were talented writers, artists and entertainers. But while French obeyed his father, however dilatorily, in becoming an engineer instead of an artist, Lover refused to become a stockbroker and was thrown out by his father, a brutal man of business.

Born at Cloonyquin, County Roscommon, William Percy French enjoyed an idyllic childhood, growing into the most easygoing of boys. A clever lad, in so many directions, it was difficult to pin his talents down. After schooling at Windermere College in England and at Foyle College in Derry, he entered the School of Engineering at Trinity College. Diversions, like the banjo, lawn tennis and watercolour painting, prolonged his course, but eventually he emerged with an engineering degree. As he said: 'I believe the Board were afraid I should apply for a pension, if I stayed any longer in TCD.'

As engineer to the Board of Works and surveyor of drains for County Cavan, Percy French familiarised himself with Irish rural character, afterwards reflected with mastery in his songs (he will always be remembered for 'The Mountains of Mourne'). He earned good money as an entertainer, and this he invested in a distillery. He became redundant and the distillery collapsed. Never downhearted, he became editor of *The Jarvey*, a weekly comic paper, and he married on the strength of it. One year later his wife died in childbirth. He married again and, as an entertainer, toured Canada, the United States and the West Indies.

Percy French was a frequent visitor at 49 Ailesbury Road, the home of his brother-in-law, Sir Alfred Irwin. Between 1894 and 1900 he lived at 35 Mespil Road. There is a memorial seat opposite the house on the bank of the Grand Canal at Wilton Place. The inscription suggests an impish humour echoing from the grave:

Remember me is all I ask
And yet
If the remembrance prove a task
Forget.

James Gandon (1743-1823)
Cannonbrook, Lucan

In 1780 Gandon had attained a high professional reputation as an architect in London. Princess Dashkof invited him to work in St Petersburg. About the same time he received an invitation from John Beresford, Chief Commissioner of the Irish Revenue, to come to Dublin to build a custom house. Gandon arrived in April 1781. He found Ireland singularly lacking in the fine arts: 'There are few painters of eminence,' he said, 'and but two architects, properly so called.'

Begun in August 1781 and completed ten years later, at a cost of £400,000, the Dublin Custom House is Gandon's masterpiece. While working on it he contended with many troubles: sea-sodden, the ground required draining, pumping and extensive pile-driving; the Dublin Corporation resented the work and passed hostile motions; the mob threatened and the drunken workers continually demanded increases in wages. For convenience, Gandon took a house at 7 Mecklenburg Street, near the site. The locality became known as 'Monto', Dublin's brothel area. The Custom House is embellished with splendid sculptures, including the Riverine Heads by Edward Smyth, Gandon's 'discovery', described by him as 'the equal of Michelangelo'.

Between 1785 and 1802 he worked on the Four Courts, which cost £200,000 to build. Meanwhile work had begun on the King's Inns. This was interrupted when Gandon prudently returned to London for the duration of the 1798 rebellion. Having developed gout, he passed the King's Inns project to his pupil, Henry Aaron Baker. He had acquired Cannonbrook, a country house in Lucan, and as his

Cannonbrook, Lucan

son James relates: 'He determined to indulge in the honourable retirement to which he had so justly earned his title by an active professional career of nearly sixty years.'

Though now in a bathchair, Gandon enjoyed the trees and lawns of his beloved Cannonbrook – his 'Tivoli' he called it. When George IV passed through Lucan to the Curragh in 1821, he intended 'to have conferred on Mr Gandon the mark of distinction to which his pre-eminent talents and useful career so well entitled him'. But unfortunately Gandon was too ill on the day. On his death the people of Lucan refused carriages, preferring to show their respect by walking the sixteen miles to and from Drumcondra Churchyard where, at his request, Gandon was buried with his life-long friend, Captain Francis Grose, the antiquarian.

Oliver St John Gogarty (1878-1957)
5 Parnell Square East
(formerly Rutland Square), 1

Gogarty was like a meteor whose white brilliance blinds the beholder. He was all things to all men: poet, pilot, politician, athlete, surgeon and wit. Like other houses in Rutland Square in the 1880s, his birthplace, No. 5, was an opulent house, backed by butlers, coachmen and servants. A prosperous Catholic doctor, Gogarty senior also owned a rural retreat called Fairfield (since demolished) on the river Tolka out by Glasnevin. In keeping with such a life-style, young Oliver was educated at Stoneyhurst, Clongowes Wood and Trinity College, Dublin. As a student he shared 'an apostolate of irreverence' with his friend James Joyce. He sometimes re-

treated to the Martello Tower in Sandycove to write his poetry. Joyce
joined him in September 1904 to work
on his novel, *Stephen Hero*. They
quarrelled and Joyce left after a few
days. Gogarty would have thrown him
out sooner but he was afraid 'if Jim
made a name some day, it would be
remembered against him'. Jim made
his name and also made Gogarty the
original of Buck Mulligan in *Ulysses*, which displeased him. Despite
the brevity of his stay, the tower has
become the 'Joyce Tower', containing a museum of Joycean memora-
bilia.

When Gogarty married and qualified – in that order – he lived at 17
Earlsfort Terrace. In 1907 he purchased a Queen Anne-style house
(since demolished), No. 15 Ely Place,
built as his home by Sir Thomas
Deane, an architect. About ten years
later he moved his consulting rooms to
32 St Stephen's Green, beside the
Shelbourne Hotel. This house bears a
plaque. Between 1915 and 1917 he
lived at Seaview, a cottage on Sorrento
Road, Dalkey. He bought Renvyle
House, Connemara, which was burnt
out in a Civil War reprisal when he
became a senator in the Free State
Government. It was rebuilt as an hotel.
Gogarty's last years were spent in an
apartment on East 61st Street, New
York.

At his request, he was buried in
Ballinakill Cemetery, half-way between Letterfrack and Cleggan in
Connemara. He composed his own
epitaph. Reading it on the windswept
hillside above Shanbollard Lake, it

comes like wisdom from one who
knows the Great Beyond:

*Our friends go with us as we go
Down the long path where Beauty
   wends.
Where all we love foregather, so
Why should we fear to join our
   friends?*

Oliver Goldsmith (1728-1774)
35 Trinity College, 2

Born at Pallas near Ballymahon,
County Longford, Goldsmith inherited his indolence from his father, the
Reverend Charles Goldsmith.
Oliver's first school report damned
him as an 'impenetrably stupid boy'.
He progressed from the village school
at Lissoy to Elphin and thence to Athlone and to Patrick Hughes's School
in Edgeworthstown. He learned Latin
and French from a priest at Ballymahon who had been educated in France.
Money was scarce, but in 1745 his
mother arranged his admission to
Trinity College as a sizar, which
meant sweeping floors and waiting on
the Fellows' table in return for board
and lodging and tuition. He lived in a
garret at the top of No. 35 (since demolished). His easy-going manner
drew the attention of his bad-tempered
tutor, the Reverend Theaker Wilder,
whose academic passions were logic
and mathematics. Goldsmith sneered:
'Mathematics seems a science to
which the meanest intellects are
equal.' Once admonished for his part
in a student rag ending in several
deaths, at the age of nineteen he was
beaten by the Reverend Wilder for
holding a noisy party in his garret.

Having acquired bad habits he was never to lose – gambling, irresponsibility and fecklessness – there was something in Goldsmith's personality that endeared him to men of distinction in London: Johnson, Reynolds and Garrick. But it was the Dubliner, Edmund Burke, who most understood the poet's failings in getting and recklessly spending his considerable literary income. At his height in 1774, he was with his friends in London's St James's Coffee House when for amusement they turned to writing one another's epitaphs. David Garrick wrote Goldsmith's:

Here lies Nolly Goldsmith,
For shortness called Noll,
Who wrote like an angel,
But talked like poor Poll.

Sadly prophetic, a few weeks later Goldsmith was dead. Joshua Reynolds and Dr Johnson arranged his funeral for Westminster Abbey. But it was then discovered that Goldsmith had left debts of £2,000. And so he was buried quietly in the Temple Burying Ground in an unmarked grave.

Maud Gonne (1866-1953)
Roebuck House, Clonskeagh, 14

A vision of beauty, a goddess moved by the lot of the underdog, an inspiration for great love poetry; indeed, the personification of Cathleen ní Houlihan herself – all this is but part of the legend that made the restless spirit of Maud Gonne. Her life complemented that of her contemporary, Constance Markievicz. The one was a leader of men; the other an inspiration to them.

Evictions in the 1880s converted her to Irish nationalism. Not even the sovereign of England could then downface this angel of Irish destiny. When in 1900 Queen Victoria treated fifteen thousand children to buns in the Phoenix Park, Maud Gonne treated thirty thousand of the hungry to bread and butter in Clonturk Park. Her campaign for free school meals pointed out that under threat of imprisonment Irish parents were by English law obliged to send their children to school, yet Ireland was the only country where no provision was made to feed the children thus taken into custody. By 1911 she was feeding two thousand children daily, and twenty years later she was still campaigning for the same cause.

In 1900 she founded *Inghinidhe na hÉireann* (the Daughters of Erin) at 32 Lower Abbey Street. Drama was included in its activities. Deeply in love with Maud Gonne, Yeats wrote the play *Cathleen ní Houlihan* for her. She consented to play the part because she considered the play good propaganda for Ireland. On 2 April 1902 on the little stage of St Teresa's Hall in Clarendon Street, hers was not a performance. She lived the part, and ever afterwards she *was* Cathleen ní Houlihan.

Having lived in France she hated the *entente cordiale*. She wanted the sympathy of France for Ireland. In 1917 she returned to Dublin and lived at 73 St Stephen's Green. The widow of John MacBride (executed in 1916), she became a familiar figure in Dublin: tall, graceful, in widow's weeds, her solemn black denoting her mourning for Ireland rather than for her husband. In 1922 she moved to Roebuck House where she lived for the rest of her life. She was jailed in 1923 for her activities on behalf of political prisoners. After a hunger-strike of twenty days she was carried from Kilmainham on a stretcher amid the cheers of faithful followers.

Roebuck House, Clonskeagh, 14

In 1938 Maud Gonne published her memoirs, *A Servant of the Queen*, the Queen being Ireland of course. When Yeats died she envied him, while she waited for release for 'the last big adventure'. She is buried in the Republican plot in Glasnevin Cemetery.

Kathleen Goodfellow (1891-1980)
4 Morehampton Road,
Donnybrook, 4

At an angle at the junction of Morehampton Road and Wellington Place stands a stately gateway leading to a grove. That this haven has escaped the 'developers' is a mystery, until one approaches the gate. On the left pier are the words 'The Grove'; on the right, 'In memory of the Donor, Kathleen Goodfellow'. A wealthy woman, and a life-long resident at No. 4 Morehampton Road, Miss Goodfellow abhorred the cutting of trees, or even flowers. On her death she bequested the triangular grove to An Taisce (the National Trust of Ireland) provided it be used as a bird sanctuary. But her philanthropy went further than the provision of birdsong for the people of the locality.

A very private person, Kathleen Goodfellow wrote poetry and fiction under the pseudonym, Michael Scott. Published by the Talbot Press in 1921, her *Three Tales of the Times* tells of life under the Black and Tans. Her real literary contribution was to the *Dublin Magazine*, not so much as a writer, but as its financial godmother. Launched in 1923, this literary journal lasted for thirty-five years, edited by its founder, Seamus O'Sullivan, the pseudonym of James Starkey, Litt.D (TCD). Married to Estella Solomons, the artist, the Starkeys found their home at the Grange, Rathfarnham, inconvenient.

56 St Stephen's Green, 2

collection of pictures which Goodfellow presented to the Sligo County Library Art Gallery.

Henry Grattan (1746-1820)
56 St Stephen's Green, 2

Eloquence and incorruptible patriotism marked the life of Henry Grattan. His passions were the liberty of Ireland and the freedom of her Catholics. Born at Belcamp House, Raheny, it was ironic that he should share the same birth-year, and the same class in school and university as John Fitzgibbon. At Trinity College they rivalled one another for academic honours. More than any man, Fitzgibbon, as the hated Earl of Clare, destroyed everything Grattan did for the good of Ireland.

A lawyer, politics attracted him. At seventeen he differed politically with his father. As a result, Grattan, though an only son, was disinherited. Writing from Belcamp after his father's death, he said: 'I write this letter from Belcamp where I am a guest, not an owner. I tell myself by way of consolation that happiness is not the gift of any one spot.' The loss of his family home was Grattan's first great sacrifice as an Irish patriot.

As a law student in London he spent much time in the galleries of the Commons and the Lords, listening to great orators. His landlady complained that at night he walked the garden addressing an invisible someone called 'Mr Speaker'. On his return Grattan lived in many Dublin lodgings: Granby Row, Kildare Street, Baggot Street and Dame Street. He

On the invitation of Kathleen Goodfellow they moved next door to her, to No. 2 Morehampton Road, a most satisfactory arrangement for all concerned, for Kathleen and Estella were long-time friends.

From this address Seamus O'Sullivan continued to edit the *Dublin Magazine* until his death in 1958. This wouldn't have been possible without the financial backing of his patron who never wanted to be seen, always insisting on remaining in the background. An only child, the daughter of a building contractor (he had built numbers 2-12 Morehampton Road), Kathleen Goodfellow was left well-off, devoting herself to writing, translating, and supporting the work of many artists. Though shy of photographers, she sat for portraits by Estella Solomons (1882-1968). Two of these may be seen in the remarkable leased temporary homes, first on Lower Rathmines Road and later at 56 St Stephen's Green, part of Mary Aikenhead's future St Vincent's Hospital. He also lived at 84 St Stephen's Green, a house later occupied by professor Edmond McWeeney of University College, Dublin. Called to the Bar, he found the Four Courts a disagreeable place. 'The lawyers', he said, 'are an ardent, rather than an eloquent, society.' In 1775 politics finally won him.

Grattan reached his political zenith in 1782. Backed by the representatives of a hundred thousand armed Irish Volunteers in College Green, he declared the independence of the Irish parliament. Dublin responded with pealing bells, bonfires and cheering crowds. Parliament rewarded him with £50,000 for his services to the nation. He bought an old coaching inn at Tinnehinch in the Dargle valley in County Wicklow, where, in the disillusionment of his old age, he remembered the Irish independence he had won – Grattan's Parliament – only to be lost eighteen years later with the Act of Union. 'I sat by its cradle,' he said, 'and I followed its hearse.'

Robert Graves (1797-1853)
4 Merrion Square South
(now 56 Merrion Square), 2

In the nineteenth century Dublin gained an international reputation as a medical teaching centre. The inspiration came principally from the Meath Hospital where it was attributable to the teamwork of two famous physicians who there perfected their method of bedside teaching. They were William Stokes and Robert Graves. Stokes, as well as William Wilde, had been among Graves's pupils. The names of Graves and Stokes are still used by doctors wherever medicine is practised.

Born in Dublin, Graves qualified at Trinity College in 1818. He then did a three-year post-graduate tour of European medical centres, covering part of his journey in the company of William Turner, the painter. He believed in continual post-graduate education and that doctors should always preserve the humility to learn from observation. 'To preserve life,' he said, 'is the noblest gift man has received from his creator.' The discovery of percussion by Auenbrugger (1722-1809) and of auscultation by Laennec (1781-1826) were new ideas which Graves brought back from the continent. He also introduced the stethoscope to Dublin.

Famine fever was prevalent in the 1820s. In 1832 there was a devastating cholera epidemic in Dublin. Graves concluded that many of these deaths had resulted from malnutrition. His treatment was in accordance, and he wished his epitaph to be: 'He fed fevers.' In 1835 he first described exophthalmic goitre, still known as Graves' Disease.

Graves is buried in Mount Jerome Cemetery.

Sir John Gray (1815-1875)
Charleville House, Rathmines, 6

A medical doctor with wider interests than medicine, John Gray was born at

Claremorris, County Mayo, and educated in Glasgow. As Dr Gray he lived at 7 Blakeney Parade, Sandymount. He became editor of the *Freemans' Journal* newspaper in 1841 and sole proprietor in 1850. He then lived at Westbourne, Roundtown, a village in Rathfarnham said to abound in handsome seats and villas. Unopposed, he was returned three times as MP for Kilkenny. As a town councillor – and as a doctor – he worked energetically for an improvement in Dublin's sanitary services and water supplies. His fame rests on his success in discontinuing the old canal supplies and substituting the purity of the Vartry water.

The Vartry scheme was begun in 1863, when Gray was chairman of the Dublin Corporation Waterworks. The four hundred-acre Roundwood reservoir was laid out to hold seven months supply of water. Passing through filter beds, the piped water then travelled twenty-two miles to a storage reservoir at Stillorgan which held eighty-four million gallons, and was situated two hundred and fifty feet above the level of Dublin's quays. The water then passed to the city boundary at Leeson Street Bridge (where the pipes can still be seen), and thence was distributed throughout the city. Completed in 1868, the cost was £550,000. For ensuring a clean water supply for Dublin, Gray was knighted by the Lord Lieutenant. About 1860 he left Rathfarnham for Charleville House, Charleville Road, Rathmines. His country retreat was The Strand, Ballybrack, County Dublin.

He died in Bath aged sixty, his early death being ascribed to overwork. Surrounded by four figures symbolising Gray's social and scientific interests, a massive bust by Thomas Farrell RHA (1827-1900), adorns his grave in Glasnevin Cemetery. Erected by public subscription, Farrell's statue of Gray holds a commanding position between those of William Smith O'Brien and James Larkin in Dublin's O'Connell Street.

Alice Stopford Green (1847-1929)
90 St Stephen's Green, 2

For eleven years, between 1918 and 1929, this house was the hospitable meeting place of intellectuals, scholars, politicians – all indeed who had ideas for the peaceful advancement of Ireland. The hostess was Alice Stopford Green, the historian. Known affectionately as Widow Green, after forty years residence in London, and at the age of seventy, she had returned to Ireland because for her, as for many, after 1916 everything had 'changed, changed utterly'.

Her house in London had been a similar meeting place. In her varied interests she had worked with John O'Leary, Bernard Shaw, Sir Roger Casement and Bulmer Hobson. It was there a committee was set up in 1914 and a fund of £1500 created – a considerable portion subscribed by Mrs Green – which led to the epic voyage of the arms-laden *Asgard* from Germany to Howth. It was also from there that she conducted her vigorous campaign to save the life of the condemned Casement in 1916.

Alice Stopford was born at the rectory in Kells. In 1875 she married the Reverend John Richard Green, who later relinquished his ministry to become an English historian. Without a degree, Alice began the study of history, and to research for her husband. After his death she became an historian in her own right. She published *The Making of Ireland and Its Undoing* (1908), a treatise showing that a flourishing Irish civilisation had been smashed by England in the sixteenth century. Her *Irish Nationality* followed in 1911. Her last book was *The History of the Early Irish State to 1014*.

No. 90 St Stephen's Green was repeatedly raided by British forces, unable to distinguish between the various shades of Irish nationalist opinion, during the Anglo-Irish War. On the foundation of the Irish Free State in 1922, Widow Green was made a senator. Like the other senators of the time, her house was threatened with burning by the Republican forces. Unlike many senators, her house wasn't burnt. A military guard was installed and the widow fed her garrison nightly with 'plain suppers'.

Lady Gregory (1852-1932)
'The Standard', Harcourt Street, 2

For the last thirty years of her life Lady Gregory was much involved as a founder and a director of the Abbey Theatre. This meant absenting herself from her beloved Coole Park, her historic mansion near Gort, County Galway. Today she would have had an apart-

ment in Dublin. In the early 1900s she 'put up at The Standard', otherwise the Standard Hotel (since demolished) which stood at the corner of Clonmel and Harcourt streets. Her home-from-home, 'The Standard', as she called it, was a warm and plush Victorian establishment which provided every comfort. Here she entertained her guests, here she brought 'the Chicks', her grandchildren, when they came from Coole to see another new play by grandma, and here she returned to rest after many a day's endurance of artistic temperaments and tiresome rehearsals.

Augusta Persse was born at Roxborough, near Loughrea, County Galway, an estate of four thousand acres. When she married Sir William Gregory, her senior by thirty-five years, in 1880 as his second wife, she moved some twenty miles up the road to Coole Park. As mistress and hostess at Coole, her forty years of widowhood were devoted to Ireland and its culture. As a motivating spirit in the Irish Literary Renaissance she thought with the thoughts of the Irish people and felt with their feelings.

Lady Gregory made Coole a cultural hothouse, and became a reputable dramatist. She had a role in the writing of *Cathleen ní Houlihan*. Her demesne, with its lakes and its seven woods, and her encouragement, provided Yeats with a spiritual home to which he responded. Of Coole he said: 'I love that house more than all houses.' He dedicated poetry to the place and to the Gregory family. Of Robert, Lady Gregory's only son, killed in the first world war, he wrote:

Soldier, scholar, horseman, he,
As 'twere all life's epitome.
What made us dream that he could
    comb gray hair?

As prophesied by Yeats, Coole was destroyed by the enemies of culture. The 'developers' spared the out-houses, where pilgrims can now take tea.

Arthur Griffith (1871-1922)
122 St Lawrence Road, 3

Music, books and walking expeditions meant much to the young Arthur Griffith. He attended Sunday afternoon concerts at the Antient Concert Rooms, and musical evenings at the Sheehans' in Belvedere Place. He fell in love with young Maud Sheehan. They were married in 1910 and settled at 122 St Lawrence Road, Clontarf, a

Arthur Griffith

house presented in recognition of his services to the nation.

Born at 4 Dominick Street (since demolished), the family moved to 4 Little Britain Street. Griffith attended Christian Brothers' schools at Strand Street and St Mary's Place. Aged fifteen, he became a printing apprentice at Underwood's in Mount Street. An avid reader, with his literary pals he talked politics and literature sitting on the steps of Simpson's Hospital in Parnell Street (afterwards Williams and Woods jam factory). In 1899 he founded *The United Irishman*, the first of many publications expounding his policy of Irish self-reliance. In 1904, when living in Summerhill, he published *The Resurrection of Hungary*. In the same year he launched Sinn Féin at 6 Harcourt Street, with Edward Martyn at its head. Thus was laid the foundation for all that followed, leading to an independent Ireland in 1922.

The Bailey Restaurant in Duke Street was Griffith's favourite haunt. He read in the National Library until ten o'clock when he repaired to the Bailey for bread, cheese and stout with his cronies. Acknowledged as their leader, he talked or played chess with Oliver Gogarty, Seamus O'Sullivan, James Stephens and James Montgomery. He had a portable chess set, which was used to pass the tedious hours in various prisons. In 1922 when the ministers of the Provisional Government were virtual prisoners in Government Buildings, food was sent in from the Bailey. For his part in the negotiation of the Anglo-Irish Treaty of 1921, Griffith was reviled by his republican opponents. He countered by expressing surprise at 'the heights of my own villainy'.

A forceful writer of propaganda, Griffith kept the authorities busy monitoring his many journals. No sooner was one suppressed than another sprang up. Even as a prisoner in Gloucester in 1918, he managed to edit *The Gloucester Diamond*, a manuscript journal named after a Dublin locality. Eight months after negotiating the Treaty, Griffith died suddenly of a subarachnoid haemorrhage. He is buried in Glasnevin Cemetery.

Arthur Guinness (1725-1803)
1 Thomas Street, 8

In eighteenth-century Ireland almost every town had its own brewery. In 1750 the first Arthur Guinness had a brewery in Leixlip, County Kildare. His brew was so appreciated by Dr Price, Archbishop of Cashel, that he left a legacy to his favourite brewer. With this the thirty-four-year-old Guinness bought Rainsfords' Brewery at James's Gate, Dublin, with a lease for nine thousand years. As well as beer, Guinness introduced the new brew, porter, a dark beer first drunk by London porters. From 1799 he concentrated on porter, making Dublin's the largest porter brewery ever. Living at No. 1 Thomas Street, now part of the main entrance to the brewery, Arthur Guinness married Olivia Whitmore, a relative of Henry Grattan. They had a family of twenty-one, of whom ten lived. The Guinness dy-

Arthur Guinness

nasty was thus firmly established.

A man of character and determination, Arthur Guinness showed a tenacity equalling that of eighteenth century bureaucrats in the shape of Dublin Corporation when, with indifference, they tried to deprive him of his essential water supply at St James's Gate. During one confrontation he seized a pickaxe from a workman and declared 'with very much improper language that they should not proceed'. They didn't. After four years of wrangling the Dublin Corporation wisely bowed out, and the Dublin public continued to enjoy Guinness.

Arthur was unselfish with his new-found wealth. He made a gift of 250 guineas in support of St Patrick's Cathedral, thus beginning the Guinness family tradition of endowment of the City of Dublin. The list is long, outstanding gifts being St Stephen's Green (see under Lord Ardilaun), the

Moyne Institute for medical research and Iveagh House, the headquarters of the Department of Foreign Affairs. Arthur Guinness was also a generous employer, supported non-sectarianism, and his social concern embraced prisoners' rights and the Dublin hospital services.

In 1764 he purchased Beaumont, a large country house beyond Whitehall. It later became a convalescent home. On his retirement he nominated as his successor his son, Arthur II (1768-1855), a wise choice, for Guinness sales trebled during the Napoleonic Wars and the brewery became the biggest in Ireland. Arthur I lived his last years at Beaumont. He lies in a vault beside the ruins of a hill-top round tower at Oughterard, near Kill in County Kildare.

Sir William Rowan Hamilton (1805-1865)
Dunsink House, Castleknock

In languages and mathematics, William Rowan Hamilton was a child prodigy. At seven he was reading Hebrew, and at thirteen he had a good knowledge of thirteen languages, including Arabic, Hindustani and Malay. Later he read Sanskrit and Persian for recreation. However, it is as a mathematician that Hamilton made his mark. The son of a solicitor, he was born at 36 Lower Dominick Street (since demolished). The use of 'Rowan' in his name was in parental admiration of Hamilton Rowan, the United Irishmen leader of 1798.

Before he had even graduated from

Trinity College – and at twenty-two years of age – he was appointed Professor of Astronomy at that College. Dr Brinkley, the astronomer, said of Hamilton: 'This young man, I do not say *will* be, but *is,* the first mathematician of his age.' A year later he became Astronomer Royal of Ireland at Dunsink Observatory. He went to live at Dunsink House and remained there until his death forty years later.

Walking into Dublin with his wife on 16 October 1843, Hamilton became inspired as he crossed the Royal Canal at Broombridge in Cabra. One hundred years later Eamon de Valera, himself a mathematician, unveiled a memorial on the bridge commemorating Hamilton, who 'in a flash of genius discovered the fundamental formula for quaternion multiplication and cut it on a stone on this bridge'.

Hamilton was knighted when he acted as secretary to the British Association during its visit to Dublin in 1835. Two years later he was elected President of the Royal Irish Academy. Yet for all his mathematical genius, he would have liked to have been a poet. From childhood he wrote poetry, and as an adult preferred the company of poets to that of mathematicians. He had a close friendship with Wordsworth, who stayed at Dunsink House. He also admired the poetry of Speranza (Lady Wilde) who was another frequent visitor.

Georg Friedrich Handel (1685-1759)
'Mr Handel's house
in Abby Street', 1

A storm raged over the Irish Sea on 18 November 1741, and the cross-channel boats to Dublin were late. However, *Faulkner's Journal* duly reported: 'The celebrated Dr Handel arrived here in the packet-boat from Holyhead, a gentleman universally known by his excellent compositions in all kinds of music.' At the time, Handel's popularity in London was suffering one of its periodic reverses.

For thirty years he had composed operas, coronation anthems and royal funeral music to order, until the royalty and his public had tired of him. Inspiration returned with his first oratorio, *Esther*. Presented in 1732, it was a success and oratorio became an established form of music in England. Then came one oratorio after another until London's musical appetite flagged again. Rejected once more, he accepted an invitation to raise funds in Dublin for Mercer's Hospital and the Charitable Infirmary, later Jervis Street Hospital. Unwittingly, he was about to make musical history, for in his baggage was the manuscript of his latest and most inspired composition. He had called it *Messiah*.

In Dublin Handel took a house 'in Abby (sic) Street near Lyffey (sic) Street'. Here he arranged his programmes and took bookings. Some citizens claimed to have watched through the windows while he composed *Messiah*. He may well have been amending his conducting score after rehearsals in the new Musick Hall in Fishamble Street, a place which pleased him greatly. 'The music sounds delightfully in this charming room,' he wrote, 'which puts me in such excellent spirits that I exert myself on the organ with more than usual success.'

Messiah was first produced on 13 April 1742. Anticipating the crowds, *Faulkner's Journal* requested 'the favour of the ladies not to come with hoops', and the gentlemen 'to come without their swords'. *Messiah* was received with rapture. The next day *Faulkner's Journal* said: 'Words are wanting to express the exquisite delight it afforded to the admiring crowded audience.' In great triumph, Handel left Dublin in August 1742. 'Certain it is,' he said, 'that this time twelve-month I shall continue my oratorios in Ireland.' Usually a man of his word, Handel never returned to Ireland, for London once again acclaimed him. His rehabilitation was complete.

Michael Healy (1873-1941)
40 Bishop Street, 8

A deeply religious and modest man, Michael Healy's attainment as an Irish stained-glass artist was considerable. Born at 40 Bishop Street, he developed a life-long artistic devotion to the poses and attitudes of people seen in the streets of Dublin. First he tried the religious life and later a career in business, before finally discovering his true vocation at the Royal Hibernian Academy of Arts. There he won prizes for his drawing from life. Later he worked at the Institute di Belle Arti in Florence before returning to Dublin.

On its foundation in 1903, Healy joined An Túr Gloine, Sarah Purser's Tower of Glass at 24 Upper Pembroke Street. Here he came under the tutelage of Christopher Whall and AE Child, distinguished English disciples of William Morris. From them he learned the intricate procedures involved in the creation of stained glass. Healy used the same aciding technique as Harry Clarke, producing the brightly-jewelled appearance characteristic of the work of both men.

Healy's windows decorate churches throughout the country, particularly Loughrea Cathedral. In Dublin his work may be seen in the Church of the Sacred Heart, Donnybrook; the Church of Ireland, Donore Avenue; and the Augustinian Church, Thomas Street, where a four-light window depicts Saint Augustine.

Michael Healy influenced and helped Evie Hone when she abandoned painting for stained glass.

T M (Tim) Healy (1855-1931)
Glenaulin, Chapelizod, 20

Tim Healy was born in Bantry, County Cork. When he was seven his father, a Poor Law Union clerk, was transferred to Lismore, County Waterford. Tim attended the local Christian Brothers' school. Largely self-educated, he published verses in the *Irish Nation*, a newspaper owned by his uncle, A M Sullivan. At sixteen he emigrated, first to Manchester, moving on to Newcastle-on-Tyne as a railway clerk. Here he involved himself in the local politics of the immigrant Irish. Seven years later another uncle, T D Sullivan, brought him to London to write parliamentary sketches for the family-owned *Irish Nation*. This was his breakthrough.

A brilliant journalist, he qualified as a barrister and became an outstanding advocate, quick, witty and intelligent. His vices included envy, malice, vanity and ruthless ambition. He became Parnell's secretary, and with him toured the US and Canada. It was Tim Healy, in one of his earliest speeches, who first called Parnell 'the uncrowned king of Ireland'. On entering Parliament he stood in awe of two men only: Gladstone and Parnell, and after Parnell's divorce, of Gladstone only. Having discovered the Chief's feet of clay, he then bitterly opposed his leadership, vindictively helping to speed him to his doom. His nickname became Tiger-Tim.

In 1905 Padraic Pearse made one of his few appearances as a barrister, to defend a farmer whom Healy accused of having his name on his cart in 'illegible' lettering. Pearse pointed out that it was in fact Gaelic lettering. The case was lost, the farmer fined one shilling, and Pearse turned away from Law for ever, calling it 'the most ignoble of all professions'.

Healy lived at 50 Great Charles Street and at 1 Mountjoy Square before he became the first Governor-General of the Irish Free State, and moved to the Viceregal Lodge, now Áras on Uachtaráin. Having served from 1922 to 1928, he then retired to Glenaulin, described by Joseph Hone as 'the always brilliantly lighted villa which he has built for himself at Chapelizod'.

Victor Herbert (1859-1924)
Maunder's Terrace, Ranelagh, 6

The civil registration of births in Ireland was introduced in 1864, five years after the birth of Victor Herbert. His biographers don't mention his birthplace in Dublin, but the available evidence suggests Maunder's Terrace, Ranelagh. His mother, Fanny Lover, was a daughter of Samuel Lover, who lived at 9 D'Olier Street. When he was seven she took Victor to the Stuttgart Conservatory to study music. He specialised in the 'cello and became first 'cellist in Strauss's orchestra in Vienna when he was twenty-three. In 1886 he married Therese Forster, a Viennese prima donna, and joined the New York Metropolitan Opera as first 'cellist.

In 1893 Herbert became bandmaster of the 22nd Regiment, New York National Guard. From 1898 to 1904 he conducted the Pittsburgh Symphony Orchestra. After 1904 he conducted his own orchestra – Victor Herbert's New York Orchestra – and appeared periodically as guest conductor with other orchestras. He was also a fluent composer of comic operas – now called musicals – to which he gave an harmonic sophistication never before attained in that genre. Though he wrote musical scores for the Ziegfeld Follies in the twenties, he is probably best remembered for his song 'Ah! Sweet Mystery of Life' from *Naughty Marietta*, the musical of 1910.

Though he never returned, he never forgot Ireland. He organised concerts and collections to relieve distress during the Troubled Times (1916-1923), and when the manuscript of *The Soldier's Song* found its way to New York, Herbert made a musical arrangement and had it published. He gave the royalties to a Father R F O'Reilly for safe transmission to Peadar Kearney in Dublin. He was active in many Irish/American societies. When he died he was President of the Friendly Sons of St Patrick and the Sons of Irish Freedom. *The Great Victor Herbert*, a biographical film incorporating his music, was a huge success on its release in 1939.

F R (Fred) Higgins (1896-1941)
Durlas, Lower Dodder Road, 6

F R Higgins was a poet – and by no means a minor poet, despite the neglect of his work. Those old enough will recall him as a tall, broad man with glasses and a Yeatsian lock falling over his forehead. Always to be seen in and around the old Abbey Theatre, he was sometimes mistaken for Yeats. More often he was taken to be his son. Apart from mutual warmth, their friendship flourished because of their common interests – poetry and, of course, the Abbey Theatre. A master of intrigue, when Higgins became a director of the Abbey in 1935 he entered zestfully into the internal power struggles of the theatre's board. If a successor had to be found to the ageing Yeats, who better than the man whom Yeats described as 'undoubtedly the finest of our younger poets; he may bring back to the Irish theatre something of its first poetic impulse'.

Born in Foxford, County Mayo, Higgins spent his youth in County Meath, his mother's native place. Of both localities he retained happy memories, particularly of the Meath countryside, often the inspiration for his poetry. Without the means to express his literary leanings he came to Dublin to become a clerk in Brooks Thomas, the builders' providers, then in Lower Abbey Street where the Irish Life building now stands. He lived nearby in North Clarence Street, off the North Strand.

It was a period when journals and magazines flourished. Higgins got a foothold by first editing a trade paper, and later a literary journal, *The Shamrock*. He was encouraged by AE (George Russell), that great nurturer of literary talent, and was soon publishing poetry. His first collection, *Island Blood*, was published in 1925. After lengthening intervals there were three further collections, the last a year before the poet's death. A member of the Irish Academy of Letters, Higgins moved in the Dublin literary circle of the time, with R M Smyllie, editor of the *Irish Times,* usually presiding in the Palace Bar in Fleet Street.

Higgins lived on Lower Dodder Road, Rathfarnham, his house overlooking the river. Having fulfilled his ambition by becoming managing director of the Abbey Theatre, he died suddenly in Dublin in 1941. He is buried at Laracor, County Meath, where Swift was the incumbent between 1700 and 1714.

Bulmer Hobson (1883-1969)
The Mill House, Rathfarnham

Of all the men who contributed to modern Irish history, Bulmer Hobson was the most self-effacing. Born in County Down of Quaker stock, he took to nationalism as a boy. In Belfast he organised various Irish-minded societies while still in his teens. In 1907 in Dublin, in collaboration with Tom Clarke, recently returned from America, Hobson led a small group in reorganising the Irish Republican Brotherhood, thus preparing the way for all that followed: the Irish Volunteers, the 1916 Rising, and ultimately the establishment of the Irish State. That his name is so little known today is due to the deliberate course he took in Easter Week 1916.

Having resigned from the Supreme Council of the IRB he was unaware until Holy Thursday of 1916 that an insurrection was imminent. Also, he differed with Pearse and Connolly regarding an armed revolt, with its inevitable loss of life. He did not believe in open insurrection unless, militarily, it could be successful. Bitterly opposed therefore to the Rising, Hobson made a last-ditch effort, on the authority of Eoin MacNeill, to prevent the outbreak of hostilities. Consequently, he was arrested on Good Friday by his colleagues and imprisoned in a house in Phibsboro. He was released on Easter Monday night *after* Pearse and his comrades, by signing the Proclamation, had signed their own death warrants. Disillusioned, Bulmer Hobson took no part in the fighting then or later. Instead, he left his seat of power for the shadows, never to return.

A literate man and an eloquent journalist, Hobson edited a number of short-lived journals devoted to nationalism: *The Republic, The Peasant, The County Dublin Observer* and *Irish Freedom,* the official organ of the IRB which he edited from 12 D'Olier Street. His books include *A Short History of the Irish Volunteers* and an updated version of Berkeley's *Querist.* In 1954 he edited the Gate Theatre Book. Until he published his last book, *Ireland, Yesterday and Tomorrow,* he had maintained his silence on the differences which beset the revolutionary

hierarchy before Easter 1916. The book begins with the young Quaker idealist teaching the 'Lord's Prayer' in Irish to small boys in Belfast and ends with the disillusioned nationalist who exiled himself to Roundstone in Connemara, where he spent his last years.

John Hogan (1800-1858)
30 Wentworth Place, 2

After twenty-five brilliantly successful years as a sculptor in Rome, John Hogan moved to Dublin, living in Digges Street. He moved to Wentworth Place, later named Hogan Place in his honour. In Dublin he suffered disappointment and disillusionment. His work was ignored, reflecting the lack of appreciation of the arts in Ireland in the nineteenth century.

Born in Tallow, County Waterford,

30 Wentworth Place (now Hogan Place), 2

John Hogan became a clerk. In his spare time he studied drawing and sculpture, the latter by copying Canova's figures and casts presented by the Prince Regent to the Crawford Institute in Cork. Through subscription he was sent to Rome for further training. There he made an instant impression with his first piece, 'The Goat Herd', modelled in plaster. His difficulty was lack of money to purchase marble.

Hogan's model for 'The Dead Christ' was first seen in Rome by a visiting Irish priest who hoped to have it commissioned in marble, although the Irish church did not patronise artists. Joyfully Hogan wrote to his parents: 'If he can raise the wind so as to enable me to purchase a fine block of marble, I should be content to live on macaroni until it could be finished ...' The commission came and the work was completed (almost) in 1829, when Hogan accompanied it to Dublin. On being unpacked the head was found to be unfinished. Hogan was challenged by the begrudgers. 'I wish to prevent jealous people from saying I got Italian help,' he replied. 'I will finish the head here under their eyes.' He did so, and 'The Dead Christ' is still where he placed it, under the high altar in St Teresa's Church, Clarendon Street.

From his arrival in Dublin in 1849 he was a victim of envy and jealousy, malicious gossip claiming he had had to flee from Italy having been a Mazzini revolutionary. In 1855 he was finally broken when his model for the Moore statue in College Street was rejected. Within days he was paralysed by a stroke and under the care of Sir William Wilde. Viewing his unfinished work he wept as he exhorted his sons: 'Finish them well, boys, I shall never handle the chisel more.' As Hogan's funeral passed Trinity College in March 1858, two hundred students, in a spontaneous tribute, joined the cortège on its way to Glasnevin Cemetery.

Joseph Holloway (1861-1944)
21 Northumberland Road, 4

Nowhere, at any time, could there have been a more indefatigable and prolific theatre diarist than Joseph Holloway. In forty-eight years of theatre-going in Dublin he produced a journal of 221 volumes. A veritable gold mine for future theatre historians, the Holloway treasure, known as *Impressions of a Dublin Playgoer*, is safely stored in the National Library of Ireland.

An architect by profession, Holloway was responsible for the conversion of the old Mechanics Theatre in Marlborough Street (itself once a morgue) into the Abbey Theatre, that fabric which served the literary renaissance of Yeats, Gregory and Synge until 1951 when it was destroyed by fire. Thus Holloway developed a particular interest in the Abbey, amounting almost to a sense of proprietorship. He attended every first night, and was often present at rehearsals. He knew every actor intimately, and recorded their gossipy gripes against the management of the day. Indeed, if there can be any criticism of the Holloway archive it is that for the occasional candid glimpses of the 'greats', some wading is necessary through much that is trite.

Holloway observed Yeats's irritating habit of pacing the Abbey auditorium during a performance. He called him 'the perpetual motion poet'. One night he found Lennox Robinson occupying his customary seat. He sat in one behind him and recorded that: 'During the progress of the piece he wriggled about like a daddy-longlegs on a pin.' Of the first production of *Riders to the Sea* in 1904 he said the acting 'resembled nature so closely that it ceased to be acting'. A good judge of form, Holloway spotted the young Cyril Cusack on his first appearance at the Abbey in 1932: 'Some day he'll do something by which he'll be remembered for ever on the Irish stage.'

An ultra-conservative, Holloway abhorred what he called 'bad language' on the stage. Here he included the language of the O'Casey plays. He thoroughly disapproved of Ernest Blythe's attempt to Gaelicise the Abbey, thus playing to empty houses. 'It is a sad fact, but true,' he said, 'that the Gaels talk a lot about artistic things but never support any.'

A bachelor, he lost part of his life when he lost Ellen, his faithful housekeeper. 'May she travel an easy road,' was his warmest wish for her.

Evie Hone (1894-1955)
The Dower House, Marley, Rathfarnham, 14

In the art of stained glass Evie Hone's reputation is international. Yet she was an outstanding painter of religious subjects before she became enchanted by stained glass at the age of thirty-eight.

Born at Roebuck Grove, County Dublin, she contracted poliomyelitis at eleven and was permanently disabled. Her training began in London in 1915. In 1920 she went to Paris with her friend, the artist Mainie Jellett.

Evie Hone

From 1924 she exhibited her pictures internationally. In 1928 she returned to Dublin permanently, but visited Paris annually. Her growing interest in stained glass prompted her to seek admission to Sarah Purser's Tower of Glass Studio at 24 Upper Pembroke Street. She was refused, but in 1933 she was admitted. Her genius was immediately apparent.

One of her first windows (1934) is in St Nathi's Church, Dundrum, County Dublin. Others may be seen in University Hall, Hatch Street; All

Hallow's College, Drumcondra; and in many churches throughout the country. 'My Four Green Fields' (1938/39), commissioned by the Irish government for the Irish Pavilion at the World's Fair, New York, now forms the centre-piece in the entrance hall of the renovated Government Buildings in Upper Merrion Street. Her own favourite piece is in St Mary's Parish Church at Kingscourt, County Cavan. It depicts the 'Annunciation', the 'Cruxifixion' and the 'Ascension'. Evie Hone's preoccupation with religious art appears to date from her reception into the Roman Catholic Church in 1939. She was received at Blackrock College by the then President, John Charles McQuaid, later to become Archbishop of Dublin.

Her Kingscourt window led to a commission to replace the East Window in Eton College Chapel (1949-1952), which had been destroyed by bombing in World War II. Depicting 'The Last Supper', the Eton College window represents a remarkable example of modern stained glass.

The Dower House, Marley, a Regency mews house where Evie Hone lived from 1928 until her death, bears a commemorative plaque.

Gerard Manley Hopkins (1844-1889)
86 St Stephen's Green, 2

It is ironic that Gerard Manley Hopkins, the Victorian poet, should be buried in Glasnevin Cemetery. Unsympathetic to Irish nationalism, life in Ireland for this patriotic English-man, this Empire-loving Jesuit professor, was a miserable academic drudgery, an exile, borne only in obedience to the rules of his Order. He hoped for the release of a recall to England, but sadly, death intervened. Like Cardinal Newman before him, Ireland and the Irish didn't match his expectations of life amongst an ardently Catholic people.

Born a High Church Anglican, Hopkins's ambition was to be a poet-painter like Rossetti. While reading classics at Oxford he was received into the Roman Catholic Church by Newman in 1866. Two years later he entered the Society of Jesus, was ordained in 1877, and in 1884, at a salary of £400 per annum, was posted to Ireland as Professor of Classics at University College, Dublin, the successor to Newman's wrecked Catholic University at 86 St Stephen's Green.

Disillusioned, Hopkins wrote, 'This house we are in, the College, is a sort of ruin. I have been warmly welcomed and most kindly treated, but Dublin itself is a joyless place.' To Newman he wrote, 'These buildings since you knew them have fallen into deep dilapidation ... Only one thing looks bright, the little church of your building.' He was referring to University Church.

Hopkins's closest Irish friend was Robert Curtis, a fellow Jesuit, whose family lived in North Great George's Street. On the invitation of a Miss Cassidy, he sometimes visited Monasterevin, from where he wrote about the river: '... the Barrow which the old Irish poets call the dumb Barrow. I call it the burling Barrow brown.' Having assisted the local priest to give Communion, Father Hopkins noted: 'the religion of the Irish hangs suspended over their politics as the blue sky over the earth without contact or interference.' His visits to Monasterevin became 'one of the props and struts of my existence'.

A poet of complex language, Ger-

86 St Stephen's Green, 2

ard Manley Hopkins was a depressive, maybe even a manic-depressive. His poetry came in bursts of inspiration. For five years he struggled with wayward Irish students of Greek. 'Five wasted years,' he called them. A victim, it is said, of defective drains, he died suddenly of typhoid at the age of forty-four. With his friend, Bob Curtis, he is buried in the Jesuit plot in Glasnevin Cemetery.

Gustavus Hume (1736-1812)
63 Dawson Street, 2

Never short of 'characters', Dublin inherited a live-wire when Gustavus Hume, surgeon, physician, and property developer, was born of the Hume family of Humewood Castle, near Kiltegan, County Wicklow. History hasn't decided whether Hume should be called a property developer who practised medicine, or a physician who developed property. However, circumstances indicate that he is more entitled to be remembered as a doctor, for he was attached to Mercer's Hospital for nearly fifty years, where he showed his talents as a paediatrician. He even became President of the Royal College of Surgeons, and attended to many United Irishmen. Oatmeal porridge, he believed, gave him his boundless energy, so it became his favourite treatment for his patients (the Humes originated in Scotland). Quick-witted Dubliners named him 'Stirabout Gusty'.

Dr Hume's remarkable energy produced another child in his family and another street for Dublin every year. As a routine, he moved his vast family into his every newly-developed street. After years of pregnancies and of traipsing after him, Mrs Hume grew tired. She took root in Harcourt Street, refusing any further moves. They parted, Gustavus moving on as usual with unabated enthusiasm. However, he called back to Harcourt Street often enough to make sure the annual addition to the population didn't dry up.

He built many houses between the east side of St Stephen's Green and Upper Merrion Street. Hence his name is commemorated in Hume Street. Ely Place was known as Hume Place until the Marquess of Ely outdid Hume by erecting the imposing mansion, Ely House, now the headquarters of the Knights of Columbanus. Not to be down-faced, Hume's reply was the erection of an equally great mansion at Merrion Square East. This was later divided into two houses.

Though Gustavus continued moving, his wife remained entrenched in Harcourt Street until her death. He finally settled in another of his own houses, No. 63 Dawson Street, one of the handsomest he ever built. Here, in a disorderly welter of children and grandchildren, he died in 1812. Though forgotten now, Stirabout Gusty's energetic life made a lasting impact: he changed the architectural face of Dublin; he furthered the interests of medicine, and last but not least, he made his mark in maintaining the population.

Douglas Hyde (1860-1949)
1 Earlsfort Place, Adelaide Road, 2

A son of the manse, Douglas Hyde was born in Castlerea, County Roscommon. His father became rector of Frenchpark, where he lived in a house called Ratra. Here young Hyde spent his formative years. Educated at home at a time when the Irish language was rapidly dying, he learned spoken Irish in the countryside around his home. From the same source he recorded folklore and lyric poetry, material he was to use in his life's work of preserving Ireland's national language.

At Trinity College, Dublin, Hyde switched from divinity to law, taking an LL.D in 1888. After one year as professor of modern languages at the University of New Brunswick in Canada, he returned to Ireland. He published poetry under the pseudonym *An Craoibhín Aoibhinn* ('the delightful little branch'). In 1893 he married Lucy Kurtz from Wurtemberg, published the *Love Songs of Connaught* and, with Eoin MacNeill, founded the Gaelic League. Non-sectarian and non-political, the League was intended to keep Irish spoken wherever it was still alive. When the League made its object 'a free Gaelic-speaking Ireland', Hyde resigned both as President and as a member.

As President of the National Literary Society, Hyde's inaugural address dealt with 'The necessity for de-Anglicising the Irish Nation'. His disgust at Irishmen speaking English was not forgiven at Trinity College. When he applied for the professorship of Irish he was rejected. Later he accepted the professorship of Modern Irish at University College, Dublin.

Hyde lived at 69 Upper Mount Street before moving to 1 Earlsfort Place. Before its demolition the address had been changed to 65 Adelaide Road. The site is now occupied by an office block, called Hyde House. Not believing that a Rising had commenced on Easter Monday 1916, Hyde set out along Earlsfort Terrace. The incessant gunfire in St Stephen's Green left him in no further doubt, and he beat a hasty retreat.

In 1925/6, and again in 1937, Hyde served as a senator of the Irish Free State. He became the first President of Ireland in 1938. On the completion of his term in 1945 he was given an official residence in the Phoenix Park.

Formerly known as The Little Lodge (see under Winston Churchill), it was renamed Ratra. Douglas Hyde died there and is buried in French Park.

John Kells Ingram (1823-1907)
38 Upper Mount Street, 2

As Professor of Oratory (1852-1866); Professor of Greek (1866-1877); Librarian (1879-1887); and Vice-Provost (1898-1899), John Kells Ingram gave some fifty-five years of service to Trinity College. His other interests included mathematics, classics, poetry and economics. Nowadays, this scholarly university professor is remembered only as the composer of a rebel song.

Ingram was born in the rectory at Templecarne, near Pettigo in County Donegal. From Edward Lyons's School in Newry he matriculated at the age of fourteen with first place at Trinity College. Never known to have nationalist leanings, his poem 'The Memory of the Dead' was written when he was nineteen, and published anonymously in *The Nation* in April 1843. After many years it became an open secret that the conservative Professor Ingram of Trinity College was the author of the rousing poem beginning:

Who fears to speak of Ninety-Eight?
Who blushes at the name?
When cowards mock the patriots'
    fate,
Who hangs his head in shame?

Lady Gregory thought it 'a strange poem of liberty for a professor in Trinity'. In prim and proper Dublin circles it was said that Ingram was ashamed of his youthful nationalistic lapse. In 1900 the professor set the record straight: 'Those who know me do not need to be told that this idea is without foundation. I think the Irish race should be grateful to men who, in evil times, however mistaken may have been their policy, gave their lives for their country. But I have no sympathy with those who preach sedition in our own day, when all the circumstances are radically altered. In my opinion no real popular interest can now be furthered by violence,' a message as pertinent today as in 1900.

John Kells Ingram died in May 1907, and is buried in Mount Jerome Cemetery.

Rex Ingram (1892-1950)
58 Grosvenor Square, Rathmines, 6

Reginald Ingram Montgomery Hitchcock was born at 58 Grosvenor Square. In Hollywood he shortened his name to Rex Ingram, a name which was to become associated with some of the greatest silent films ever made.

Educated at St Columba's College, Rathfarnham, Rex Ingram entered Trinity College Law School, but left

58 Grosvenor Square, Rathmines, 6

without a degree. Aged nineteen, he went to America and entered the Yale School of Fine Arts. He acquired his first knowledge of the cinema as a small-part actor in one-reel films. In 1916 at the age of twenty-three he graduated to film directing for Univer-

sal. By 1918 he had directed ten films. The titles alone are reminiscent of the 'flicks' of the time: *Broken Fetters, Chalice of Sorrow* and *The Flower of Doom*. Later on Ingram joined Metro Pictures Corporation (later Metro Goldwyn Mayer), and made three films before winning international recognition in 1921.

The best-selling Spanish novel, *The Four Horsemen of the Apocalypse*, was published in the United States in 1918. It was about a young man, Julio, who refused to join the French army in the 1914-18 War. Hun atrocities eventually drove him to do so and he was killed. Metro Pictures adapted the story, chose the creative Rex Ingram to direct, and gave the part of Julio to an unknown actor called Rudolph Valentino.

While *The Four Horsemen* (War, Conquest, Famine and Death) was a contemporary novel, Ingram gave it spectacular symbolism, with the horsemen galloping through the sky over a war-torn world. His treatment made cinematic history. The film was an instant success when it opened in New York in 1921. Overnight, Ingram had become a director of world stature, and of course, Valentino had rocketed to stardom.

An imaginative pioneer, with a flair for filming exotica, Rex Ingram's films of the silent twenties blazed a trail that was followed in the sound-filled thirties by the mammoth productions of the likes of Cecil B de Mille, and still later by the wide-screened epics of today.

With his film-star wife, Alice

Terry, Ingram moved to Nice in 1925. After becoming a Mohammedan he returned to America where he died in 1950.

Mainie Jellett (1897-1944)
36 Fitzwilliam Square, 2

The Jellett sisters, Mainie and Bay, set out to be musicians. Bay, the violinist, became the leader of the Gate Theatre orchestra, and later conductor of the Gaiety Theatre orchestra. At twenty-two Mainie abandoned the piano for painting. With Elizabeth Bowen, she had received her earliest lessons from Elizabeth (Lolly) Yeats, after which she studied under William (later Sir William) Orpen at the Metropolitan School of Art in Dublin. In 1917 she went to the Westminster School under Walter Sickert, a direct descendant of the French impressionists. In 1920, with her great friend Evie Hone, she went to Paris where they worked in the studio of Andre Lhote, the Cubist painter. There Mainie Jellett learned what she called 'the pure creation of form for its own sake'.

Jellett and Hone returned to Dublin where their new-fangled painting drew harsh criticism from a public unused to Cubist ideas. Their mutual understanding and friendship sustained them against this unfriendly reception in their native city. But they had been warned in Paris that the Cubist path was a thorny one. Both turned to religious subjects, Evie Hone eventually becoming an artist in stained glass. Mainie Jellett was noted for her application of abstract painting to re-ligious themes. Her 'Descent From the Cross', 'Madonna of Eire' and 'Assumption' are all notable pictures.

An encouraging teacher, she trained many young artists in her Dublin studio, and she organised the first Irish Exhibition of Living Art to enable them to show their work. She exhibited regularly in Dublin, London and Paris. Mainie Jellett's pictures are now highly-prized possessions amongst collectors.

Denis Johnston (1901-1984)
Etwall, Lansdowne Road, 4

Trundling trams, close-cut lawns and the waterchute in Herbert Park were the outside world of a small boy's life at 54 Wellington Road in Edwardian Ballsbridge. As a teenager, when the family lived at Etwall, Lansdowne Road, Denis Johnston saw his father's house ripped asunder to make an outpost for the Volunteers in Easter Week, 1916. The experience helped to make a man of many parts.

Johnston had four professions: the law, the theatre, war correspondence and the academic. The first was the most enjoyable, he claimed, but theatre people were the best company. Educated at Cambridge and Harvard, he became an able seaman on a tanker before beginning practice in the Four Courts Law Library. Then *The Old Lady Says 'No'* burst upon the scene, the first of many plays. In 1936 he joined the BBC to become a pioneer of television. As a war correspondent with the Eighth Army he reported from Alamein and later from Buchenwald. When BBC television resumed, Johnston became Programme Director, before leaving to begin an academic career in the United States teaching English literature. After ten years he came back to Ireland for conversation.

In 1934 Denis Johnston played in the film version of Synge's *Riders to the Sea*, financed by Gracie Fields. Two years later he appeared in Lord Longford's *Armlet of Jade* in London. He helped to make the film *Guests of the Nation*, from a short story by Frank O'Connor. That film is now treasured in the archive of the Irish Film Institute.

Apart from radio and television plays, Denis Johnston wrote seven plays for the theatre, every one of which made an impact. But it was *The Old Lady* (rejected by the Abbey Theatre) as done by the new Gate Company in 1929 that threw the Dublin theatre world into a tizzy of guesswork and mystery.

His first wife was Shelah Richards, the Abbey actress. After a divorce he married the actress Betty Chancellor. On retirement they lived on Sorrento Terrace in Dalkey overlooking Killiney Bay. Betty died in April 1984 and Denis three months later. They are buried in the Close of St Patrick's Cathedral in the heart of the playwright's 'wilful city of savage dreamers'.

Francis Johnston (1760-1829)
64 Eccles Street, 7

An eminent architect, and the son of an architect, Francis Johnston was born in Armagh where he practised for some years. He moved to Dublin in 1793 and was employed by the Board of Works. He adapted his house in Eccles Street, doubling its width to include a portion adorned with decorative panels, one of which depicts Michelangelo's 'Moses'. In the back garden he built a campanile to accommodate his bells. He enjoyed ringing them until his neighbours complained, so he donated them to nearby St George's Church, his own architectural masterpiece. No. 64 Eccles Street was later occupied by another noisy tenant, Isaac Butt, who used to play his organ at unsociable hours.

Johnston built St George's (1802-13) on a commanding height and gave it a spire two hundred feet high. In appearance it resembles the church of St Martin-in-the-Fields in London. Edward Bunting (1773-1843), the pioneer collector of Irish music, was organist. No longer a place of worship, St George's is now destined to become a multi-purpose entertainment and conference centre. Built about the same time, Johnston's Chapel Royal at Dublin Castle is a contrast in church architecture. The exterior carvings are by Edward Smyth.

Of Johnston's design for Dublin's General Post Office, only the classical facade survives. After the Act of Union, when the parliament building in College Green was sold by the British government to the Bank of Ireland, Johnston was commissioned in 1802 to make suitable external alterations so as to reconcile the Irish people to the loss of their parliament.

He designed a number of 'big houses' throughout the country. Between 1801 and 1806 he castellated and embellished Tullynally Castle in County Westmeath, and remodelled Killeen Castle in County Meath. He founded the Royal Hibernian Academy in 1813.

When Francis Johnston died his own bells were tolled at his own church.

Martello Tower, Sandycove

James Joyce (1882-1941)
41 Brighton Square, Rathgar, 6

The eldest of eight children, James Joyce was born on 2 February 1882 at 41 Brighton Square, Rathgar. He was two when the family made its first move on its non-stop trek from one Dublin address to another. Thus Joyce became saturated in Dublin's geography. He claimed that if the city were destroyed, it could be rebuilt from a study of his works. Of his fifty-eight years, he spent thirty-six living in Pola, Rome, Trieste, Paris and Zurich. Only his first twenty-two years were spent in Dublin, in which time he lived at almost as many addresses. Yet he remained in permanent communion with every nook and cranny of his native city, and never wrote a line about any other place. The list below is probably incomplete.

1884-87	23 Castlewood Avenue, Rathmines
1887-91	1 Martello Terrace, Bray

In 1888 Joyce went to Clongowes Wood College, County Kildare.

1892-93	Leoville, 23 Carysfort Avenue, Blackrock
1893-94	14 Fitzgibbon Street and 29 Hardwicke Street

From 1893 to 1898 Joyce was at Belvedere College, Dublin.

1894	2 Millbourne Avenue, Drumcondra
1895	17 North Richmond Street
1896-99	29 Windsor Avenue, Fairview
1899	7 Convent Avenue, Fairview
1899-1900	15 Richmond Avenue, Fairview
1900-01	8 Royal Terrace (now Inverness Terrace), Fairview
1902	32 Glengarriff Parade, North Circular Road
1902-03	7 St Peter's Terrace, Phibsboro

In 1902 Joyce left for Paris to study medicine. He returned in 1903 when his mother was dying.

1904	60 Shelbourne Road, Ballsbridge
1904	35 Strand Road, Sandymount
1904	103 Strand Road, Sandymount

1904 September – Martello Tower, Sandycove, with Oliver Gogarty. The first episode of *Ulysses* is set in the Tower. Gogarty is caricatured in the book as Buck Mulligan – a portrayal with which he was not pleased. The Tower is now the Joyce Museum.

1904-Oct.	Joyce left Dublin with Nora Barnacle.
1909	Joyce visited Dublin and stayed at 44 Fontenoy St.

During this visit he established Dublin's first permanent cinema, the Volta, in Mary Street. Aged thirteen, Austin Clarke saw the first programme on Christmas Eve, 1909. Dealing with incest, the main film was *The Tragic Story of Beatrice Cenci*, supported by *La Pouponniere* or *The First Paris Orphanage*.

1912	Joyce paid his last visit to Dublin, along with Nora and their children, also visiting Galway. In Dublin they stayed at 17-21 Richmond Place, North Circular Road.

The best-known Joycean address is, of course, No. 7 Eccles Street (since demolished), immortalised in *Ulysses*. From here Leopold Bloom stepped forth on 16 June 1904 to play his part for eighteen hours in the fictional life of Dublin. The date has become Bloomsday, so named by Sylvia Beach, Joyce's guardian angel, and the first publisher of *Ulysses*. Bloomsday is observed in Dublin by a coterie of intellectuals, but as with his writings, the plain people have never quite caught up. They still marvel that so much American resource and academic effort can be expended on researching what the author spent a lifetime forging in the smithy of his soul, clearly intending that it should remain that way.

As with so many Irish writers, AE (George Russell) had a hand in the making of Joyce. On reading his poems in 1902 he said, 'Young man, there is not enough chaos in your mind.' Then he advised simple stories, and *Dubliners* resulted. The chaos came later.

With the invasion of France in World War II, Joyce left Paris for Zurich. He died there on 13 January 1941. With Nora, his beloved, he is buried in Fluntern Cemetery above Zurich.

Patrick Kavanagh (1904-1967)
62 Pembroke Road, 4

Parnassus for the poet Patrick Kavanagh was the bank of the Grand Canal at Baggot Street Bridge where, as requested, he is commemorated with 'a canal bank seat for the passersby'. Tiring of the 'barbaric life of the Irish country poor', Kavanagh, aged thirty-five, migrated from his birthplace – Mucker, Inniskeen, County Monaghan – to begin his 'begging and scrambling around the streets of malignant Dublin'. In a bed-sitter on Drumcondra Road he slept on a

41 Brighton Square, Rathgar

62 Pembroke Road, 4

stretcher bed, and his hunger exceeded his purchasing power. But mental stimulus abounded once he discovered the literary delights of the Palace Bar in Fleet Street, where porter and poetry flowed copiously. To Kavanagh it was an education, a sort of university extension course.

Another migration brought the poet from north to south Dublin where, like Joyce, he had many addresses, but unlike Joyce they were mostly in the same area:

1939	35 Haddington Road
1942	122 Morehampton Road
1942	9 Lower O'Connell Street
1943-58	62 Pembroke Road
1958-59	19 Raglan Road
1959	110 Baggot Lane
1960	1 Wilton Place
1963	37 Upper Mount Street
1965	136 Upper Leeson Street

Kavanagh's happiest and longest tenancy was his 'lonely shieling on Pembroke Road'. On leaving that house in 1958 he said, 'If the truth must be told, I wept.' He even claimed his ghost might be found on Pembroke Road.

Prose helped to subsidise poetry – once he interviewed the Beatles. His *Kavanagh's Weekly* lasted four months before dying in debt. In 1939 Gogarty took a libel action, making Kavanagh's novel, *The Green Fool,* a best-seller. Once he was questioned by the Gardaí about so-called obscenities in his most celebrated poem, *The Great Hunger.* His novel, *Tarry Flynn,* was banned, later to become a successful Abbey Theatre play.

On a simple cross over the poet's grave at Inniskeen is inscribed: 'Pray for him who walked apart on the hills loving life's miracles.'

Peadar Kearney (1883-1942)
68 Lower Dorset Street, 7

When 'The Soldier's Song' reverberates at Croke Park or the jumping enclosure at Ballsbridge, few remember the two young Dublin working-men who combined their talents to make a rallying song and, incidentally, to give

Peadar Kearney

Paddy Heeney died in poverty shortly afterwards, and is buried in an unmarked grave in Drumcondra Churchyard.

With the foundation of the Volunteers in 1913 the Fenian anthem, 'God Save Ireland', was replaced by 'The Soldier's Song'. It was sung on route marches, and after 1916 in the internment camps whence its popularity spread. Hearing it in New York, Victor Herbert, himself a Dubliner, made a musical arrangement, and had it published. On locating the author, the accumulated royalties were sent to him in Dublin in 1917.

Like his famous nephew, Brendan Behan, Kearney was a house-painter, but he preferred to work as a stagehand at the Abbey Theatre. Despite the hardships of the 1913 strike, he married and settled in a furnished room at 17 Russell Place, North Circular Road. In 1916 he fought in Jacobs' Factory with Thomas MacDonagh. In 1920, while living at 3 Richmond Parade, North Circular Road, Kearney was arrested and interned at Ballykinlar, County Down. He died at 25 O'Donoghue Street, Inchicore, in 1942 and is buried in the Republican Plot in Glasnevin Cemetery.

the new Ireland a national anthem. Peadar Kearney, who wrote the words, was born at 68 Lower Dorset Street. A plaque marks the house. After his father's death at forty-three, the family moved to Marino, then to Summerhill. Other addresses were 49 Dolphin's Barn Street, 49 Capel Street and 10 Lower Dominick Street. Paddy Heeney of 101 Mecklenburg Street was young Kearney's pal. He played his melodeon as they tramped together through the Dublin mountains. They made their own marching songs, trying them out on their friend, Nellie Bushell, well known for many years as an Abbey Theatre usherette. The words of 'The Soldier's Song' by Kearney and the music by Heeney were first heard together at Nellie's house, 19 Newmarket Street, in 1907.

Luke Kelly (1940-1984)
Lattimore Cottages,
Sheriff Street, 1 (since demolished)

Like love and marriage, the names of Luke Kelly and The Dubliners will always go together. One remembers rollicking pub sessions with rousing ballads heard through porter fumes and smoke and the clatter of pint glasses. But one remembers too the wistful, lonesome, heart-tearing emotion generated by Luke Kelly's singing of 'Raglan Road' and 'The Foggy Dew' and a hundred other ballads from his inexhaustible repertoire.

Born in Lattimore Cottages in Sheriff Street, Kelly always identified with the down-trodden, the victims of injustice. The family moved to St Laurence O'Toole flats and later to Glen Cloy Road in Whitehall, where Luke thought he had landed in outer space. As a young man he loved football, soccer or Gaelic. He loved music too, any music, and was always willing to perform. His idol was Frank Sinatra. As a Dubliner he grew up singing the Dublin ballads before ballad-singing and the *bodhrán* gained respectability.

When he emigrated at seventeen in search of work, he was comforted to hear Englishmen singing 'The Ould Triangle'. Brendan Behan with *The Quare Fella* had got there before him. Recognised as a natural ballad-singer, Luke became popular in the pubs and clubs of England where he learned what left-wing politics were about.

Luke Kelly returned to Dublin and joined The Dubliners in time to revel in the ballad boom triggered by the Clancy Brothers and Seán Ó Riada. From weekly gigs in Howth's Royal Hotel, they were soon commanding London's Albert Hall filled with home-sick emigrants.

Pubs were important venues for The Dubliners. Belting out ballads and incessant world travel became a bore.

Relaxation was necessary. Inevitably, they gained a reputation as hard-drinking paddies. Luke Kelly developed symptoms of illness. Unfortunately, they were attributed to alcohol. Eventual collapse led to the late

Luke Kelly

diagnosis of a brain tumour. From his home in Dartmouth Square he was admitted to hospital where several operations failed to save his life. He died in January 1984.

Luke Kelly's recordings will give pleasure far into the future. Who could not be moved by the man's palpable emotion when he sang 'Scorn Not His Simplicity', a special song composed by his friend Phil Coulter?

As a tribute, Ballybough Bridge over the Tolka was named after Luke Kelly.

Charles Kickham (1828-1882)
2 St John's Terrace, Blackrock

Charles Kickham was born over his father's shop in Mullinahone, County Tipperary. In that same house as a boy he had an accident involving an explosion of gunpowder. Deafened and almost blinded, it was natural that for self-expression the young man should turn to writing. He loved a Protestant girl in Mullinahone, but he never married. To her he wrote the haunting song he called 'Slievenamon'. But the gentle, poetic Kickham was also a revolutionary activist, denouncing co-operation with constitutionalists. As a Fenian he rose to the highest heights – chairman of the Supreme Council of the Irish Republican Brotherhood.

With John O'Leary, Thomas Clarke Luby and James Stephens, Kickham worked as joint editor of *The Irish People*, the IRB propaganda newspaper published from 12 Parliament Street, Dublin. A tidy man himself, O'Leary was critical of what he called 'the considerable ignorance of the practical working of a newspaper office'. Nevertheless, the newspaper was making its mark sufficiently for the office to be raided and wrecked in 1865. With James Stephens, the Fenian leader, Kickham escaped, taking refuge at Fairfield House, Herbert Road, Sandymount, where a month later they were arrested. Despite the impairment of his sight and hearing, Kickham was sentenced to fourteen years' imprisonment. In fact he served four years in Pentonville.

Still popular, Kickham's novel, *Knocknagow*, is based on life around Mullinahone, his beloved birthplace. From his home in Blackrock, where he died, his coffin was followed by a thousand people, swelling to ten thousand by the time it reached Kingsbridge Railway Station. His reputation ensured him an even more massive demonstration of love and loyalty at his funeral the next day in Mullinahone.

Arthur Wolfe, Lord Kilwarden
(1739-1803)
Newlands House, Clondalkin

Arthur Wolfe, 1st Viscount Kilwarden, came from Forenaughts, County Kildare. A barrister, he soon became an influential citizen in the Ireland of his time. In 1787 he became Solicitor General. Two years later he rose to the position of Attorney General. From 1783 to 1798 he was an MP in the Irish parliament and in 1798 he was given a peerage as Baron Kilwarden. In all his legal dealings Arthur Wolfe was a humane and generous man, qualities rare in the judiciary of his time. Indeed, he was known as 'the justest judge in Ireland'.

At the height of his success Lord Kilwarden lived in what became the clubhouse of Newlands Golf Club. His country residence, many of the original features have been preserved, including the massive drawing-room with its magnificent ceiling and fireplace. Swift was often a guest. A figure of Hibernia decorated the front of Kilwarden's town house, No. 5 Leinster Street (since demolished).

Kilwarden's concern with social

welfare led to his appointment in 1776 as a governor of the Hospital for Incurables in Donnybrook. In straitened circumstances at the time, once Kilwarden became the hospital's treasurer things changed dramatically. Donations flowed in, one anonymous benefactor contributing £4000, a massive sum in the eighteenth century.

Kilwarden's influence was also responsible for the hospital receiving its charter from King George III in 1800. It opens thus: 'Our right trusty and well beloved counsellor, Arthur Lord Baron Kilwarden, Chief Justice of our Court of King's Bench in our Kingdom of Ireland ...' The hospital's welfare was of course grievously affected by the fate which overtook the gentle Kilwarden.

Robert Emmet's ill-organised Rising broke out on 23 July, 1803. That night, accompanied by his daughter and his nephew, Kilwarden was being driven home through Vicar Street, off Thomas Street. Mistaking him for one of his notorious legal colleagues, the carriage was set upon by a riotous mob. With his nephew he was dragged to the street. Both were brutally piked to death. The horror of the tragedy appalled the hapless Emmet, convincing him of how dreadfully wrong his insurrection plans had gone. In despair he left Dublin, his own fate soon to catch up with him.

Sir Hugh Lane (1875-1915)
Clonmell House, 17 Harcourt St., 2

The product of an unhappy marriage, Hugh Lane was born at Ballybrack House, Blackrock, Cork, the son of the Reverend J Lane and Adelaide Persse, a sister of Lady Gregory. In addition, Lane was disadvantaged by delicacy and a lack of formal schooling. Yet he lived to become a rich man and one of Ireland's most generous benefactors. In addition to thirty-nine French impressionist pictures ('the Lane pictures'), the other pictures given by him to Dublin galleries are beyond valuation.

As a young man Lane learned about pictures by working for a pittance in London galleries. He eventually took a room at 2 Pall Mall and began dealing. His life's ambition was to give Dublin a gallery of modern art. At his own expense he leased Clonmell House, an eighteenth-century mansion in Harcourt Street, and in 1908 made it into a temporary gallery where he exhibited his priceless treasures, pending a permanent home to be provided by Dublin Corporation.

The wavering of the Dublin philistines exhausted Lane's patience, and he then willed his French impressionists to the National Gallery in London. However, before leaving for America in February 1915 he had second thoughts. He wrote a codicil, 'The Codicil of Forgiveness', again leaving the pictures to Dublin, provided a suitable gallery was built. The codicil was not witnessed, and three months later Lane was drowned in the sinking of the *Lusitania*. Observing the letter of the law, rather than a sense of decency, London retained the Lane pictures.

After years of wrangling an arrangement was made in 1959 for half the pictures to be exchanged between

London and Dublin at five-yearly in-
tervals. In Dublin they are displayed at
Charlemont House, now known as the
Sir Hugh Lane Gallery of Modern Art.
As Augustus John said of Hugh Lane,
'He was one of those rare ones who,
single-handed, are able to enrich and
dignify an entire nation.'

James Larkin (1876-1947)
41 Wellington Road, Ballsbridge, 4

Like a flaming figure of destiny, in
1913 James Larkin raised the workers
of Dublin from their knees and set
them on their feet. A myth in his own
lifetime, he was a passionate dema-
gogue who preached with immense
conviction. 'You are strong, you are
powerful, you are of some importance
in the world,' he insisted. 'Do not allow yourselves to be trampled on.'
With Big Jim as their inspiration, the
workers undertook to fight the des-

potic rule of the capitalist employers
of Dublin, personified by the handsome and urbane William Martin
Murphy. At first the Dublin strike of
1913 brought only hunger and despair.
'Larkin will meet his Waterloo,' declared Murphy's newspaper, *The Independent.* 'Murphy will reach St
Helena,' retorted Larkin's newspaper,
The Irish Worker.

After its baptism of fire, the Irish
labour movement sprang into action,
bringing new meaning to the lives of
Dublin workers. Unity, Solidarity, and
direct action were the watchwords of
Larkin, then secretary of the Irish
Transport and General Workers' Union. Now headquartered in Dublin's
tallest building, that union was
founded in 1909 in a tenement room
in Townsend Street, with 'a table, a
couple of chairs and a candle'. Out of
the same strike came the Irish Citizen
Army. With Sean O'Casey as secretary,

54 Upper Beechwood Avenue, Ranelagh

it had been founded to defend locked-out workers against police brutalities and eviction. With James Connolly as its leader, the Citizen Army became a nationalist force, fighting in the General Post Office in 1916.

Born in Liverpool in poor circumstances, Larkin suffered much for his outspokenness, including imprisonment. On his first arriving in Dublin he lived on the North Circular Road. In 1913 he lived in Auburn Street, from where he was evicted with his wife and family. They moved to Creighton House, North Strand. In 1923 he lived at 54 Upper Beechwood Avenue, Ranelagh, until he moved to live with his sister Delia, at 17 Gardiner Place. His last home was 41 Wellington Road, Ballsbridge.

When Larkin died in January 1947 he was honoured with a lying-in-state at the Thomas Ashe Memorial Hall (since demolished) in College Street. His immense funeral travelled through snow and slush to Glasnevin Cemetery. Dramatically poised, a statue of Larkin by Oisin Kelly stands in O'Connell Street.

Edward Hartpole Lecky (1838-1903)
Cullenswood House, Ranelagh, 6

Lecky was the eminent Irish historian who declined the Chair of History at Oxford. He wrote an eight-volume *History of England in the Eighteenth Century*, half of which concerns the history of Ireland. At Trinity College, Dublin, his books constitute the Lecky Library in New Square, and his statue flanks the campanile in Front Square.

Some authorities give Newtown Park, County Dublin, as Lecky's birthplace. Writing about St Enda's College, then based at Cullenswood House, Padraic Pearse in *The Story of a Success* says: 'William Edward Hartpole Lecky was born at Cullenswood House on March 26th 1838. So our school-house has already a very worthy tradition of scholarship and devotion to Ireland; scholarship which even the most brilliant of our pupils will hardly emulate, devotion to Ireland, not indeed founded on so secure and right a basis as our own, but sincere, unwavering, life-long.'

This is faint praise, grudgingly given, Pearse perhaps remembering that though Lecky favoured the release of Fenian prisoners and the establishment of a Catholic university, he opposed Home Rule.

Lecky died in London and was cremated, his ashes being buried in Mount Jerome Cemetery. With the proceeds from his land in County Carlow, his widow endowed the Lecky Chair of History at Trinity College.

Joseph Sheridan le Fanu (1814-1873)
70 Merrion Square, 2

In the twenty years of le Fanu's residence in Merrion Square, his genius brought forth some of the most blood-curdling tales of darkest terror to be found in English literature. While his wife, Susan, lived they had been genial hosts. There was warmth and comfort, and in the big dining-room the chandelier lit the portraits of the famous

Sheridan family (Richard Brinsley Sheridan was a grand-uncle). But after Susan's death le Fanu retreated more and more into himself and even his oldest friends, like Charles Lever, were refused admission. He became a recluse, writing from midnight to dawn, the candles throwing shadows, grotesque and weird, on the walls around him. Tea helped him to concentrate on suspense and horror and the darkest passions of the human soul. When sleep came, it was tormented by shivering nightmares and dreams of impending death, always the same vision of violent death under the ruins of a tumbling house.

Whether le Fanu's strange living conditions helped to induce the supernatural for him, or whether his ghostly creations eventually took possession of him, remain questions more properly answered by a psychoanalyst than by a Victorian reader mesmerised by the horror related in his matter-of-fact style.

A barrister who never practised, le Fanu was born at the Royal Hibernian School, Phoenix Park (now St Mary's Hospital). He had a happy childhood in Chapelizod, the setting for his *The House by the Churchyard*, and later in Abington, County Limerick, when his father was Dean of Emly.

On his marriage in 1844, le Fanu lived at 2 Nelson Street, Dublin. He moved to the south side, living first at 1 Warrington Place before moving to 15 Warrington Place. In 1851 he made his last move, to 70 Merrion Square (then 15 Merrion Square South), the house symbolic of his repeated night-

mare, the house that was to crush the life out of him. It bears a plaque. Joseph Sheridan le Fanu is buried in Mount Jerome Cemetery.

Charles Lever (1806-1872)
35 Amiens Street, 1

If Charles Lever hadn't been a doctor and a novelist he could have been an actor. He was born in a house in the North Strand, later to become No. 35 Amiens Street, and finally demolished to make way for Connolly Railway Station. His father, an English architect and builder, came to Dublin to help James Gandon with the erection of the Custom House. He soon moved to the country where he built Moatfield House, a villa at Coolock. Young Charles grew up in the surrounding fields and lanes. In 1955 the villa was demolished and replaced by Cadbury's Chocolate Factory.

As a medical student Lever lived at No. 2 Chambers in Trinity College, and at Lisle House, 33 Molesworth Street, then a fashionable hostel. At Dr Steevens's Hospital he was taught by Abraham Colles, and William Wilde was a contemporary. In 1832 he set up in practice in Dublin and worked throughout the cholera epidemic. Ten years later he became a full-time author and editor of the *Dublin University Magazine*. To stimulate his writing he travelled extensively. 'You can't keep drawing wine off the cask, and putting nothing in,' he said, 'this is my way of replenishing it.' Lavish extravagances, including gambling, meant he had to write too much and too rapidly. His collected works number thirty-seven volumes. 'You ask me how I write,' he said. 'My reply is just as I live – from hand to mouth.'

When he lived in the mansion, Templeogue House (now occupied by the Maynooth Mission to China), he entertained his friends, Trollope, Carlyle and Thackeray, who later dedicated his *Irish Sketch Book* to Lever, 'a friend from whom I have received a hundred acts of kindness and cordial hospitality'. Later he moved to Oatlands, Stillorgan, now a Christian Brothers' monastery.

Over-talented and always restless, Lever eventually moved to Italy, where in 1858 he was appointed British Consul at Spezia. Nine years later he was promoted consul at Trieste where he died.

Edward, 6th Earl of Longford (1902-1961)
Christine, Countess of Longford (1900-1980)
Grosvenor Park, 123 LeinsterRoad

At least twice in its lifetime the Gate Theatre all but died. On each critical occasion it was saved by financial injections from the same source. To the interest, energy and generosity of Edward Longford and of his wife, Christine, Dublin owes the continued existence of 'the Gate'. When their outlay had exhausted family resources, they sold their books, their bric-a-brac, even their clothes, Edward then resorting to a begging bowl in the streets. But they succeeded – the foundations of the Gate Theatre are now as solid as those of the Rotunda complex in which it is housed.

The Longfords' interest in theatre began as undergraduates in Oxford. Three years after its foundation, Edward joined the Board of the Gate Theatre. Working with Hilton Edwards and Mícheál MacLiammóir, the Longfords learned their theatre, both contributing original plays. Edward's *Yahoo* is probably the best of many plays on Swift, and Christine contributed mostly plays based on Irish history. His belief in plays which should have been seen in Dublin often involved Edward in heavy personal losses. Friction resulted in a breach. In 1936 Edward founded Longford Productions, which toured Ireland annually, educating the populace to a greater appreciation of classical theatre.

As a schoolboy at Eton, and with only *O'Growney's Grammar*, he had taught himself Irish. He translated from Greek and French, and his translation from Irish includes his version of Merriman's *Midnight Court*. For two years he served in the Senate. A successful novelist, Christine's work, set in the 1930s, cries out for republication.

Commuting from Tullynally Castle, County Westmeath (then called Pakenham Hall) for every Dublin first-night prompted the Longfords to purchase a town house in 1927. After five years at 143 Leinster Road they moved a little further up the road to a stucco villa called Grosvenor Park. Thinking the name too West-British and snobbish, they preferred to use the address, 123 Leinster Road. After Edward's death Christine lived at 21 Herbert Street (now the Cheshire Barrett Home) and at 81 Ailesbury Road.

Samuel Lover (1797-1868)
9 D'Olier Street, 2

A memorial in St Patrick's Cathedral aptly summarises the achievements of the highly talented Samuel Lover: 'Poet, painter, novelist and composer, who, in the exercise of a genius as distinguished in its versatility as in its power, by his pen and pencil illustrated so happily the characteristics of the peasantry of his country that his name will ever be honourably identified with Ireland.'

Lover was born at 60 Grafton Street. He went to Samuel Whyte's famous school at 79 Grafton Street (now Bewley's Cafe). He wanted to be an artist, but his father insisted on a business career. Sydney Owenson (later Lady Morgan) advised her protégé: 'If I had a son and he even desired to become a highwayman, I should make him a present of a pair of pistols and a good horse, and say, since the gallows is your vocation, in heaven's name pursue it.'

Samuel left home and soon he had become well-known for his portraiture, especially his miniature painting. By 1830 he was secretary of the Royal Hibernian Academy, and had set himself up comfortably at 9 D'Olier Street, where he gave lavish musical entertainments.

In addition to his pictures, novels, ballads and songs poured from his pen. His songs were as popular as they were humorous:

> *O, I'm not myself at all, Molly dear,*
> >   *Molly dear,*
> *My appetite's so small,*
> *I once could pick a goose, but my buttons is no use,*
> *Faith my tightest coat is loose, Molly dear.*

Lover's musical talent was passed to his grandson, 'The Great Victor Herbert', whose compositions for Hollywood's extravaganzas of the 1930s are still popular. Lover is remembered for his novels, *Rory O'Moore* and *Handy Andy*. When his reputation as a miniaturist spread to London he decided to move there. He prospered and never returned to Ireland.

Kathleen Lynn (1874-1955)
9 Belgrave Road, Rathmines, 6

Born at Cong, County Mayo, the daughter of a canon, as a child Kathleen Lynn saw poverty at close quarters. 'The local doctor was the fount of help and hope,' she said, 'so I decided to become a doctor.' Schooled in Dublin, England and Germany, she qualified as a doctor in 1899. The first woman to be elected a resident doctor at the Adelaide Hospital, prejudice prevented her from going into residence. Despite such anti-feminism, she became a Fellow of the Royal College of Surgeons in 1909, one of the first women to do so.

A confirmed republican, Dr Lynn was appointed Surgeon-General to the Irish Citizen Army, and in 1916 attended the wounded, including Sean

Connolly, the Abbey Theatre actor and the first fatal casualty of the rebellion. She was imprisoned in Kilmainham and deported, but released in 1918 to assist in fighting the influenza epidemic of that year.

Shocked by social conditions in Dublin, Dr Lynn, with Madeleine ffrench-Mullen, founded St Ultan's Childrens' Hospital in 1919 with £70 and two cots. Although 'on the run', she carried on her work. 'I evaded capture by dressing like a lady, in my Sunday clothes and feather boa and by walking instead of cycling.' She voted against the Treaty. In 1923 she was elected to Dáil Éireann, but never took her seat in Leinster House. Countess Markievicz bequeathed her cottage in Glenmalure to Dr Lynn, who, in turn, bequeathed it to An Óige. It is now a youth hostel.

Dr Lynn named her new hospital after St Ultan who succoured the orphan children of County Meath. Often I was privileged to accompany her to St Ultan's Well at Ardbraccan near Navan. She presented me with her treasured copy of Sir William Wilde's *The Beauties of the Boyne* which she had used in 1919 in locating the forgotten holy well. In it she wrote: 'To Dr Cowell because he appreciates, from Kathleen F Lynn, 1953.'

Philip Lynott (1949-1986)
85 Leighlin Road, Crumlin, 12

A coloured Irishman over six feet tall with a swinging gait and a shock of black curls – these were the characteristics which marked Philip Lynott

for his fans, denying the Rock'n'Roll idol of the 1970s the privacy he often craved. If fame meant anything to this man, it meant music. His other car wasn't a Porsche – he never even learned to drive!

Born in Birmingham to an unmarried Irish mother, she and her coloured child suffered much in the prejudiced era of the 1950s. Aged four, the boy came to live with his grandparents in Leighlin Road in Crumlin. There he became an Irishman, indeed a bornagain Dubliner. His grandfather glimpsed the future showman, likening Philip to Sammy Davis, junior. After a commendable record in the Christian Brothers' School, Philip Lynott became a Crumlin celebrity, playing with the Black Angels' Band. Then came the Black Eagles, Skid Row and the Orphanage leading to Thin Lizzy and, like a streaking meteor, the

Philip Lynott

emergence of Philip Lynott as a Rock'n'Roll legend.

World tours followed one another. In 1977 in a tour of the United States he was unimpressed with the New World. 'They're all plastic,' he concluded. In the same year for his twenty-eighth birthday he entertained three hundred guests at Castletown House, Celbridge, County Kildare.

On his marriage to Caroline Crowther, daughter of the actor Leslie Crowther, he bought a house in Richmond, Surrey. However, his devotion to Ireland impelled him to send his wife to Dublin's Holles Street Hospital for the births of their children. As a refuge from incessant Rock'n'Roll adulation, he bought Glen Cor, a secluded house in Howth where he escaped whenever possible. Nearby he bought another house as a fiftieth birthday present for his mother.

With the split-up of Thin Lizzy, Philip's world began to fall asunder. His marriage failed and illness caught up. Admitted to hospital as an emergency, it then transpired – too late – that long-time drug addiction had undermined the idol of the teenagers. Philip Lynott died suddenly in Salisbury in 1986, aged thirty-six.

My Boy, his biography written by his mother, Philomena Lynott, should be read by every teenager throughout the world. It is a truly tragic exposé of the destruction of talent wrought by drug-addiction.

Catherine McAuley (1778-1841)
House of Mercy, Lower Baggot St., 2

From an opulent background, Catherine McAuley became the foundress of the nursing and teaching congregation of the Order of Mercy in Dublin. The work she began in 1831 was to become the largest congregation of nuns in the world. By a current reckoning twenty-three thousand of her Sisters of Mercy are ministering for the good of mankind in over fifteen hundred foundations.

Born at Stormaston House, a mansion in the Ballymun district, Catherine McAuley was orphaned at seventeen. At first she lived with an uncle, Owen Conway, a surgeon in East Arran Street. She was then adopted by William Callaghan, Director of the Apothecaries' Hall, then at 149 Mary Street. When he and his wife moved to Coolock House, Catherine lived with them for nineteen years, until their deaths, when she inherited the house and £25,000, a vast sum at that time. Moved by the poverty she witnessed, she sold the house, and for £4000 purchased a site at the corner of Lower Baggot Street and Herbert Street. Here her House of Mercy was built for the education of poor girls.

Inspired by the work of Mary Aikenhead, and her Irish Sisters of Charity, Catherine McAuley decided to found a religious order. She fulfilled a noviceship at the Presentation Convent, George's Hill. In 1831 she opened the first Convent of Mercy, and the Baggot Street House of Mercy became the Motherhouse of the Order, which it remains today. Specialising in educating the poor, convents were opened throughout Ireland. In 1841, supported by English Catholic aristocrats, they spread to England. Before the end of the century, the Sisters of Mercy were working throughout the world.

Catherine McAuley died in 1841 at the Baggot Street Convent. On a lawn at the rear in a leafy quadrangle, surrounded by the graves of forty of her nuns, she lies under a Gothic memorial oratory to which visitors come 'from all quarters of the world', people fascinated by the incalculable good wrought by one woman in her brief lifetime. In April 1990 her name was elevated in the church calendar: she is now the Venerable Catherine McAuley.

P J McCall (1861-1919)
25 Patrick Street, 8

In the widening of Patrick Street in Dublin's Liberties some historical houses were lost. No. 25, a one-time pub and grocery, was the birthplace of a ballad-maker whose work is preoccupied with County Wexford. His mother was responsible, having originated in South Wexford, and having nurtured her son on the bravery of the battles of 1798. Who hasn't heard sung the firey words of 'Boolavogue', or 'Kelly the Boy from Killane'? They were the ballads that sustained the Volunteers through the years of the War of Independence.

A patriot and a republican, Patrick J McCall worked for the Library Association of Ireland where he became associated with James Connolly, Arthur Griffith and Sean T O'Kelly. A part-time writer, his stories are forgotten, but his ballads live on: 'Haste To The Wedding', 'Follow Me up to Carlow' and 'Redmond O'Hanlon'. Of them all it is 'Boolavogue' that evokes something of the fighting spirit of the men of Wexford in 1798:

Then Father Murphy, from old Kil-
*   cormack,*
Spurred up the rocks with a warning
*   cry;*
"Arm! Arm!" he cried, "for I've
*   come to lead you,*
For Ireland's freedom we live or
*   die."*

The house in Patrick Street bore a plaque in memory of P J McCall. Appropriately, it was put there by the '98 Commemoration Committee. Even more appropriately, it was unveiled by his friend Sean T O'Kelly, by then President of Ireland. Now in safe-keeping, it is hoped it will be suitably re-erected in the locality.

Count John McCormack (1884-1945)
Glena, Rock Road, Booterstown

The musical triumphs, the fabulous earnings and the exotic travels of John McCormack read more like high-flown fiction than the real-life story of an Irish operatic tenor turned ballad singer. For thirty years he was the world's most beloved concert performer, mobbed by his idolators, and festooned with honours by church and state. One ambition was never fulfilled – he owned a string of racehorses, yet he never won the Derby.

Born in Athlone and educated at

Count John McCormack

the Marist School there and at Summerhill College, Sligo, his dream was to become a singer. He worked as a clerk while he trained with Dr Vincent O'Brien, Choirmaster of Dublin's Pro-Cathedral Choir. Beating another tenor, one James Joyce, he won the Dublin Feis Ceoil, after which admirers made it possible for him to go to Maestro Vincenzo Sabatani in Milan. 'I can do little,' said the Maestro, 'except teach this boy how to use his voice properly. God has done the rest.'

By 1912 he had made his Covent Garden debut, and had toured the world. Once he said, 'If my reputation as a singer is to be judged by any particular record, I am willing to stand or fall by *Il Mio Tesoro*.' He was criticised for 'wasting' the perfection of his voice and technique as a ballad recitalist. John McCormack's answer was unequivocal: 'The popular ballad is as vital today as it ever was, for the hearts of men and women do not change.'

Moore Abbey, Monasterevin, County Kildare, was McCormack's home for twelve years. There he kept his racehorses, and there he made his film, *Song of My Heart*, in which Maureen O'Sullivan made her debut. In all, his wife set up twenty-eight homes in different countries during her husband's career. Their move to Glena in Booterstown in 1944 was their last. There in the twilight of his life he entertained his friends, played his recordings, and listened to the special birthday tributes broadcast in his honour.

A bronze bust surmounts McCormack's massive marble tombstone in Dean's Grange Cemetery.

F J McCormick (1891-1947)
16 Palmerston Gardens, 6

Time was when an account of an evening at the Abbey Theatre ended with '... but F J McCormick was magnificent'. In the sense that greatness in the theatre is recognisable, but indefinable, McCormick was indeed the greatest character actor ever produced by the Abbey Theatre. When he was a Roman he *was* a Roman, or a Cockney or a Corkman. When he invoked them, his body, his hands, his eyes spoke for him – the technique known today as body language. As 'Joxer', his favourite part, he summoned every human instrument at his command to create the most supreme bowsie of them all. Yet for all his greatness he scorned pretentiousness and show, preferring the grind of weekly rep in Dublin to the tempting offers of film contracts that repeatedly came his way.

Peter Judge (his real name) was born at Skerries, County Dublin, the son of a farmer. He became a civil servant, first in London in the Savings Bank Department and later in the Irish Department of Education. His first stage appearance was in the York Street Workingmens' Club. He later appeared at Edward Martyn's Hardwicke Street Theatre, graduating to Boucicault melodrama at the Queen's Theatre (since demolished), where he rehearsed during his lunch-break, and where he adopted his stage-name to avoid parental disapproval. In 1918, he resigned his 'safe job' and joined the Abbey Theatre, where in thirty years he played some five hundred parts. In 1925 he married Eileen Crowe, the Abbey Theatre actress. She died in 1978.

In the film *Odd Man Out*, McCormick's performance as the vicious little slum rat called 'Shell' was making him an international reputation when he died suddenly in Dublin.

Siobhán McKenna (1922-1986)
40 Highfield Road, Rathgar, 6

International fame, if not fortune, followed the Irish actress Siobhán McKenna. At home comparative indifference denied her the appreciation her art deserved. Like Cyril Cusack's, her name in Dublin will always be associated with *The Playboy of the Western World,* with which she had a life-long love affair. Even her dogs were called Christy Mahon and Pegeen Mike.

Two accents came naturally. Siobhán was born off the Falls Road in Belfast and grew up in Shantalla in Galway. Her father, a lecturer in mathematics, encouraged study. She responded, first with a scholarship to University College, Galway, and then another to University College, Dublin. After graduation she joined the Abbey Theatre and met an actor called Denis O'Dea. They married and lived in Harcourt Street, later moving to his old home, 52 South Richmond Street.

In 1953 two greats came together in *The Playboy*, Cyril Cusack as Christy Mahon and Siobhán McKenna as Pegeen Mike. Cusack's habitual underplaying allowed Siobhán, at least for once, to 'capsize the stars', as her biographer Mícheál Ó hAodha describes it. Although they afterwards appeared together periodically, Cusack and McKenna never stopped playfully needling one another.

Shaw's *Saint Joan* with a Connemara accent came as a surprise. Dublin 4 couldn't understand it. London W1 had no difficulty. It ran there for five months before touring Paris and the United States. Siobhán McKenna appeared in many plays with great success wherever English was spoken.

Donal Donnelly played opposite her in the 1960 Dublin Theatre Festival production of *The Playboy*, which later went to London. Bernard Levin, the English critic, enthused: 'Miss McKenna touches her words and they burst into flame. She tosses her head and the stars dance. She wrings indignation from a look, love from a gasp, and infinite ravishing beauty from every syllable she utters.' If that isn't praise, what is? Only of a great actress could it be written.

Siobhán's Dublin home was 23 Highfield Road, Rathgar, until she moved up that road to No. 40. Her retreat was a cottage on Burrough Road in Sutton. Her last appearance was in May 1986 as a bed-ridden old woman called Mommo in Tom Murphy's *Bailegangaire*. She died in November 1986 and is buried in Rahoon cemetery in her beloved Galway.

Anew McMaster (1893-1962)
57 Strand Road, Sandymount, 4

'All I ask of Ireland is a living, just a living. God knows it's not much to ask.' Against the better judgment of his friends, Anew McMaster, the Irish actor, was about to abandon a brilliant international career to bring Shakespeare to Sligo and to Skibbereen. 'Fit-ups, dear, with a black velvet background and great splashes of colour ... and Shakespeare's words ...' An actor of immense range and power – as he had proved in the great cities of the world – McMaster upheld the tradition of grandeur even in the humblest halls in the backwoods of Ireland. He was the saviour of every sixth-year English class, and reverend mothers adored him. In due time he could say: 'My name in Ireland has become that ghastly thing, a household word!'

Born in Monaghan, he grew up in Warrenpoint, County Down. 'Mac', as he was known amongst theatre people, remembered nothing of his mother who died aged twenty-seven. At sixteen he ran away to follow his heart's desire – to be an actor. In 1911 he made his debut on the London stage in *The Scarlet Pimpernel* at the New Theatre. He married Marjorie Willmore, and it was he who brought her brother – now his brother-in-law – Mícheál MacLiammóir, back to Ireland. Later he employed a London actor called Hilton Edwards. Thus he was instrumental in introducing the two men destined to become the founders of the Dublin Gate Theatre.

A production of *Othello* was scheduled for the Dublin Theatre Festival of 1962 with 'Mac' as the Moor and Edwards as Iago. But fate intervened. As MacLiammóir explained, 'I think it was the news that his health forbade that he should play Othello in the Festival that was the direct cause of his death.'

Leonard McNally (1752-1820)
22 Harcourt Street, 2

Ireland's many attempts to overthrow the domination of Britain frequently ended abortively through the activities of government informers. To this day, 'informer' is a pejorative word in Ireland, connoting somebody lower than the lowest Judas. Nor were these traitors always 'common informers'. There were men of status and position whose double-dealing only came to light after their deaths. One such was

Leonard McNally. Born in Dublin, he became a grocer in St Mary's Lane. Ambitious, he was called to the Irish Bar in 1776, and to the English Bar in 1783. He posed as a popular and democratic barrister, and he joined the United Irishmen. In addition, he was a successful playwright, his comedies being produced at Covent Garden.

On the day that Lord Edward Fitzgerald was arrested, and mortally wounded – as a result of the work of another informer, the Dublin barrister Francis Magan, of 20 Usher's Island – the Viceroy and his Court were attending a gala performance of Leonard McNally's comic opera, *Robin Hood*, at the Theatre Royal.

McNally acted officially as defence counsel for United Irishmen, while at the same time acting as Dublin Castle's paid spy. The facts emerged after his death in 1820, when his heir claimed the continuation of his secret service income of £300 a year which McNally had drawn since 1798. The betrayer of Robert Emmet is buried in the vaults of Adam and Eve's Church, Merchant's Quay.

Seán MacBride (1904-1988)
Roebuck House, Clonskeagh, 14

A son of Maud Gonne and Major John MacBride (executed for his part in the 1916 rebellion), Seán – as he liked to be known – was educated in France (French was his first language), and at Mount St Benedict, Gorey. Aged thirteen, Yeats said he could pass for eighteen. Hence his activity as a schoolboy in the Anglo-Irish War. He accompanied the Treaty delegation to London in 1921 as private secretary to Michael Collins. Taking the republican side in the Civil War, he afterwards became one of the wild men of the IRA (of which he became Chief of Staff), and was imprisoned in 1927 and 1929. He worked as a journalist on the *Irish Press*, and was called to the Bar in 1937. In 1946 he founded the political party Clann na Poblachta. In 1947 he was elected a TD, and as Minister for External Affairs in the first coalition government (1948-51) he became a politician of international repute, while acting vigorously at home against the partition of Ireland. In 1957 he left politics and pursued a distinguished career at the Irish Bar.

MacBride became a much admired international statesman, his concerns being nuclear disarmament, human rights and equality in the Third World, while always championing the cause of Irish nationhood. He was a founder-member of Amnesty International and of the International Commission of Jurists. In 1974 he was awarded the Nobel Peace Prize, in 1977 the Lenin Peace Prize, and in 1981 the Dag Hammarskjoeld Prize for International Solidarity. He worked for the Anti-Apartheid Movement and acted as the United Nations Commissioner for Namibia. He travelled widely to secure the release of political prisoners.

A world-acclaimed champion of peace, Seán MacBride remained a controversial figure in Ireland. Many, it seems, distrusted his broken accent. However, he lived to see the Irish

State, born in violence, become a fully-fledged democracy, while the declaration of the Irish Republic took place during his tenure as Minister for External Affairs. Like his contemporaries 'on the run' in the Troubled Times (1916-1923), he had many Dublin addresses of convenience, but Roebuck House remained his permanent home. His myriad interests were reflected in the legal, political and artistic diversity of those who paid their respects as his coffin, draped in the UN flag, was taken to the Republican Plot in Glasnevin Cemetery.

Seán MacDermott (1885-1916)
16 Russell Place, Jones's Road, 3

The drama played out in Dublin in Easter Week 1916 owed everything to one man's genius for revolutionary conspiracy. Seán MacDermott re-

Seán MacDermott

vealed his mind to no man. His strategic importance as the link between the Irish Republican Brotherhood and the Volunteers only became evident in the last few frantic days before the Rising.

Born at Kiltyclogher, County Leitrim, MacDermott spent his early years in Scotland and the United States. On his return to Ireland he became a nationalist, joining every prominent nationalist organisation. He was trained in republicanism by Bulmer Hobson in Belfast, after which he became a full-time organiser at thirty shillings a week. For this, and despite lameness, he took to the road, cycling thousands of miles throughout the country in all weathers in his recruitment campaign. With his good looks, his dedication, and his captivating charm, he easily influenced young men.

From 1910 he organised and edited *Irish Freedom*, the IRB organ. His first publishing office was at 5 Findlater's Place (since demolished). He later transferred to 12 D'Olier Street (which bears a plaque). MacDermott's capacity for secret manipulation ensured that by the eve of the Rising he had become its absolute stage-manager. Then the prophetic words he had spoken a year earlier came to pass: 'We'll hold Dublin for a week, but we'll save Ireland.'

In 1916 Dublin Castle recorded MacDermott's address at 500 North Circular Road. Executed on 12 May 1916, he is buried with the other leaders in Arbour Hill Cemetery.

Mícheál MacLiammóir (1899-1978)
4 Harcourt Terrace, Adelaide Road, 2

Mícheál MacLiammóir claimed to have been born in Cork, where he had begun school before his family moved to London. Although his Irish nationality was accepted throughout his life, some doubt has arisen since his death. It is certain, however, that his introduction to the theatre was as a child actor in London. As a youth he studied painting. News of the 1916 Rising aroused a sense of indignation. Aided by a copy of Padraic Pearse's *The Mother* he joined the Gaelic League in London. Ever after he was to say, 'I believe passionately in the Irish language.' On his travels through Europe he learned Spanish, French and German. His was a love-hate relationship with Ireland: he loved the countryside; he hated Irish amateurism and its sneering disregard for professional perfectionism.

In the 1920s he joined the theatrical company of Anew McMaster, his brother-in-law. In 1928 he met Hilton Edwards, and their life-long partnership began with the foundation of the Dublin Gate Theatre. Multi-talented, MacLiammóir was by turn actor, dramatist, director, set-designer, costume-designer, translator and accountant. The work of the Gate revolutionised Irish theatre, exposing it for the first time to international influences.

When he first returned to Ireland he lived at Ardana, York Road, Dun Laoghaire, and later at 57 Strand Road, Sandymount. For some years he lived with relatives in a cottage on

Mícheál MacLiammóir

Howth Hill. Up to 1944 he shared a flat with Edwards over a hardware shop at 13-15 Dawson Street. Then they purchased a Regency house in Harcourt Terrace where they lived out their lives. The house bears a plaque.

4 Harcourt Terrace, Adelaide Road, 2

MacLiammóir was a highly-honoured man. He received awards from the Irish Academy of Letters and Irish Actors' Equity. Trinity College conferred an honorary D.Litt. He was made a Freeman of the City of Dublin, and France made him a Chevalier of the Légion d'Honneur. He died in March 1978, six months before the celebration of the golden jubilee of the Dublin Gate Theatre.

Eoin MacNeill (1867-1954)
43 Lower Hatch Street, 2

A lesser-known issue of Easter Week 1916 is the conflict which existed between the Irish Republican Brotherhood (represented by Padraic Pearse) and the Irish Volunteers (represented by Eoin MacNeill). This rivalry for authority over the Volunteers reached its climax on the eve of the Easter Rising and wrecked any chance of a military success. In founding and leading the Irish Volunteers MacNeill had intended them as a defensive rather than a revolutionary force. Pearse held an opposite view. In deceiving MacNeill, Pearse put what he considered to be the national interest above everything else.

Born at Glenarm, County Antrim, Eoin MacNeill began his career as a civil servant in the Four Courts in Dublin. Through his friendship with Father Eoghan O'Growney, the Gaelic scholar, he learned the Irish language. He became Professor of Early and Medieval Irish History at University College, Dublin. With Professor Douglas Hyde (later first President of Ireland), he co-founded the Gaelic League in 1893, a non-political organisation devoted to the study of Irish. In 1913 he was instrumental in founding the Irish Volunteers at an historical meeting in the Rotunda. He was elected their President and Chief of Staff.

It was at his brother's house at Woodtown Park, Ballyboden, in the foothills of the Dublin mountains, in the early hours of Good Friday 1916 that MacNeill was roused and informed that an insurrection was planned for Easter Sunday. Many were afterwards to blame the MacNeill countermand for the immediate failure of the Rising.

Other addresses at which MacNeill lived were 19 Herbert Park, 4 and 3 South Hill Avenue, Booterstown.

Richard Madden (1798-1886)
4 Booterstown Avenue, Booterstown.

Richard Robert Madden, historian of the United Irishmen, was born in Bridge Street, near Oliver Bond's house. In 1829 he qualified as a doctor in London, and worked there as a surgeon before taking a post as special magistrate to administer the Abolition of Slavery statute in Jamaica. He later worked in Havana and Australia before returning to Dublin in 1848 where he became a voluminous writer of history. *His Lives and Times of the United Irishmen* alone runs into seven volumes.

He befriended Anne Devlin when he discovered her living in poverty. She died while he was abroad, and was buried in a pauper's grave in Glasnevin. On his return, he had her exhumed and reburied near the O'Connell Tower. The headstone he erected records her bravery as a faithful friend of Robert Emmet. He co-operated with Thomas Davis in marking Wolfe Tone's grave in Bodenstown. His family owned the fairground in Donnybrook, the site of the infamous Donnybrook Fair, now Bective Rangers' Football Club. He brought cypress trees from Napoleon's grave at St Helena to place round his family grave in Donnybrook.

In his later years, in addition to his writing, Dr Madden worked on behalf of the Irish peasantry, as he had worked on behalf of the slaves and the exploited settlers in Australia. His house in Booterstown Avenue is marked with a plaque. He is buried in Donnybrook Cemetery.

Sir John Pentland Mahaffy
(1839-1919)
38 North Great George's Street, 1

On being knighted in his eightieth year, Mahaffy said: 'I won't be called Sir John, but Sir Provost of Trinity.' An apt remark, for the two words 'Sir' and 'Provost' summarised his life's ambitions. While honours poured in upon him from European universities, Mahaffy suffered only setbacks at Trinity College. When eventually he attained the Provostship at seventy-five, he remarked: 'Ten years too late!'

Born in Switzerland, he grew up partly in Newbliss, County Monaghan, and partly in Dorset Street, Dublin. After graduating from Trinity he took Holy Orders, but he never played the role of cleric convincingly. Once he was asked was he really a clergyman. 'Yes,' he replied, 'but not in any offensive sense of the term.' His epigrams may have influenced his pupil, Oscar Wilde. 'In Ireland the inevitable never happens,' he said, 'and the unexpected occurs constantly,' and 'An Irish atheist is one who wishes to God he could believe in God.'

Mahaffy opposed a revival of the Irish language, believing it would be 'a return to the dark ages'. Amongst nationalists he is remembered for his refusal to join the platform party at the Thomas Davis Centenary Celebrations (20 November 1914) because of the presence of 'a man called Pearse'.

In 1877 Mahaffy brought the youthful Wilde to Greece. Oscar duly acknowledged his debt, calling Mahaffy 'my first and last teacher, the scholar who showed me how to love Greek things'. But when the scandal broke, Mahaffy said, 'We no longer speak of Mr Oscar Wilde.'

Mahaffy loved the nobility. At a stretch a lord would do, but dukes and kings were irresistible. He lived opulently in North Great George's Street, where, as his wife declined social occasions, he became something of a bachelor with all home comforts. When affluence allowed him a second house he acquired Sea Lawn, Sutton. Later he purchased Earlscliff, Howth, which a wag suggested might better be called Dukescliff.

Lieutenant Michael Malone
(1891-1916)
25 Northumberland Road, 4

A typical hero of the 1916 Rising, Michael Malone spent the last three days of his life in the defence of 25 Northumberland Road, at the corner of Haddington Road. As Commander of the Third Battalion of the Irish Volunteers, with headquarters in Boland's Mill, Eamon de Valera had organised outposts to defend Dublin City against British reinforcements coming from Kingstown (now Dun Laoghaire). Due to an extreme shortage of men and munitions, their distribution was planned most prudently. Two men, Michael Malone and James Grace, were assigned to No. 25 Northumberland Road, which dominated the gate of Beggar's Bush Barracks and the length of the road towards Ballsbridge. With the arrival of several thousand British Sherwood Foresters, Malone's became the front line outpost of the Third Battalion.

Three days earlier, wearing his best overcoat and carrying his umbrella and his single-shot rifle, Malone had reported to Commandant de Valera that in their particularly exposed outpost he and Grace would require a fast-firing weapon. De Valera divested himself of his own treasured Mauser pistol, entrusting it to Malone together with some additional four hundred rounds of ammunition. With this, and their superhuman courage, Malone and Grace set themselves to hold the might of the British army from the corner of Haddington Road.

The Battle of Mount Street Bridge is now enshrined in Irish history. It is commemorated by a monument on the bridge. Fourteen indomitably courageous Irish Volunteers firing their puny rifles from Clanwilliam House, the nearby Parochial Hall and No. 25 Northumberland Road, inflicted casualties numbering two hundred and thirty-four officers and men. The Sherwood Foresters retired to regroup in the grounds of the Royal Dublin Society in Ballsbridge. Next day they made their final assault on the bridge. The corner house was taken only when Michael Malone was shot dead at his post, Grace managing to escape. The house bears a plaque.

James Clarence Mangan (1803-1849)
3 Fishamble Street, 2

Born at 3 Fishamble Street (since demolished), Mangan was christened James. He added the 'Clarence' himself. His homelife was cold, cruel and loveless. He left school early to help his family, who remained a burden and helped in his undoing. Scrivening in Dublin offices provided bread. In his spare time he read and wrote and studied Irish and other languages. Serious writing began in 1834 with his first contribution to the *Dublin University Magazine*. He sympathised with the Young Ireland Movement, and the first issue of *The Nation* (15 October 1842) contained poetry by Mangan. Impressed, Thomas Davis found a London publisher for Mangan's *Oriental Nights* and *Anthologia Germanica*.

George Petrie took Mangan to work with him on the Ordnance Survey in his own home at 21 Great Charles Street. Mangan carried a bottle of tar water which he constantly sipped, his humour ranging from silence to puns and jokes. Six years later he became a clerk in Trinity College Library, where John Mitchel recorded what he saw: 'It was an unearthly figure in a brown garment – the same garment (to all appearance) which lasted till the day of his death. The blanched hair was totally unkempt; the

corpse-like features still as marble; a large book was in his arms, and all his soul was in the book ...'

Mangan fell in love with a woman who led him on, but who turned out to be married. Heartbroken and humiliated, he turned to drink, never again escaping from the slippery slope. He lived at 3 Parliament Street and at 6 York Street (since demolished). He was found dying of cholera in a cellar at 2 Bride Street. After his death in the Meath Hospital, Dr William Stokes called in the artist Sir Frederick Burton who made a drawing now to be seen in the National Gallery.

Oliver Shephard, the sculptor, made a bust of Mangan which now stands in St Stephen's Green. Sara Allgood, the actress, unveiled it and recited Mangan's poem about himself:

Roll forth, my soul, like the rushing river,
That sweeps along to the mighty sea;
God will inspire me while I deliver
My soul to Thee.

Guglielmo Marconi (1874-1937)
Montrose House, Donnybrook, 4

A happy coincidence links Marconi, the inventor of wireless telegraphy, with Montrose, now the headquarters of Ireland's national radio and television services. Montrose was built in 1836 by James Jameson of the Dublin distillery. His daughter, Annie, went to Italy to study music. In 1864 she married Guiseppi Marconi. To their second son, Guglielmo, the idea of wireless telegraphy was always so real, he could not believe it wasn't equally real to everybody else. Because

Countess Constance Markievicz

because it was the nearest point across the Atlantic from the Marconi Station on Cape Breton Island. The station was steam driven, its boilers being fired with turf (peat). Clifden Station was the first point-to-point wireless service in the world.

And that is how Guglielmo Marconi, Nobel prizewinner and grandson of the Jamesons of Montrose, Donnybrook, invented radio and thereby 'put a girdle round about the earth'.

Countess Constance Markievicz
(1868-1927)
Surrey House, 49B Leinster Road, 6

A gazelle with a gun, an avenging angel, Countess ní Houlihan, the Joan of Arc of Ireland. Police reports called her 'The woman known as Countess Markievicz'. But no label could summarise this woman's boundless energy, her passionate contradictions, and her burning dedication to the cause of Ireland. The daughter of Sir Henry Gore-Booth of Lissadell, County Sligo, Constance was born at Buckingham Gate, London, in 1868, the year Gladstone pronounced that 'the final hour was about to sound' for all England's problems in Ireland. Had Gladstone been right, one shudders to think of the boring life which might have been the lot of Constance Markievicz.

his father disapproved of nonsense, it was his mother who encouraged the boy to experiment in the attic of the Villa Grifone, the family home outside Bologna. Here one day, with his brother Alfonso and his home-made apparatus, they managed to pass a message from one end of the attic to the other. Wireless telegraphy had been born!

Again, it was his mother in 1896 who took Guglielmo to London, where his invention was developed. By 1901 signals sent out from Cornwall were heard by Marconi in Newfoundland, 2,100 miles away. In 1903 a message transmitted by President Roosevelt from a radio station at South Wellfleet, Massachussets, was received at Poldhu in Cornwall where it was answered by King Edward VII.

Marconi in 1905 chose Clifden, County Galway, for a radio station

Horsemanship, beauty and courage marked her youth. Presented at Court, she remembered the Queen as a dumpy little woman in black, her fingers festooned with diamond rings. Twenty-nine years later the débutante in white satin was sentenced to death by shooting. Breaking with the 'big house' tradition, Constance went to Paris to paint. There she married a Polish count. They set up home at St Mary's, Frankfort Avenue, Rathgar, a wedding present from her mother. In a painting retreat – a cottage at Balally, Sandyford – she read through copies of *Sinn Féin*, which fired a sense of patriotism. In 1909 she moved to 9 St Edward's Terrace, Rathgar, and also leased Belcamp Park, Raheny, as a training centre for her Fianna Boy Scouts. From Belcamp she moved to 15 Lower Mount Street.

In the 1916 Rising she fought with the Citizen Army at the Royal College of Surgeons. She was the only woman to have a gun and to wear a military uniform. At the surrender she kissed her gun before giving it up, and then marched away at the head of her men to her court-martial.

Surrey House was her last home. When she was condemned to death it was vandalised. The Court recommended the prisoner to mercy solely on account of her sex, and her death sentence was commuted, but she never again had a home of her own. Between 1916 and 1924 she endured five long terms of imprisonment. In the intervals she stayed with friends. She died in a public ward at Sir Patrick Dun's Hospital.

While a prisoner in Holloway in 1918, Constance Markievicz was elected to the British House of Commons. She never took her seat. Elected in 1919, Lady Astor was the first woman to take her seat.

Archbishop Narcissus Marsh
(1638-1713)
St Sepulchre's Palace,
Upper Kevin Street, 8

As for Guinness's Brewery, so for Marsh's Library – more visitors to Dublin know the history and geography of these institutions than do the citizens of Dublin. Born in Wiltshire, and educated at Oxford, Narcissus Marsh was brought to Dublin in 1679 as Provost of Trinity College. Theologically, he never looked back. In 1683 he became Bishop of Ferns and Leighlin. Driven from his See, he fled to England, but in 1690, after the Battle of the Boyne, he returned to Ireland. He became Archbishop of Cashel in 1691, and of Dublin in 1694. In 1703 he went to Armagh as Primate.

As Archbishop of Dublin Marsh lived in the medieval archiepiscopal Palace of St Sepulchre, close by St Patrick's Cathedral. The magnificent pair of granite gate-piers, which once led to the palace, now lead to the forecourt of the Kevin Street Garda Station which stands on the site, and which incorporates part of the old palace walls.

In the garden of St Sepulchre's, alongside St Patrick's Cathedral graveyard, Marsh in 1701 built one of the first free public libraries in Europe. To it he bequeathed his collection of books. In addition, it contains the collection of twenty-five thousand books bequeathed by Edward Stillingfleet, the seventeenth-century Bishop of Worcester. Archbishop Marsh gave Swift his first seat in the chapter of St Patrick's Cathedral. Swift frequented

Archbishop Narcissus Marsh

Marsh's Library, sometimes annotating volumes with his acerbic observations.

An historical gem of both scholarship and architecture, Marsh's Library deserves to be better known by the descendants of those Dubliners for whom Archbishop Marsh created it two hundred and ninety years ago.

Edward Martyn (1859-1923)
4 South Leinster Street, 2

Born at Tulira Castle, County Galway, Edward Martyn was the 'dear Edward' of George Moore's *Ave Atque Vale*. When he wasn't playing the organ at Tulira, or writing plays in the style of Ibsen, he was holding court in his two little rented rooms over a tobacconist's close by the Kildare Street Club – 'the only place in Dublin where I can get caviar'. Though an over-conscientious Roman Catholic, Edward Martyn was also a lover of good fare.

While he was a preparatory schoolboy at Belvedere College, his domineering mother supervised affairs by moving to a house in Dublin. But Edward escaped her when he went to Beaumont and Cambridge. As an adult his ambition was to attempt to impose some cultural good taste on those most in need in Ireland. In this he gave priority to the Roman Catholic Church. As a result, Loughrea Cathedral provides evidence of what the ecclesiastical use of Irish stained glass can do in creating an atmosphere of devotion. Disgusted by the execrable standard of Irish Roman Catholic church music, Martyn founded, and endowed, the Palestrina Choir at Dublin's Pro-Cathedral where he regularly worshipped.

At his own expense he also founded the Irish Theatre, which flourished at 38½ Hardwicke Street between 1914 and 1920. As a playwright, he thought it only reasonable to give priority to his own plays. They were about the Irish middle class and were intended to counteract the Abbey Theatre's perpetual peasant comedy. In running his theatre he was assisted by Thomas MacDonagh and Joseph Plunkett, both signatories of the 1916 Proclamation. Many destined for fame made their first appearances in Martyn's theatre, including Jimmy O'Dea (in *The Cherry Orchard*, the first-ever Ibsen play in Ireland), Mícheál MacLiammóir and F J McCormick. Martyn excused a cold, cheerless auditorium: 'We are more concerned with the picture than the frame,' he said.

Although apolitical, Martyn was a

founder-member of Sinn Féin. Thus the Hardwicke Street Theatre became politically suspect, particularly after 1916. At every performance two detectives sat in the back seats. Martyn's ultimate generosity was to donate his body to the Cecilia Street Medical School for dissection by medical students. He was buried with six paupers in an unmarked grave in Glasnevin, the only ceremony being the singing of the *'Benedictus'* by his Palestrina Choir.

Father Theobald Mathew (1790-1861)
Capuchin Friary, Church Street, 7

Ireland's partiality to alcohol is of long standing. Bound up with occasions of joy and sorrow, one excuse is as good as another for 'a jar'. Living conditions in the nineteenth century were such that resort to any measure was welcome if it induced forgetful relief. Social upheavals, like the cholera epidemic of 1832, and the Famine of 1847, were followed by increased consumption of alcohol, providing an enormous source of revenue for the government. Out of the resultant moral chaos arose an apostle of temperance with a charisma envied by politicians.

Theobald Mathew was born at Thomastown Castle, County Tipperary, one-time seat of the Mathews, Earls of Llandaff. He entered Maynooth College, but on breaking the rules he left, entering the Capuchin Order at Church Street, Dublin, where he was ordained in 1814. He worked in Cork for twenty years. There he

won a reputation as a preacher. He mobilised local youth to work amongst the deprived. At the time, due to alcohol, political meetings were often occasions of physical violence. Daniel O'Connell wasn't amused.

In 1838 Father Mathew founded the temperance movement, and made himself its head. Fearless and untiring, he stomped the country preaching against the demon drink. To all who took the pledge he gave a medal. Debt to the supplier of the medals caused his arrest, losing him the possibility of the Bishopric of Cork. He toured England and America gathering large sums for his crusade. In Washington he became the second foreigner invited to take the floor in the US Senate. His attraction in Ireland was magnetic. Thousands took the pledge. In two days in Limerick he enrolled one hundred and fifty thousand members. Political meetings became more peaceful, and O'Connell was duly grateful.

Post-Famine eviction, starvation and emigration damaged the work of Father Mathew. By then he was ailing following a stroke. He died at Cobh, and is buried in St Joseph's Cemetery in Cork. He is commemorated by statues in O'Connell Street, Dublin; Patrick Street, Cork; and at Thomastown Castle, the latter unveiled in 1939 by his great-nephew, Archbishop David Mathew.

Charles Robert Maturin (1782-1824)
37 York Street, 2

A graduate of Trinity College and an uncle of Lady Wilde, Maturin took

Holy Orders and was a curate at St Peter's Church, Aungier Street (since demolished). His clothes depended upon his current fortune, but he always kept his wife well dressed. Mangan, the poet, was a neighbour; he noted the reverend's occasional preference for a boot on one foot and a shoe on the other.

Maturin wrote lurid Gothic novels, full of detailed horror. When he was engaged on his writing, he pasted a red wafer on his forehead to warn his family he wasn't to be disturbed. His most famous novel was *Melmoth the Wanderer,* which influenced both Balzac and Baudelaire. After his imprisonment, Oscar Wilde adopted the names of a Christian martyr and a character from a Maturin book – Sebastian Melmoth. Maturin was also a dramatist. Produced at Drury Lane in 1816, his play *Bertram* was admired by Scott and Byron. It earned him £1000 and he returned to Dublin a celebrity. He spent the money in having clouds and eagles painted on his ceilings, as well as scenes from his novels.

Dancing was his greatest passion. He organised morning parties and danced quadrilles all day, keeping the window curtains drawn and the candles lit to preserve the illusion of night. Though he rarely went visiting, he seldom missed Lady Morgan's evenings. When Sir Charles Morgan helped him with his chronic debts, Maturin's letter of thanks included a request that Lady Morgan should use her influence with Edmund Kean, the actor, regarding a play Maturin had sent him. The actor replied that he had

let friendship outweigh prudence too often already. The success of Lady Morgan's novel, *The Wild Irish Girl*, inspired Maturin to write one called *The Wild Irish Boy.*

The unique Charles Maturin died at the early age of forty-two.

Mary Mercer (? - 1735)
Great Ship Street, 2

A medical student called George Mercer came to Dublin from Lancashire in the 1660s. After a brilliant academic career in Trinity College, he had an equally successful career as a doctor. At his death he left his fortune to his only child, a daughter called Mary.

Concerned with the plight of poor girls, Mary Mercer decided to devote her wealth to their welfare. In 1724 she leased, for 999 years, a dilapidated site in Stephen Street, once the situation of the Chapel of the Leper Hospital of St Stephen. There in the old churchyard she built an alms house where she intended to care for and to educate her girls. But for whatever reason, Mary Mercer lost interest, and while the project lapsed her name lived on.

The need was great for a hospital in the locality. A group of philanthropists made plans, and looked at the alms house in the Stephen Street churchyard. Shortly before her death, Mary Mercer willingly transferred her lease to the trustees of what became a hospital. Opened in 1734 with ten beds, in deference to her they called it Mercer's Hospital. Eight years later the hospital benefitted financially

8 Ontario Terrace, Canal Road, Charlemont Bridge

from the first production of Handel's *Messiah,* performed at Fishamble Street Music Hall.

Dublin was served for two-and-a-half centuries by Mercer's Hospital until it was closed in 1983 in the rationalisation of the hospital system. But, phoenix-like, Mercer's Hospital was to rise again. Acquired by the Royal College of Surgeons, it was extended and updated and is still serving medical science. It now accommodates the College library, the Mercer's Institute for Research into Ageing, the Mercer's Foundation, and a hostel for overseas students. Most importantly, the Mercer's complex houses the Royal College of Surgeons Department of General Practice, which provides training for students and a medical service for the locality.

With Mary Aikenhead, Kathleen Lynn, Catherine McAuley and Grizel Steevens, Mary Mercer takes her place in that pantheon of women whose inspiration provided Dublin with a hospital service.

John Mitchel (1815-1875)
8 Ontario Terrace, Canal Road,
Charlemont Bridge, 6

'Wherever the British flag throws its poisonous shadow, I may find a prison or a grave; but a home never.' Such was the literary style – and the sentiments – of John Mitchel, the nonconformist solicitor from Newry who became a convicted felon for Ireland. On 27 May 1848, he sailed from Dublin on a British warship to begin his sentence of fourteen years' transportation for seditious journalism, inciting rebellion in Ireland, published in the *United Irishmen*, his 'physical force' paper.

On the same date Mitchel made the first entry in his *Jail Journal*: 'At Charlemont Bridge, in Dublin, this evening there is a desolate house – five little children, very dear to me; none of them old enough to understand the cruel blow that has fallen on them this day, and above all – above all – my wife.' Three years later his wife and children joined him in exile in Van Diemen's Land. Two years later they escaped to America. On arrival in New

York on 26 November 1853, Mitchel wrote: 'Without entering the city at all, we pass straight over to Brooklyn, where my mother awaits our arrival; and here ends my journal.'

Today John Mitchel is probably best remembered for his *Jail Journal*, a book that ranks with the greatest Irish literature of the nineteenth century. Pearse considered it 'the last gospel of the new testament of Irish nationality, as Wolfe Tone's autobiography is the first'. Arthur Griffith published an enlarged edition in 1913, and it was reprinted three times in the ensuing years. Excluding all else he did for Ireland, as the author of the *Jail Journal*, John Mitchel justified his life.

John Rawdon, 1st Earl of Moira (1720-1793)
Moira House, 9 Usher's Island, 8

John Rawdon, 1st Earl of Moira, for whom Moira House was built in 1752 was, in Dublin, second only to Lord Charlemont for artistic taste, charm and intelligence. For years Moira House was 'the seat of refined hospitality, of good nature and good conversation'. Here Henry Grattan was often a guest. Here Lord Edward Fitzgerald and his Pamela danced. Here came Wolfe Tone (Francis Rawdon, the second Earl, was godfather to one of Tone's children, Francis Rawdon Tone). John Wesley was a guest in 1775. He was surprised to find 'a more elegant room than any I ever saw in England. It was an octagon having one window, the sides of it inlaid with mother of pearl reaching from the top of the room to the bottom. The ceiling, sides and furniture were equally elegant.'

On the death of the 2nd Earl in 1826, Moira House became the Mendicity Institute, and was scalped of its top storey, its fine decorations and its garden. The remainder of the house has since been demolished, leaving only the three front entrance gates and the railing. The site is occupied by an uninspiring erection containing an Eastern Health Board day centre.

In Easter Week 1916 the Mendicity Institute became an outpost of the Four Courts garrison, the First Battalion, Dublin Brigade of the Volunteers. Because of the poor response to the call-up, Commandant Edward Daly promoted the twenty-year-old Sean Heuston (the nearby railway station is named after him) as commandant in charge of the Mendicity. With twenty men he pinned down a large contingent of British troops in the Royal (now Collins) Barracks, holding out for the better part of a week. A plaque over the right-hand gate records the battle. Heuston was executed with the leaders of 1916.

George Moore (1852-1933)
4 Upper Ely Place, 2

Born at Moore Hall near Ballinrobe in County Mayo, George Moore represents a reassurance to worried parents with difficult sons who cannot count or spell. George Henry Moore, MP, received a report on his son's progress at Oscott College, Birmingham: 'George is deplorably deficient and it is by no means easy to see how his defects are to be supplied ...' At the age of eighteen, on his father's death, he inherited Moore Hall and £2000 a year. He went to Paris in a futile attempt to become a painter. There he cultivated Zola, Degas, Manet, Renoir and other giants of the time, and he became fashionably irreligious. He turned to writing, and at thirty-five had published *A Modern Lover, A Mummer's Wife* and *A Drama in Muslin*. He moved to London and there completed *Esther Waters*.

Moore liked to believe he heard the voice of Cathleen ní Houlihan calling him back to Ireland. Hatred of the Boer War drove him to Dublin in 1901. Settling at 4 Upper Ely Place he wrote *The Lake* and his famous Dublin trilogy, *Hail and Farewell*. A bachelor, he surrounded himself with comfort – French impressionists on the walls, servants on the stairs, and good food on the table. But Irish literary love-hate relationships drove him to Ebury Street, London, in 1911. After Easter 1916 he saw the ruins of Dublin as 'a city that has passed away, shapeless mounds that might be Babylon'. Then Moore Hall, his old home to which he was devoted, was burnt out by the anti-Treaty forces, a gesture against his brother, Colonel Maurice Moore, who had become a senator in the Free State government.

George Moore made his own funeral arrangements. Opposite Moore Hall on Castle Island in Lough Carra, he was to be placed on a pyre, the wood to be brought from the estate. Later he modified his needs: he must be cremated and his ashes scattered on Castle Island. He warned: 'Mind the wind that it doesn't blow the ashes back into the boat.' In fact he was cremated, and the urn placed in a rocky cavity on his favourite Castle Island.

No. 4 Ely Place bears a plaque.

4 Upper Ely Place, 2

Thomas Moore (1779-1852)
12 Aungier Street, 2

Moore's birthplace was a house of family entertainment given, as her son recalled, 'by my joyous and social mother. Our front and back drawing-rooms were on such occasions distended to their utmost capacity, and the supper table in the small closet was always the most merry.' Robert Emmet was an undergraduate friend at Trinity College. Moore too had revolutionary ideas, but wisely, his mother packed him off to London after graduation in 1799. There he took the drawing-rooms by storm. As Lady Morgan observed: 'He was the guest of princes and the friend of peers.' On a visit to his parents she added tartly, 'From royal palaces and noble mansions he had returned to his family seat at a grocer's shop.'

But Moore had a loving affection for his old home. Forty years later, at the height of his fame, he came again to Aungier Street. He was received coolly until he revealed himself to the new owner: 'But the moment I mentioned who I was, his countenance brightened with the most cordial feeling, and seizing me by the hand, he pulled me along to the small room behind the shop (where we used to breakfast in old times), exclaiming to his wife, "Here's *Sir* Thomas Moore, who was born in this house, come to ask us to let him see the rooms. And it's proud I am to have him under the old roof".'

Moore visited every room, and concluded sadly: 'The many thoughts that came rushing upon me in thus visiting, for the first time since our family left it, the house in which I passed the first twenty years of my life, may be more easily conceived than told.'

On his last visit to Dublin, Moore was driving with George Petrie when he asked to proceed through Aungier Street. Opposite No. 12 he asked for the car to stop. Gazing at his old home, he wept. 'I am looking, Petrie,' he explained, 'for the little gable window by which I penned my earliest verses, the Melodies.'

Moore died in Wiltshire and is buried there. The house in Aungier Street bears a plaque.

Sydney Owenson, Lady Morgan
(1783-1859)
35 Kildare Street, 2

Sydney Owenson was born on a crossing between England and Ireland. Her father, Robert Mac Owen (changed to Owenson for professional purposes), was an actor, born in County Sligo, and a friend of Garrick and Goldsmith. Related to the Croftons, Sydney as a girl spent much time at their home, Longford House, Beltra, County Sligo, where often she felt moments 'of such felicity as childhood only experiences, when we feel that we are happier than we know'. She was an inveterate writer: poetry, novels, pamphlets. It was at Longford House she wrote her most famous novel, *The Wild Irish Girl*, which ran into seven editions, and made her the toast of Europe, a position she filled with poise and charm. Feeling threatened no doubt, Jane Austen had something to say: 'If the warmth of her language could affect the body, it might be worth reading in cold weather!'

Staying with the Marquess and Marchioness of Abercorn at Baronscourt, Newtownstewart, County Tyrone, she met her husband, Sir Thomas Morgan, a doctor. They lived at 39 Kildare Street, Dublin. The number was later changed to 35. Now demolished, the site is occupied by the Setanta Buildings. When Dublin became a deprived city following the Act of Union in 1800, Lady Morgan created a salon which became one of the brightest in the city. A liberal and a Gael (her father had taught her Irish), she sympathised with the plight of Catholics and her house became a meeting place for intellectuals of every view. Once she recorded in her diary how 'fifty philosophers passed through my rooms last night'. Less than four feet tall, and draped in shawls, Lady Morgan played the Irish harp. She did her writing with a gold pen set with mother of pearl. 'Our destiny in this world is such a wretched one,' she said, 'that I try to forget it in writing.'

In 1837 she was awarded a pension of £300 a year by Lord Melbourne 'for services rendered to the world of letters'. After eighteen years in Kildare Street the Morgans moved to Belgravia, where Thackeray became a frequent visitor. Many believed the little lady inspired the character of Becky Sharp. Lady Morgan is buried in Brompton Cemetery. She left £100 for a tablet to be placed in St Patrick's Cathedral in memory of Turlough O'Carolan, the blind harper, whose music she admired.

The Misses Morkan
(Of uncertain age)
15 Usher's Island, 8

James Joyce's great-aunts, Julia Lyons and Ellen Callanan, lived at 15 Usher's Island. He used their address fictionally, making it the gracious home of his spinster characters, the Misses Morkan – the bossy Miss Kate and the meek Miss Julia – in 'The Dead', the last, the longest and the greatest story in *Dubliners*. No longer young, the Misses Morkan were ladies of gentility. They were devoted to music, and to such finer things in life as floors that shone with the dint of polished beeswax, and a picture of the balcony scene in *Romeo and Juliet*, and another of the murdered princes in the Tower that Miss Julia had worked in blue and brown wools when she was a girl.

They were hospitable at all times of the year but, as with Joyce's great-aunts, it was their Christmas dance for which they were most admired amongst their friends and relatives. The tables burgeoned, the guests danced gracefully, some perhaps getting more tiddily than the Misses Morkan found acceptable. But it was the songs of the soloists that stirred memories, scenes from the past flooding in to merge in a melange of bittersweet remembrances of Christmasses long past.

It was against this event that Joyce

so poignantly unveiled the lasting feelings of a happily-married woman for her youthful romance with a long-dead boy who used to sing 'The Lass of Aughrim'. Rarely has a film director translated to the screen such sensitive writing as that with which Joyce concluded his story. It was accom-

The Rotunda Hospital

plished in 1987 by the dying John Huston in his version of *The Dead*, his last film, made while he was linked to an oxygen cylinder. And rarely does one leave a cinema haunted by the sight of snow gently falling on the leafless branches, the crooked crosses and the leaning headstones in a lonely Connemara graveyard – the burial place of the dead boy-lover.

Joyce's story will be read into the far future. Huston's film will live alongside it, making real the old-world gentility of the Misses Morkan, so characteristic of Victorian Dublin.

Dr Bartholomew Mosse (1713-1759)
9 Cavendish Row, Parnell Square, 1

Born in Maryborough (now Port-laoise), Dr Mosse was the son of a clergyman. Having qualified as a doctor at twenty-one, he travelled widely in Europe studying the practice of midwifery. Returning to Dublin, he found conditions pitiable. Expectant mothers were 'generally in cold garrets, open to every wind, or in damp cellars subject to flooding from excessive rains; destitute of attendance, medicines, and often proper food, by which hundreds perish with their little infants, and the community is at once robbed of the mother and child.'

Moved to action, Dr Mosse secured the old theatre of Madame Violante in George's Lane (now South Great George's Street), which had fallen on lean times since the departure to London of Peg Woffington, its star attraction. Soon the make-do hospital proved too small for the demand. Mosse then acquired 'four acres and one rood plantation measure', the site of the present Rotunda Hospital. Mosse's efforts in fund-raising resulted in a wrongful accusation of embezzlement. He was jailed, escaped, and took refuge in the Welsh mountains until things cooled and he could vindicate himself. Between 1751 and 1757 Richard Cassels, the German architect, built the first lying-in hospital in the British Isles. Dr Mosse became its first Master.

Pleasure gardens were laid out to provide an income, like the Vauxhall Gardens in London. Ever since, pleasure and parturition have been closely associated in and around the Rotunda, the complex comprising the Gate Theatre, the Ambassador Cinema and a ballroom. The greatest artistic treasure within the hospital is its chapel with its uniquely flamboyant baroque decoration.

The trials experienced in the creation of the Rotunda Hospital soon told on the physique of Bartholomew Mosse. Two years after its opening he became ill. He went to stay with his friend Alderman Peter Barré at Cullenswood House in Ranelagh. Two weeks later, aged forty-six, he died. He is buried in an unmarked grave in Donnybrook Cemetery.

T C Murray (1873-1959)
11 Sandymount Avenue, 4

Thomas Cornelius Murray, always known as T C Murray, was one of the greatest of the Abbey Theatre's great playwrights. Lennox Robinson said of him: 'He never seemed to have had to learn his craft, his genius just happened.' Like Robinson, Murray's interest in theatre began with visits to the old Cork Opera House. His plays showed his deeply penetrating obser-

vation of rural life in the Ireland of his time. In an Irish setting, his themes were universal: loveless marriage, the ambitions of mothers for their sons, the horrors of old age. In his writing Murray never flinched at realism – a spade was a spade – and his plays could always be relied upon to fill the Abbey Theatre. Of his first play, *Birthright*, produced in 1911, Joseph Holloway, architect of the Abbey and critic *par exellence*, said, 'Of late the Abbey has earned for itself the title of "the house of drama of bad language", and *Birthright* caps all previous efforts in this direction.' On the other hand, Yeats said the play was 'as perfect as a Chopin prelude'.

The son of a shopkeeper in Macroom, County Cork, T C Murray first became a student-teacher in St Patrick's Training College, Drumcondra (1891-93). He was appointed head master of the Inchicore Model Schools in 1915. At that time he lived at Gortbeg, 136 South Circular Road, Kilmainham. He had reached middle age when he began to write for the theatre. He wrote fifteen plays, not one of them negligible. In *Maurice Harte* (1912) and *Autumn Fire* (1924) he encompassed all the frustration, the unspoken and terrifying tragedy of Irish rural life, that authoritarian and stifling ethos that helped to fill those immense cold, grey mental hospitals which still bestride our land.

T C Murray's versatility was recognised in 1949 when the National University of Ireland conferred an honorary D.Litt. There is a plaque on his house in Sandymount Avenue.

Cardinal John Henry Newman (1801-1890)
6 Harcourt Street, 2

Lead, Kindly Light, amid the encircling gloom,
Lead Thou me on!

Newman wrote his hymn on the spur of the moment in 1832. In another context he once said, 'England, surely, is the Paradise of little men, and the Purgatory of great ones.' Both quotations are apposite in the light of his subsequent experience of gloom and little men in the Dublin of his time. Born an Anglican, he took Holy Orders at Oxford. He had charisma, his sermons exerting extraordinary power. In 1845 he converted to Catholicism, and in 1847 he was ordained in Rome.

To provide university education for Catholics, the Irish hierarchy decided to found a Catholic University. Newman's prestige appealed to Dr Paul Cullen, Archbishop of Dublin, so he was invited to become Rector. From his arrival in Ireland in 1852 until his retirement in 1859, nothing but gloom and little men beset the hapless Newman. He saw the University as a centre of Catholic influence and culture for all nationalities, under lay authority; Cullen saw it as a seminary for Irish students under clerical control. Newman realised he had been brought to Dublin under false pretences – as a political and ecclesiastical weapon against non-denominational education. Nevertheless, he patiently tried to make progress.

The Catholic University was established at 86 St Stephen's Green, while No. 6 Harcourt Street (St Mary's University House) became the students' residence. Here Newman carved daily for some thirty students with whom he shared. 'It is odd, I should begin to keep house at fifty-three,' he said.

To influence through preaching, Newman saw the need for a university church. Cullen disagreed, and refused his assistance. Newman undertook the project himself. 'My idea was to build a large barn,' he said, 'and decorate it in the style of a basilica, with Irish marbles and copies of standard pictures.' University Church in St Stephen's Green is a barn, but only in the sense that the Sistine Chapel is a barn.

Newman was created a cardinal in 1879, and died in Birmingham in 1890.

Alfred Charles Harmsworth, Lord Northcliffe (1865-1922)
Sunnybank, Chapelizod, 20

A boy of seven called Alfred Charles William Harmsworth was given a toy printing set which fascinated him. Was it symbolic? For little Alfred of Chapelizod was destined to become the self-made and greatest British presslord of all time, the first Viscount Northcliffe of St Peter-in-Thanet, and Baron Northcliffe of the Isle of Thanet. In the heyday of his newspaper empire, Lord Northcliffe as good as ruled England. His success was his recognition that the masses had been compulsorily taught to read, so he catered for this newly literate people. Thus he swayed public opinion.

Sunnybank, Chapelizod, 20

Politicians feared him. 'I would as soon trust a grasshopper,' said Lloyd George – a case of the kettle calling the pot black.

A teacher at the Royal Hibernian Military School in the Phoenix Park, his father, following a Fenian raid, moved the family to Hampstead. Alfred attended Henley House School, where H G Wells taught chemistry. On leaving school he borrowed £500 and launched a magazine called *Answers.* His arithmetic was bad, so he recruited his brother, Harold (the future Lord Rothermere), who became a financial wizard. Together they were an unbeatable team. The launch of *Comic Cuts* brought profits of £25,000 per annum. *The Evening News* brought in £14,000 in its first year. Launched in 1896, Harmsworth's *Daily Mail,* sold at a halfpenny a copy and trumpeting British imperialism, reached a circulation of over one million per day. This newspaper popularised the song 'Tipperary' amongst the British Expeditionary force in France in 1914.

As a promotional stunt the *Daily Mail* offered £1000 to the first man to fly the English Channel. Bleriot did so in 1909. Then came £10,000 prizes for a London to Manchester flight, and a round-Britain air race. It was Northcliffe's transatlantic prize which encouraged Alcock and Brown to undertake the first flight of the Atlantic from Newfoundland to Clifden, County Galway, on 14-15 June 1919.

Lord Northcliffe retained an interest in his native country. He purchased the house in Chapelizod in which he was born, and in 1921 he agitated for a cessation of the Black and Tan campaign. Burnt out after a dynamic life, he died aged fifty-seven, and was honoured with a Westminster Abbey funeral service.

Sean O'Casey (1880-1964)
422 North Circular Road, 7

Born at 85 Upper Dorset Street (the site is now occupied by a bank), John Casey was the youngest of thirteen children, 'the shake of the bag' as he called himself. The family moved to 9 Innisfallen Parade, between Lower Dorset Street and Mountjoy Prison. John attended St Mary's National School, 25 Lower Dominick Street (since demolished). On his father's death poverty struck. The family moved to 22 Hawthorne Terrace near the East Wall Road. This area is dominated by St Barnabas's Church, whose rector 'was the first to give the small clasp of friendship to the author'. The next move was across the railway, to 18 Abercorn Road, when John was seventeen. Here on 12 November 1918 (the day after Armistice Day), despite all his loving care of her, his mother died. Meantime he had become a nationalist and, learning Irish, had become Seán Ó Cathasaigh. In 1923, when *The Shadow of a Gunman* was produced, the Abbey Theatre playbills made him Sean O'Casey.

Leaving his noisy brothers, Sean moved into one room at 35 Mountjoy Square. His final move was to 422 North Circular Road, where he wrote four plays, including *Juno and the Paycock* and *The Plough and the Stars*, the plays by which the Abbey Theatre survived financially until the government began to subsidise it. O'Casey's hatred of war crystallised in *The Silver Tassie*, the play which Yeats refused to produce. Disillusioned with Dublin's literary begrudgery, O'Casey proclaimed 'Innisfallen, fare thee well!' and left Ireland forever.

O'Casey's finest characters are his tragic women. His great plays all reach the same conclusion: the brave are always the women – Juno Boyle, Bessie Burgess, Minnie Powell. His insight came from his mother to whom he was close. To her he dedicated *The Plough and the Stars*: 'To the gay laugh of my mother at the gate of the grave.'

After nearly

422 North Circular Road, 7

forty years of self-imposed exile, O'Casey died in Devon aged eighty-four.

Daniel O'Connell (1775-1847)
58 Merrion Square, 2

As a rising barrister, and a spokesman for Catholic Emancipation, in 1814 Daniel O'Connell moved into 30 Merrion Square (now 58 Merrion Square). From the time of his arrival, his neighbours were rarely without excitement. When Mr O'Connell's coach wasn't being towed home in triumph by a cheering crowd, Mr O'Connell was being driven away in a Black Maria amidst an angry crowd. Elated or defeated, crowds outside No. 30 became a feature of the place.

O'Connell liked to use insulting language against his opponents. His supporters liked it even more. His reference to the 'beggarly Corporation of Dublin' annoyed Alderman D'Esterre, a pork butcher from Bachelor's Walk. A duel ensued, ending in D'Esterre's death. O'Connell's remorse was great. Duelling was banned by the Catholic Church, so he sent an apology to Archbishop Murray. The reply read: 'Heaven be praised! Ireland is safe!' No lesson learned, O'Connell insulted Robert Peel, the Chief Secretary, who challenged him to a duel. Disgusted, his wife fled to Derrynane, the family home in County Kerry. O'Connell wrote to her: 'My darling heart, here I am surrounded by my babies and thinking of my own darling, their mother.' Their reconciliation ended O'Connell's duelling.

Its shelves packed with books, O'Connell's study had a crucifix on the wall. Strewn over the floor were the red-taped files with his briefs. Rising at four in the morning, he was at work by five. At ten-thirty he walked to the Four Courts, returning home to dine at four pm and to work on to bedtime. Only adherence to a strict regime for twenty-five years enabled him to attain his vast achievements.

With Catholic Emancipation in 1829 Daniel O'Connell became Ireland's 'Liberator', but he failed to gain repeal of the Act of Union. An old man when Famine struck in 1847, he struggled to the House of Commons. 'Ireland is in your hands, in your power,' he pleaded, 'if you do not save her, she cannot save herself.' His opponents remained obdurate. Three

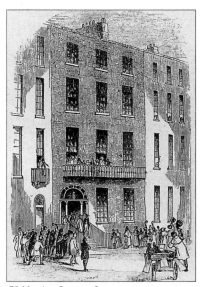

58 Merrion Square, 2

Daniel O'Connell

Frank O'Connor (1903-1966)
Court Flats, Wilton Place, 2

Michael O'Donovan, otherwise Frank O'Connor, was born in Douglas Street, Cork. His childhood homes in Cork were 251 Blarney Street (since demolished), and 9 Harrington Square. His biography, *An Only Child,* recalls his spartan life up to his teenage participation in the Anglo-Irish and the Civil wars. Though he was largely self-educated through his own wide reading, his formal education was at the North Monastery Christian Brothers' School (Cork's famous 'North Mon'). His teacher, Daniel Corkery, sowed the first literary seed that was to blossom so brightly, making Frank O'Connor one of the world's great short story writers.

After internment in 1923 he became a librarian, serving in Sligo, Wicklow and Cork, before his appointment as municipal librarian at Ballsbridge. At first he lived in 'digs' in Sandymount Green 'in a big house kept by a Donegal man and his sister who had retired to enjoy themselves in the great city'. While in lodgings in Ranelagh in 1931 he wrote *Guests of the Nation,* his first book of short stories. He then fulfilled an ambition: he moved into a flat and shared it with his mother. It was on Anglesea Road, close to the library. Here in 1932 he wrote his novel *The Saint and Mary Kate.* Henceforward his literary success was assured.

In 1935 Frank O'Connor became a director of the Abbey Theatre, with which he had a stormy relationship. He resigned in 1939 in disagreement

months later he died at Genoa on his way to Rome.

The statue of O'Connell near O'Connell Bridge is by John Henry Foley. The winged figures are by Thomas Brock who completed the monument eight years after Foley's death. Some of the figures are pierced by bullet holes sustained in the twentieth-century battles fought in O'Connell Street.

with the theatre's policy, but meanwhile, two of his plays had been produced there. For the next twenty years he lectured at American universities. He returned to Ireland in 1960, and made his last home at the Court Flats, Wilton Place, where a plaque commemorates his residence. He is buried in Dean's Grange Cemetery.

Jimmy O'Dea (1899-1965)
11 Lower Bridge Street, 8

Jimmy O'Dea was born in Lower Bridge Street, beside the house of Oliver Bond, where the leaders of the United Irishmen were arrested in 1798. His first public appearance was as an altar-boy at the nearby Augustinian Church. When the family moved across the Liffey to Capel Street he became the playmate of Jack Lemass, ie Seán Lemass (1899-1971), the future Taoiseach. They acted together in Sheridan's *The Rivals* and T C Murray's *Autumn Fire* at the Father Mathew Hall. Then Jimmy graduated to Edward Martyn's Hardwicke Street Theatre and to Ibsen's *The Cherry Orchard*. At twenty-one he qualified as an optician, and set up in business. But it was a case of no business like show business. Jimmy made three films with Irish Photo Plays Ltd. It was then his Chaplinesque appeal began to show.

In 1920, over two bottles of stout and a handshake, his thirty-five year partnership with Harry O'Donovan began. In the Queen's, the Olympia and the Gaiety theatres a spate of theatrical creations burst upon Dublin,

Jimmy O'Dea and Maureen Potter

and O'Dea became Dublin's supreme comedian. He could convulse an audience with a well-timed pause and a look of mock surprise. His war-time 'Irish Half-Hour', a BBC programme broadcast from Bangor, North Wales, commanded a fifteen million listenership. His fame spread further when he played Finian in the Hollywood version of *Finian's Rainbow*.

To his company he was 'the Governor'. He presided like a father, proud of his talented family. In September 1964, as the curtain fell on *Finian's Rainbow* at the Gaiety Theatre, Jimmy O'Dea spoke his last lines on any stage: 'Farewell, my friends, I'll see you all one day in Gloccamorra.' His last Dublin home was at 75 Pembroke Road, Ballsbridge.

John O'Donovan (1809-1861)
36 Upper Buckingham Street, 1

Born at Attateenmore, County Kilkenny, and educated in Dublin, the name of John O'Donovan is linked enduringly with the history of Celtic scholarship. He began life full of hope for the resurgence of true Irish learning. He worked for a period in the historical section of the Ordnance Survey, and later catalogued Irish manuscripts in Trinity College. He edited the principal publications of the Irish Archaeological Society. O'Donovan's greatest work was editing and translating the *Annals of the Four Masters*, which were published in seven volumes between 1848 and 1851. These were the Annals of the Kingdom of Ireland compiled at Bundrowes, a Franciscan community near Bundoran, County Donegal, between 1630 and 1636 by four Franciscans, the 'Four Masters': Michael O Clery, Peregrine O Clery, Peregrine Duignan and Fearfasa O Mulconry. At the instigation of Sir William Wilde, a memorial commemorating the Four Masters was erected in 1876. It stands on a triangular lawn opposite the Mater Hospital.

For his services to literature O'Donovan was honoured by the Royal Irish Academy, by Trinity College and by the Royal Academy of Science at Berlin. Joined by Eugene O'Curry (1796-1862), his brother-in-law and a self-made scholar without formal education (who in 1854 became Professor of Irish History and Archaeology at Newman's Catholic University), O'Donovan began the translation of the *Seanchus Mór* (the Ancient Laws of Ireland). He died before its completion. Six months later O'Curry was dead. Both men died in poverty. In response to a request from the Royal Irish Academy, the Glasnevin Cemetery authorities provided free grave spaces. Fifteen years passed before a group of academic admirers erected handsome tombstones over these distinguished scholars.

Sean T O'Kelly (1882-1966)
55 Wellington Street, 7

With his twin sister, Sean T O'Kelly was born at 55 Wellington Street, and christened at St Michan's Church, Halston Street. The family moved to 4 Berkeley Road where their father ran a shoe shop and here the young 'Sean T' grew up. As an altar boy at Berkeley Road Church he became friendly with Matt Talbot. His first school was the Mountjoy Street Convent. Later he attended the Christian Brothers' School, Mary's Place, graduating to the O'Connell Schools on the North Circular Road. As a young assistant in the National Library he was influenced by Thomas Lyster, the Librarian, and by Edward Dowden, Professor of English at Trinity College.

In 1903 Sean T became closely associated with Arthur Griffith in the foundation of Sinn Féin, of which he became secretary from 1908 to 1910. In 1913 he helped to found the Irish Volunteers. He fought in the General Post Office in 1916, where he was appointed Staff Captain to Padraic

Pearse. Afterwards he suffered his first of sixteen terms of imprisonment. At that period he lived at 27 Upper Rutland Street. Here he sheltered the brothers, Padraic and William Pearse, for the two nights preceding the Easter Rising.

Sean T was the first diplomat of the Irish Republic. Accredited in 1919 by Dáil Éireann as Envoy to the Peace Conference then in progress in Paris, he attempted to put Ireland's case as a small nation to Woodrow Wilson, President of the US. He failed because British influence militated powerfully against a hearing of Ireland's claim.

Sean T helped in the foundation of Fianna Fáil, and served as a Minister of State in several governments led by de Valera. He lived at 38 Anglesea Road, Ballsbridge until he became the second President of Ireland (1945-1959), and moved to Áras an Uachtarain. On his retirement Sean T O'Kelly lived at Roundwood, County Wicklow.

John O'Leary (1830-1907)
11 Warrington Place, 2

Born in Tipperary town of well-to-do parents, John O'Leary first attended the local grammar school before becoming a boarder at Carlow College, where one of his teachers was Father Thomas Croke, later Archbishop of Cashel and a founder of the GAA. During the Famine the college kitchen became a communal feeding place. O'Leary contracted relapsing fever and was sent home.

While convalescing he read the poems and essays of Thomas Davis, which changed his life. At sixteen he met James Stephens, the Fenian leader, and the revolutionary die was cast. He became an active, if not the most exceptional, Fenian – he never took the oath. As editor of the *Irish People*, the Fenian newspaper, he was arrested in 1865 and deported. He spent five years in Portland Prison, and the next fifteen in exile in Paris. Always an avid reader, it was then he began to collect books.

In 1885 O'Leary returned to Ireland a free man. With his books he set up home at 40 Leinster Road, Rathmines. Five years later he moved to 134 Rathgar Road, and a year later to 30 Grosvenor Road, then to Drumcondra. He later lived at 53 Mountjoy Square and at 17 Temple Street. When the

John O'Leary

Yeats family moved to London, leaving WB behind, he shared with O'Leary, living at Lonsdale House, St Laurence Road, Clontarf. His final move was to 11 Warrington Place (since demolished), near Mount Street Bridge. O'Leary never assessed a house for its comfort, but rather for its capacity to accommodate his collection of ten thousand books.

An inspiration for young Irish writers, O'Leary encouraged a fourteen-year-old schoolboy called Arthur Griffith. Then he met the twenty-year-old Willie Yeats, who was trying to be a poet in the English tradition. Recognising genius, O'Leary channelled it from English to Irish literature. Yeats remembered his debt: 'From O'Leary's conversation and from the Irish books he lent or gave me has come all I have set my hand to since.'

O'Leary always remained a critical admirer of James Stephens. They are buried side-by-side in Glasnevin Cemetery under identical Celtic crosses.

Brian O'Nolan (1911-1966)
4 Avoca Road, Blackrock

Better known by one or other of his many *noms-de-plume*, Brian O'Nolan was born in Strabane, County Tyrone. His father was an official in the Customs and Excise Service, so the family moved frequently, living in Dublin (Inchicore), Strabane again, Tullamore and back to Dublin, at Herbert Place, and 4 Avoca Road, Blackrock. Brian had a brilliant career as a student at University College, Dublin, where he wrote for *Cothrom Féinne*, a college magazine, and edited another called *Blather*. He was prominent in the Literary and Historical societies. On graduation in 1932, he studied in Germany before returning to Ireland to become a civil servant in the Department of Local Government. Eventually he resigned to concentrate on his writing. Under the *nom-de-plume* 'Myles na Gopaleen' he created the famous Cruiskeen Lawn column in the *Irish Times,* which ran for twenty years. With satire and humour he dealt appropriately with the establishment, and with institutions and current events, like 'The Emergency', otherwise the World War of 1939-45, when bureaucrats blossomed even more luxuriantly than in peacetime.

As Flann O'Brien, O'Nolan

11 Warrington Place (now demolished), 2

published *At Swim Two Birds* in 1939, a novel blending satire, fantasy and farce and which James Joyce thought 'a really funny book'. *An Béal Bocht*, written in Irish, and a satire on Irish Irishry, appeared in 1941. *The Dalkey Archive* came in 1964, and *The Third Policeman*, although written in 1940, wasn't published until 1967. His play *Faustus Kelly* was produced at the Abbey Theatre in 1943.

A brilliant talent was cut short with the death of Brian O'Nolan in 1966.

The O'Rahilly (1875-1916)
40 Herbert Park, 4

Born in Ballylongford, County Kerry, to well-to-do parents, Michael Joseph O'Rahilly found his own way to patriotism. After local schooling, and Clongowes Wood College, and a stint as a medical student, young O'Rahilly had a holiday romance with Nancy Browne, one of five beautiful and wealthy American sisters just then touring Europe under their mother's tutelage and as part of their education. O'Rahilly followed her to America where they married in her home town of Philadelphia.

On their return to Ireland in 1900 they lived at Wilfort Cottage, a rambling house on the Dublin Road near Bray. In 1904 they moved to Brighton before returning to Philadelphia. In 1909 they came back to Dublin and lived at 38 Upper Leeson Street before moving to 40 Herbert Park in 1912. It was from this home that The O'Rahilly drove away in his famous green car on the morning of Easter Monday

1916, never to return.

It was as part of Douglas Hyde's de-Anglicisation policy, popular at the turn of the century, that Michael O'Rahilly assumed the title 'The O'Rahilly'. By this title he is known to history.

It was The O'Rahilly, with Bulmer Hobson, who first proposed the institution of the Irish Volunteers in 1913. He believed, with Eoin MacNeill, that insurrection was not the way the Volunteers could best sustain the cause of national independence in 1916. Accordingly, he drove to Limerick with MacNeill's countermanding order in the early hours of Easter Sunday. Yet, when the Insurrection broke out on Easter Monday, while he still disagreed with it, The O'Rahilly then felt it his duty to go to the General Post Office to fight beside the men he had trained.

On Friday 28 April 1916 he wrote a note as he lay dying: 'Darling Nancy, I was shot leading a rush up Moore Street. Took refuge in a doorway ... Tons and tons of love dearie to you and to the boys ... It was a good fight anyhow. Please deliver this to Nannie O'Rahilly, 40 Herbert Park, Dublin. Good bye darling.' Found in his breast pocket, the note had been pierced by a bullet.

Sir William Orpen RHA (1878-1931)
Oriel, Grove Avenue, Blackrock.

Born to be an artist, 'Orpsie' enjoyed an idyllic childhood in a wealthy family. They lived in a fashionable suburb, still surrounded by tall trees and green fields, between the Dublin mountains and the sea. At eleven he went to the Dublin Metropolitan School of Art where he won every prize. His gift for drawing meant he received little other education. At nineteen he went to the Slade School in London where, again, he won all before him. Augustus John, a fellow student, became a life-long friend. John was tall, 'Orpsie' small. 'The chief thing that impressed me in my youth,' he said, 'was my ugliness.' In his picture, 'The Dead Ptarmigan – Self Portrait', in the National Gallery of Ireland, Orpen has spared himself nothing in the depiction of his ugliness.

He kept in close touch with Ireland, making frequent visits to take life-classes, and sometimes to fulfill portrait commissions. Holidays at The Cliffs, Howth, resulted in airy, sunlit pictures like 'A Breezy Day, Howth' and 'A Summer Afternoon'. His huge picture, 'The Holy Well', in the National Gallery, shows naked Irish pagans drinking from a well and thus being transformed into Christian and costumed Aran islanders, and his friend, the bearded Sean Keating, surveying the scene from a rocky height.

As well as helping James Larkin to fight starvation in the Dublin strike of 1913, Orpen inspired his friend Hugh Lane to launch his Municipal Gallery of Modern Art at 17 Harcourt Street. In 1914 Orpen turned his back on Ireland. By then he was living a double life, his marriage eventually failing.

England meant unparalleled success. Orpen couldn't cope with the demand for portraits. In World War I he became an official artist with the rank of Major in the Royal Army Service Corps. These pictures are in the Imperial War Museum in London. In 1918 he was knighted. By the late twenties he had painted over six hundred portraits in oils and many thousands of figure studies, drawings and watercolours. An income of £50,000 a year, a Rolls and a life of luxury failed to bring happiness. 'The struggling man is a joke,' he said, 'the successful man is a far greater joke.' At fifty-three alcoholism hastened the death of a great artist.

Walter Osborne (1859-1903)
5 Castlewood Avenue, Rathmines, 6

Reared in the atmosphere of his artist father's brushes and paint, there was never a doubt as to the future career of Walter Osborne. At seventeen he entered the school of the Royal Hibernian Academy in Lower Abbey

5 Castlewood Avenue, Rathmines, 6

Street (destroyed in 1916). The Taylor Scholarship in 1881 brought him to Antwerp Academy where, shortly afterwards, Van Gogh was to be a pupil. In 1883, at twenty-four, he became an Associate of the Royal Hibernian Academy, and at twenty-seven a full member.

Osborne worked in Brittany and Southern England. From 1877 he exhibited annually at the Royal Hibernian Academy. He first exhibited at the Royal Academy in 1886. After 1891, for family reasons, he spent more time in Ireland, and had his studio at 7 St Stephen's Green. After he had cast off academic constraints, Osborne's working method became a compromise between realism and the spontaneity of impressionism. His work in Ireland, particularly in the Dublin Liberties, shows a fascination with children and animals, and the vagaries of sunshine and shadow. To live, he had to respond to the demand for portraiture. However unhappily, he produced the cliches. Bram Stoker commissioned a portrait of his wife, Florence Balcombe, once the girlfriend of Oscar Wilde. It was hung in the Royal Academy and bought by Stoker for £75. An Osborne picture today costs nothing less than a ransom.

A modest man, Walter Osborne refused a knighthood in 1900. Three years later he died aged forty-four.

Father Paul Mary Pakenham
(1821-1857)
10 Rutland Square (now Parnell Square), 1

Charles Reginald Pakenham, the fourth son of Thomas, second Earl of Longford, was born at 10 Rutland Square, the town house of the Earls of Longford. Charles's aunt, Kitty Pakenham, married the Duke of Wellington in the drawing-room of the same house.

Charles Pakenham was educated at Winchester and at the Royal Military College, Sandhurst. By 1846 he had become a captain in the Grenadier Guards. An inveterate reader, he became attracted by the Oxford Movement, and particularly by the conversion of Newman to Roman Catholicism. In 1850 Charles was himself received into the Roman Catholic Church by Cardinal Wiseman. Though discouraged by his family, by his friends, and by the Passionist Fathers, he decided to enter that Order at their monastery at Broadway in the Cotswolds. On resigning his commission, his uncle, the Duke of Wellington, advised him: 'You have been a good soldier, Charles, strive to be a good monk.'

Implicitly, Charles obeyed. As a novice in 1851, he became Brother Paul Mary. Four years later he was ordained at Oscott College in Birmingham. With the approval of Cardinal Cullen of Dublin, the Passionist Fathers decided to spread to Ireland, and in 1856 Father Paul Mary Pakenham became the founder of the

Passionist Order in Ireland, and the first Rector of Mount Argus Monastery. Renowned as a preacher, Father Paul Mary led an austere and self-sacrificing life. Ill-health soon intervened, and in 1857 his premature death caused 'all Dublin to mourn over him with an almost universal sorrow'. Beyond the wall, in Mount Jerome Cemetery, lies his kinsman, Edward, sixth Earl of Longford, and his wife Christine. To her I am indebted for these notes on the life of Charles Reginald Pakenham.

Anna (1842-1911) and Fanny (1847-1882) Parnell
7 Hume Street, 2

The contribution to Irish history of the sisters, Anna and Fanny Parnell, has been eclipsed by the fame of their brother, Charles Stewart Parnell. That is as he would have wished it. The activities of his socially-minded sisters were an embarrassment to him. Educated privately at Avondale, the family home in County Wicklow, Fanny took to writing poetry for nationalist journals, while Anna dabbled in painting and observed the poverty of the people.

The Land League, founded by Michael Davitt in 1879 to fight landlordism, was eventually banned, and its leaders gaoled. It was then the Parnell sisters founded the Ladies' Land League with their headquarters at 39 Upper O'Connell Street. While Fanny toured the US raising money, Anna distributed £70,000 of food, clothing and shelter for evicted families. The Land League huts they built to house the homeless were ruthlessly destroyed by the police. Even the Archbishop of Dublin, Dr McCabe, condemned the Parnell sisters for outraging feminine modesty. The British authorities charged that their League was a front for Fenian activities: burning, shooting and maiming of human beings and cattle. When Davitt's Land Leaguers were released, Parnell found the activities of his sisters even more embarrassing. He refused to pay a debt of £500 incurred by Anna, something for which his sisters never forgave him. The fame of Anna and Fanny Parnell was snatched from them by an ambitious and jealous brother. They, and their good works, were to fade into comparative oblivion.

Fanny continued her fund-raising in the US, and lecturing on Ireland's wrongs. Devoted sisters, her death in New Jersey in 1882, aged thirty-five, left Anna a devastated woman. She became an oddity, a recluse, living in solitude, mostly in England. While swimming at Ilfracombe in Devonshire in 1911 she was drowned at the age of sixty-nine. As feminist leaders, born before their time, history has never adequately recognised the greatness of Anna and Fanny Parnell.

Charles Stewart Parnell (1846-1891)
14 Temple Street, 1

The Dublin home of the Parnell family became an address of notoriety in the 1860s. Under continuous police surveillance, it was raided repeatedly. It had become a hiding place for wanted Fenians. The young, silent and sultry Charles Stewart Parnell, then an undergraduate at Cambridge, disapproved. The trouble lay with his widowed and colourful American mother, Delia Tudor Stewart Parnell, who never paused to clarify her politics or her philosophy. Men with secret missions used her house, and in her drawing-room veteran Irish-American officers organised for the Fenian Rising. Her daughter, the beautiful and temperamental Fanny, wrote patriotic poetry for John O'Leary, the handsome editor of *The Irish People* and the romantic Fenian leader with whom she was currently in love. All the while, Mrs Parnell managed to remain an intimate friend of the Viceroy, Lord Carlisle. Disapproving of his mother's revolutionary activities, Charles, home from Cambridge, removed himself from 14 Temple Street (then Upper Temple Street), to his County Wicklow inheritance to become the lonely young squire of Avondale.

With the arrest of the Fenian leaders in 1865, a long series of trials for high treason began at Green Street Courthouse. The prisoners were defended by the great barrister Isaac Butt, whose fees were met by Mrs Parnell. It was then, in his mother's house, that Charles first met Butt, the man he was ruthlessly to oust as leader of the Home Rule Party. By 1867 Fenianism had lost its challenge for Mrs Parnell. She left Dublin to live in Paris.

Parnell's fifteen years of splendid

Charles Stewart Parnell

political service to Ireland made him her Uncrowned King. In 1891, after the divorce scandal, he married Catherine O'Shea. Four months later he died suddenly in Brighton. Aged eighty-three, Mrs Delia Parnell died accidentally in a fire at Avondale in 1898. She was buried in Glasnevin with her distinguished son.

Padraic Pearse (1879-1916)
27 Great Brunswick (now Pearse) Street, 2

An English stone carver, Pearse's father came to Ireland to join the boom in church building following Catholic Emancipation. James Pearse became a Roman Catholic and married an Irish girl. They lived in Macken Street (then called South Clarence Street). They moved to 27 Great Brunswick Street

Padraic Pearse being arrested following the 1916 Rising

Gaelic League newspaper, *An Claidheamh Soluis*. His first ambition was fulfilled.

Increasing affluence brought the family to 5 George's Ville, Sandymount Avenue, a few doors from the birthplace of WB Yeats. The next move was to Lisreaghan Terrace, Sandymount. In 1904 they moved to 39 Marlborough Road, Donnybrook, and in 1907 to Brookville, Sallymount Avenue. This address was adapted to read 'Cuil Chramach, Leeson Park', the park being a more socially acceptable locality.

In 1908 Pearse fulfilled his second ambition by founding St Enda's College at Cullenswood House on Oakley Road, Ranelagh. In 1910 he transferred the College to the Hermitage, Rathfarnham, a gracious house beautifully situated at the foot of the Dublin mountains. Cullenswood House then became St Ita's Girls' School. Pearse called the Irish educational system a 'murder machine'. Reluctantly, he admitted that Irish children showed a

where the patriot brothers, Patrick and William (1881-1916) were born. The house bears two plaques and the name of the street has been changed to Pearse Street. A rise in the world enabled the family to move to Newbridge Avenue, Sandymount. While at the Christian Brothers' School in Westland Row, Patrick set himself three ambitions: to edit a bilingual newspaper, to found a bilingual school and to start a revolution. Before he was twenty-four he was lecturer in Irish in the Catholic University, had gained his BL degree, and was editor of the lack of respect for the truth, and cruelty in their treatment of animals. Yet for all the cultivation of the Pearse myth by Irish educators, it is remarkable how they avoid his ideas on the reformation of the system so as to produce more upright, honest citizens of character and individuality.

His third ambition was realised on Good Friday 1916 when, with his brother Willie, Pearse cycled away from St Enda's College for Liberty Hall and the General Post Office, never to return. He was executed in Kilmainham Jail on 3 May, Willie on 4 May 1916.

George Petrie (1789-1866)
21 Great Charles Street, 1

An archaeologist, writer, musician and artist, George Petrie was the son of a Scottish miniature painter who settled in Dublin. Petrie spent a long and intensively active life collecting and preserving the art, music and literature of Ireland. His working day was never long enough for the tasks he set himself. In fact he was interested in everything Irish, and was responsible for making Irish Christian archaeology a subject for serious study. A member of the Royal Hibernian Academy, and of the Royal Irish Academy, he worked in the museum and library of the latter. As well as the twelfth-century Cross of Cong, Petrie bought and presented to the Royal Irish Academy a manuscript of the second part of the *Annals of the Four Masters*.

His official work was the Ordnance Survey of Ireland, which was carried out in the little back parlour of his house at 21 Great Charles Street, off Mountjoy Square. Here he was assisted by the scholars John O'Donovan and Eugene O'Curry, and here he recruited the poet James Clarence Mangan as another assistant. In 1858 Petrie moved to 7 Charlemont Place, 2, on Dublin's southside.

In a paper written in 1833, entitled 'On the Origins and Uses of the Round Towers of Ireland', Petrie attempted to explain these peculiarly Irish structures. In 1851, when the O'Connell monument in Glasnevin Cemetery was being planned, he proposed that it should comprise a group of buildings, including a chapel like that of Cormac on the Rock of Cashel (ie, the Glasnevin mortuary chapel), a high cross like those at Monasterboice and Clonmacnoise and, lastly, an accurate reproduction of a round tower. The O'Connell Tower is the highest round tower in Ireland. For lack of funds Petrie's design was never completed.

Petrie helped in the foundation of the Society for the Preservation and Publication of the Melodies of Ireland. *The Petrie Collection of the Ancient Music of Ireland* contains one hundred and forty-seven airs, including 'The Londonderry Air'. But for the work of George Petrie, Ireland's culture would be the poorer.

Richard Pigott (1835-1889)
7 de Vesci terrace, Monkstown

A sleazy journalist and the proprietor of several third-rate and insolvent newspapers illicitly acquired (*Shamrock, Flag of Ireland* and the *Irishman)*, Richard Pigott also ran a photographic business on Lower Ormond Quay where he did a rewarding line in pornography and blackmail. A man who couldn't go straight, Dick Pigott required a substantial income to meet his expensive tastes in wine, women and song. He was devoted to his young family – his only redeeming feature. In 1881 Parnell needed a newspaper as a mouthpiece. For £3000 Pigott was glad to make a sale, his newspapers becoming *United Ireland* under the aegis of Parnell. In the course of this transaction Parnell had to sign some business letters. Ingeniously, Pigott was to preserve this correspondence for use later on.

Pigott wrote a pamphlet, *Parnellism Unmasked*, purporting to link Parnell with crime in Ireland, particularly with the Phoenix Park murders. *The Times* of London became interested, commissioning Pigott to obtain more evidence. He obliged by inventing documents to which he forged Parnell's signature. Believing them genuine, *The Times* published a facsimile of a so-called Parnell letter incriminating himself. The political world was stunned, for Parnell was at his political peak at the time. He hankered to take a libel action against *The Times*, but his private life forbade it. A special commission of enquiry with three judges was set up. The government was shocked when, under cross-examination by Sir Charles Russell (later Lord Russell of Killowen), Pigott was revealed as an inveterate liar – though he didn't admit the forgeries.

The commission adjourned for a week. Meanwhile, Pigott absconded to Paris from where he sent his confession of guilt. He then went on to Madrid. As the police there closed in, he 'had a big revolver in his hand, placed the muzzle against his mouth, drew the trigger, and fell to the ground a horribly mutilated corpse'.

The collapse and flight of Pigott placed Parnell on a pedestal, from which all too soon he would topple. He received £5000 damages from *The Times*, and the cost to that newspaper was £200,000 and the loss of its reputation.

George Noble, Count Plunkett (1851-1948)
Muckross Park, Donnybrook, 4

George Noble Plunkett was the son of Patrick Plunkett, the nineteenth-century developer who built all those South Dublin roads with English names: Wellington, Marlborough, Elgin, Clyde, etc. A barrister, a bibliophile and a journalist, George Plunkett once edited his own magazine, *Hibernia*. He became Director of the National Museum, where in 1905 he figured in a controversy, suggesting that a picture by Corot, which Hugh Lane hoped to include in his collection for Dublin, was a fake. The episode became a *cause célèbre*, with Susan Mitchell writing a parody in contemporary verse:

And John B Yeats stood near the gates
With mischief in his gaze,
While W.B. the poet, he
Pondered a telling phrase,
You'll find it in the Freeman
After a day or so

*And Moore was there – the same
      who is
High Sheriff for Mayo.*

Interested in politics, George Noble was the father of Joseph Plunkett, executed as a 1916 leader. Though once an applicant for the Under-Secretaryship at Dublin Castle, George Noble Plunkett, as the father of three 1916 men, one a martyr, was in 1917 elected a Sinn Féin MP for North Roscommon. He never took his seat. His electoral success was the first open defeat inflicted by the physical force men on the constitutional Irish Party since the beginning of Parnell's day. A month later Plunkett was conferred with the Freedom of Sligo. He had already been given a Papal title.

In 1884 he married Josephine Cranny. They lived at her family home, Muckross Park, Donnybrook, now the Dominican College. Later they lived at Kilternan Abbey, Kilternan; at 40 Elgin Road; and at 26 Upper Fitzwilliam Street.

Sir Horace Plunkett (1854-1932)
Kiltieragh, Foxrock

A younger son of the thirteenth Baron Dunsany, Horace Plunkett was an enigmatic idealist. A Unionist, he yet supported the Gaelic League and the Gaelic Athletic Association. After Eton and Oxford, pulmonary tuberculosis sent him to ranch in Wyoming for ten years. He returned to Ireland full of plans for the reformation of its stagnant agriculture, and ready to invest his American earnings in providing technical back-up for such a project.

He served as MP for South Dublin from 1892 to 1900. In proposing a Board of Agriculture and a Technical Education Bill, Plunkett made a plea not inappropriate to the Ireland of to-day: 'We Unionists without abating one jot of our Unionism and the Nationalists without abating one jot of their Nationalism, can each show our faith in the cause for which we have fought so bitterly and so long by sinking our party differences for our country's good.' In 1894 Plunkett's co-operative movement, the Irish Agricultural Organisation Society, was set up at 84 Merrion Square (now called Plunkett House), where his assistants were George Russell (AE, the philosopher) and Susan Mitchell, the witty poetess. By 1899 Plunkett's ambition was fulfilled: the Irish Department of Agriculture came into being. Irish agriculture was transformed.

A patron of the arts, Horace Plunkett's home in Foxrock was an open house to co-operative workers, writers and artists. Three nights before his fatal journey to Cork, Michael Collins dined at Kiltieragh with Horace Plunkett, Lady Lavery and Bernard Shaw. Plunkett was nominated to the Senate in December 1922. As a result, his home was bombed by the republican forces in January 1923, and completely destroyed by fire on the following night. Kiltieragh, with all its artistic treasures, was sacrificed as part of the republican campaign to destroy the homes of every Irish senator.

Joseph Plunkett (1887-1916)
Larkfield, Kimmage Road, 12

Joseph Plunkett was a son of Count Plunkett and a grandson of Patrick Cranny, a building developer who lived at Muckross Park, Donnybrook. Educated at the Catholic University School, Belvedere College, Stonyhurst and University College, Dublin, Plunkett travelled widely in southern Europe and North Africa in an effort to cure pulmonary tuberculosis. In appearance he was a most unlikely revolutionary, but his pallor concealed a steely resolution.

His interests ranged from history, politics and economics to chemistry, poetry and Egyptology. He was also a critic, poet and editor of *The Irish Review*. In 1914 with Edward Martyn and Thomas MacDonagh he founded the Hardwicke Street Theatre. He acted under the pseudonym 'Luke Killeen', and one of his plays, *The Dance of Osiris,* was produced there. He left the theatre when Strindberg's *Easter* was produced, believing it unsuitable on religious grounds.

In 1915 Plunkett acted as an emissary to Germany. From Chancellor Bethman-Hollweg he obtained the promise of a cargo of arms to reach Ireland on Easter Sunday 1916. On his return he was appointed Director of Military Operations. Said to be in a dying state following an operation for tuberculous glands, he left his bed and went out to fight on Easter Monday 1916. A Marconi enthusiast, Plunkett had constructed his own radio set and was responsible for broadcasting the true facts of the Rising; he contradicted the British version that it had been merely 'a small riot'.

Four hours before his execution on the morning of 4 May 1916 Joseph Plunkett married his fiancé, Grace Gifford, in the chapel of Kilmainham Jail.

Dr Dorothy Price (1890-1954)
10 Fitzwilliam Place, 2

Born at Newstead, Clonskeagh, County Dublin, Dorothy Price née Stopford came of a Protestant/Unionist family. On the death of her father in 1902 the family left Wyvern, Bushy Park Road, Rathgar, for 65 Campden Gardens, West Kensington. Then aged 12, Dorothy attended St Paul's Girls' School where her interests were social science, art and the theatre. Encouraged by her aunt, the Irish historian, Alice Stopford Green, she first learned about Ireland. In 1915 she returned to Dublin and studied medicine at Trinity College. Through his friendship with Alice Stopford Green, Dorothy met Sir Matthew Nathan, then Under-Secretary. As his guest she was marooned in the Under-Secretary's Lodge in the Phoenix Park throughout Easter Week, 1916.

The brutal aftermath of the Rising converted her from West Britishism to Irish nationalism. She joined Cumann na mBan and she qualified in 1921, 'in spite of martial law and the army of occupation'. Appointed dispensary doctor at Kilbrittain, County Cork, she helped the IRA both before and after the Treaty. In 1924 she was appointed physician to St Ultan's Hospital, Dublin, where she specialised in tuberculosis in children. In 1925 she married District Justice, Liam Price, and set up home and practice at 10 Fitzwilliam Place.

The ravages of tuberculosis turned Dorothy Price's mind to the prevention of a preventable disease. She visited Vienna and Gothenburg and studied the new BCG vaccination. Her use of BCG at St Ultan's was interrupted by World War II. Her post-war results encouraged the government to set up the National BCG Committee and a country-wide vaccination campaign began in 1949. I was privileged to be appointed its medical director. Sadly, Dorothy Price suffered a stroke in 1950 (at which point they moved to 8 Herbert Park, 4) but happily she lived to see her dream – the control of tuberculosis in Ireland – coming true.

Thomas Prior (1681-1751)
Bolton Street, 1

Two boys called George Berkeley and Thomas Prior became firm friends at Kilkenny College. When Berkeley (1685-1753) became Bishop of Cloyne he called Prior 'the promoter, founder and guardian of the Dublin Society', later known as the Royal Dublin Society. When the RDS acquired the stately house, once the Masonic Girls' School, at the corner of Merrion and Simmonscourt roads, they called it Thomas Prior House in memory of the man whose cultural and educational legacy to Ireland is incalculable.

It all began when, early in the eighteenth century, in almost a spirit of defiance, the Anglo-Irish developed a sense of Irish nationality. They were reacting against the restrictive enactments of the English parliament which militated against the Irish economy. In June 1731 fourteen men of Anglo-Irish stock met in the rooms of the Philosophical Society in Trinity College and founded the Dublin Society to improve husbandry, manufacture and other useful arts. Thomas Prior was appointed secretary, a post he held for twenty crucial years. Future meetings were held in the Lords' Committee room at Parliament House in College Green. Meetings of various working committees took place in Prior's house in Bolton Street where, a bachelor, he lived quietly attended by a couple of man servants.

In addition to his pioneer work in creating the Royal Dublin Society, it was Thomas Prior who acquired for Dr Bartholomew Mosse the ground on which he built his Rotunda Lying-in Hospital.

Prior was born at Garrison, Rathdowney, County Laois (formerly Queen's County). Garrison was the estate he inherited from his father, and where he died in 1751. He is buried in the local churchyard.

Sarah Purser (1848-1943)
11 Harcourt Terrace, 2

From being a poor girl, Sarah Purser, through her own initiative, made herself unique – a rich artist in her own lifetime. Born at Dun Laoghaire (then Kingstown) when her mother was on holiday, the family lived at Dungarvan, County Waterford, where in 1875

11 Harcourt Terrace, 2

their fortunes failed. After their move to Dublin, Sarah borrowed thirty pounds, went to Paris and learned to paint. On her return she opened a studio at 2 Leinster Street. Her earliest commission came from Lady Gore-Booth of Lissadell, County Sligo, to paint her daughters, Constance and Eva. Her reputation as a portrait painter was made. Her portraits of personalities of the Irish Literary Renaissance now hang in the Dublin galleries. Indeed, the Sir Hugh Lane gallery of Modern Art is Purser's greatest memorial, for it was she who persuaded President W T Cosgrave and his new Free State government to hand over Charlemont House to Dublin Corporation. The Friends of the National Collections of Ireland (funded by herself) then converted the Georgian mansion into a magnificent picture gallery.

Around 1900 Edward Martyn sought vainly for Irish stained glass for Loughrea Cathedral, then being built. Sarah Purser remedied the situation in 1903 by launching An Túr Gloine (the Tower of Glass) at 24 Upper Pembroke Street. This became a most important institution for stained glass, for there a team of artists (including Evie Hone) produced Irish glass which has found its way to many countries. The most representative collection in Ireland is in Loughrea Cathedral.

Sarah Purser lived and worked at 19 Wellington Road for ten years. In 1887 she moved to 11 Harcourt Terrace, a Regency house near the Grand Canal. It bears a plaque. After twenty years she moved to Mespil House, a seventeenth-century mansion with a park, a lake and a stream. The site now accommodates the Mespil Flats in Sussex Terrace. Until her death 'Miss Purser's second Tuesdays' took place in the grand drawing-room under its magnificent ceiling, afterwards re-erected in Áras an Uachtarán.

John Redmond (1856-1918)
7 Belvedere Place, 1

Born at Ballytrent on the coast of County Wexford, John Redmond as a boy knew many who had shouldered pikes in 1798, those to whom Rebel was a name of honour. Though himself a potential rebel, Redmond was no revolutionary. He was a constitutionalist, and led the Irish Parliamentary Party after the death of Parnell. Educated at Clongowes Wood and Trinity College, the Jesuits taught him how to debate, even how to declaim, attributes he put to good use from the age of twenty-four when he was first elected an MP. On the day he took his oath and his seat at Westminster, he made his maiden speech (one of protest) and was suspended, being carried from the House by the Sergeant-at-Arms in one of the demonstrations regularly enacted by the Irish Parliamentary Party.

Under Parnell's leadership, Redmond's career was inconspicuous. It was in 1914 as leader of the Party that he gained notoriety when the long-awaited Home Rule Bill was passed, but suspended until the end of the War. In blind gratitude, Redmond made a speech at Avoca pledging Irish support to England's war effort until Home Rule could come into effect. His speech split Ireland, and spelled Redmond's political doom. He was accused of imbecility, idle vanity, corrupt bargaining, and every unworthy motive, including that of buying Home Rule with the blood of young Irishmen.

In the 1890s John Redmond lived at 15 Upper Fitzwilliam Street. In the 1900s he moved to 7 Belvedere Place. As a barrister, these were houses of convenience, not homes. The home he loved was Aughavannagh on the slopes of Lugnaquilla in County Wicklow, a one-time military barracks, later Parnell's shooting lodge, and now the Aughavannagh Youth Hostel. The election of the first Sinn Féin candidate (George Noble Count Plunkett) in 1917, and the death of his younger brother William, an MP, on active service in France, were mortal blows to Redmond. He retreated to the now-lonely house at Aughavannagh. But the mountains, the streams and the lakes no longer comforted him. He died in 1918.

Lennox Robinson (1886-1958)
Sorrento Cottage, Vico Road,
Dalkey

The most prolific playwright ever found by the Abbey Theatre, Lennox Robinson ('Lynx' to his friends) was born at Douglas near Cork. His father being a clergyman, the family moved in 1892 to 5 Fisher Street, Kinsale, and in 1900 to a spacious rectory at Ballymoney near Bandon. Robinson's education was a musical one, and he played the violin and the organ. While politics had no part in life at the rectory, unionist principles were of course inculcated. One hot afternoon in August 1907 he went to the Cork

Opera House where the Abbey Theatre was presenting Yeats's *Cathleen ní Houlihan* and Lady Gregory's *The Rising of the Moon*, with the Fay brothers, Sara Allgood and Máire O'Neill. Young Robinson underwent a catharsis. Unionist precepts instantly gave way to a new and fervid nationalism. 'That strange Irish thing,' he called it, 'the commanding force in my life.' He went home and wrote *The Clancy Name*, the first of his many plays for the Abbey Theatre.

On first coming to Dublin Lennox Robinson lived in furnished rooms at 2 Upper Mount Street where farthings figured largely in his bills. Appointed manager at the Abbey Theatre, he went with the company on tour to America. By living on a dollar a day for food he saved thirty pounds in six months. On his return to Dublin he bought some furniture and took unfurnished lodgings in Lower Baggot

Street. Then he moved into the lodge at Kiltieragh, Sir Horace Plunkett's place at Foxrock. Increasing affluence allowed him to purchase Sorrento Cottage in 1925. In its terraced gardens above the sea he made theatrical history with his open-air productions of Greek plays. His last home was 20 Longford Terrace, Monkstown. On his death Lennox Robinson was honoured with a grave in the precincts of St Patrick's Cathedral.

George Russell (AE) (1867-1935)
17 Rathgar Avenue, 6

Born in Lurgan, County Armagh, when George Russell was eleven his family moved to Dublin. 'I have never been sufficiently grateful to Providence,' he said, 'for the mercy shown to me in removing me from Ulster.' At first the Russells lived at 33 Emorville Avenue, South Circular Road. In 1885 they moved to 67 Grosvenor Square, and later to 5 Seapoint Terrace. Meanwhile George had got a clerkship in Pim's store in South Great George's Street, where he earned forty pounds per annum, and looked from the high windows at the heavens longing for freedom. At night he attended the Metropolitan

17 Rathgar Avenue, 6

School of Art where he met another spiritually-minded young man called Willie Yeats. Theosophy was their common interest. With periodic estrangements, their friendship lasted for life.

On his marriage in 1898 Russell moved to 10 Grove Terrace and later to 66 Calderwood Avenue. His next home, 28 Upper Mountpleasant Avenue, became the first of his famous meeting places for intellectuals. He continued the custom at 25 Coulson Avenue, but it was at 17 Rathgar Avenue that his Sunday evening at-homes became part of the Dublin literary and artistic scene. In his book-lined living room, Moses-like, with shaggy beard and steel-rimmed spectacles, this twentieth-century prophet welcomed allcomers, provided they had intellectual interests. His literary protégés were numerous, many afterwards becoming famous.

The new Irish Free State exercised a puritanical censorship of writers. Intellectual claustrophobia drove George Russell to live in England. When he died in 1935 his coffin was brought to Plunkett House, 84 Merrion Square, where it lay in state before his burial in Mount Jerome. It was in Plunkett House that AE had worked for many years with Sir Horace Plunkett in the Irish Agricultural Organisation Society.

Cornelius Ryan (1920-1974)
33 Heytesbury Street, 8

The literary achievements of Cornelius Ryan, based on events in World War II, have been acclaimed throughout the world. First there was *The Longest Day*, then *The Last Battle*, and finally *A Bridge Too Far*, all of them world best-selling books. Subsequently they were filmed in 'epic' versions, *A Bridge Too Far* alone costing twenty-five million dollars to make. In Ireland these mammoth attainments by a local boy were rather taken for granted. But then in Ireland World War II never happened. What *did* happen was a lesser event called 'The Emergency'.

Cornelius Ryan was born at 33 Heytesbury Street, a stone's throw from his school round the corner in Synge Street. He became a journalist, and left Dublin to become a war correspondent, first in Europe and then in the Pacific. For *The Longest Day* Ryan interviewed some seven hundred D-day survivors in America, Canada, Britain, France and Germany. He did not consider himself a military historian. *The Longest Day*, which sold sixteen million copies, owed its popularity to the sources of his information – the participants. *The Last Battle* sold ten million copies in nineteen languages, and had thirty-one different editions.

A Bridge Too Far, dealing with the slaughter at Arnhem, took seven years to research. In a race against death, Cornelius Ryan refused pain-killing drugs for cancer in order to keep himself alert to complete this, his last book. He died shortly afterwards at Ridgefield, Connecticut, where he had lived on his farm.

Sir Walter Scott (1771-1832)
9 St Stephen's Green, 2

In 1825 Scott came to Ireland for three reasons: to see Killarney, to visit his friend Maria Edgeworth (he was her 'noblest and gentlest of lions') and to celebrate his fifty-fourth birthday with Walter, his married son, then living at 9 St Stephen's Green (now the St Stephen's Green Club). Another cause for celebration was that Walter junior had just been gazetted captain in the Fifteenth Hussars then serving at Dublin Castle. The fact that he could rent a stately home in Dublin for £150 per annum was an after-affect of the Union of 1800 and the exodus of Anglo-Irish society to London. Yet Sir Walter found Dublin 'splendid beyond my utmost expectations'.

When he called in to Mr Richard Milliken's bookshop, 104 Grafton Street, he spent sixty pounds on books on Irish history and antiquities. The great novelist was recognised and mobbed: 'I begin to think there is something about me which I never suspected before and give Pat great credit for having discovered it.' Scott was overwhelmed at the admiration of the Irish for his works. The Royal Dublin Society gave a public dinner; Trinity College conferred an LL.D, and the Royal Irish Academy elected him a member. 'I had been most thoroughly unprepared for finding the common people of Dublin so alive to the claims of any non-military greatness.'

For all his admiration for the Irish, Scott summed them up pretty aptly: 'I never saw a richer country, or a finer people; the worst of them is the bitter and envenomed dislike which they have to each other.'

Sir Ernest Shackleton (1874-1922)
35 Marlborough Road,
Donnybrook, 4

Only coincidence can account for two things which occurred on 15 February 1874. The *Challenger,* the first steamship to enter Antarctic waters, photographed the icebergs of Antarctica for the first time, and established that further south lay a great continent on which, so far, no human foot had trod. On that same day, at Kilkea House, between Castledermot and Athy in County Kildare, Ernest Henry Shackleton was born, the boy destined to conquer that new continent. His father abandoned farming in 1880 and adopted the study of medicine at Trinity College. It was then the family settled at 35 Marlborough Road, Donnybrook. Young Ernest saw the sea and the great ships at Dublin docks. He read of Spanish pirates and life with the Eskimos, and he dug a shaft in the back garden as the shortest way from Ireland to Australia. His first voyage was from Kingstown (now Dun Laoghaire) to Holyhead en route for London where his father, now a doctor, set up in Sydenham. At Dulwich College Ernest's brogue earned him the name of Mike.

In 1902 Shackleton made his first voyage of exploration, in the *Discovery* with Scott of the Antarctic. In 1907, aboard the Nimrod, he travelled three hundred and sixty-six miles further South than any previous expedition. On his return to England he was knighted. Shackleton's ambition was frustrated when Amundsen, a Norwegian, beat him to the South Pole in 1912, shortly to be followed by Scott who died on the ice on his return journey.

In 1914 Shackleton led an expedition to cross the mountains of the Antarctic continent. Aboard the *Quest*, in 1922, on his fourth expedition to

35 Marlborough Road, Donnybrook, 4

the Antarctic, Shackleton died suddenly at Grytviken, South Georgia. There he was buried, in the shadow of the mountains he had been the first to cross, and within sound of the wild Antarctic seas, beneath a cairn built by his comrades from his last expeditionary ship, the *Quest*.

George Bernard Shaw (1856-1950) 33 Synge Street, 8

As a small boy at 33 Synge Street, Shaw once had a strange dream. From the back garden he saw the sky filled with a bright light, and in the centre was God. But suddenly God became King Billy sitting on his horse. This reveals something of family life in Synge Street, which made Shaw 'violently and arrogantly Protestant by

family tradition'. He recorded his own description of his birthplace: 'It had, in the basement, kitchen, servants' bedroom and pantry; the *rez de chaussee*, parlour (dining-room), nursery and return room (my bedroom and my father's dressing-room, over the pantry) and on the first (top) floor, drawing-room and best bedroom. My sisters slept in the nursery when we grew out of it. We moved into 1 Hatch Street, and after my mother went to London, and I lived in lodgings with my father at 61 Harcourt Street. Torca Cottage, on Dalkey Hill was our country house.'

Little 'Ginger' was not a happy child. His father was a drunkard and his mother was preoccupied with her music. At first he went to the Central Model School in Marlborough Street, where he came in contact with the

Catholic children of Dublin shopkeepers and tradesmen. To Shaw it was a disaster, something he decided to hide away as a terrible secret. Later he attended Wesley College in St Stephen's Green (since demolished). But Shaw's erudition came from no seats of learning. He was self-educated. He adored the theatre, particularly Barry Sullivan in Shakespeare. 'I am one,' he said, 'whose whole life was influenced by the Dublin National Gallery for I spent many days of my boyhood wandering through it and so learned to care for art.' He repaid the debt. Today the gallery is enriched from his royalties. His statue stands in the forecourt proclaiming the happy arrangement.

Always very much an Irishman, Shaw cultivated his Dublin accent to the end. Yet he never wished to return. 'One always loves best the country one has conquered,' he said, 'and I have conquered England.'

Henry Sheares (1753-1798) and John Sheares (1766-1798) 128 Lower Baggot Street, 2

Both barristers, the Sheares brothers came from a wealthy Cork family. On the death of Henry's first wife in 1791, his four children were taken to France to be reared by her parents. In 1792 Henry, accompanied by John, visited the children. The brothers found themselves attracted to the revolutionary principles then popular in France. On their return to Dublin they both joined the United Irishmen.

In May 1798 they were involved in preparations for the rebellion. Captain Armstrong, a new but trusted ally, heard the plans after a dinner party in Baggot Street. The second Mrs Henry Sheares played the harp to entertain him, while he dandled her children on his knee. He had wormed himself into the affections of his victims – for Armstrong was an informer. Next morning John and Henry Sheares were arrested. In the house the hated Major Sirr discovered a draft proclamation in John's writing, ending with the words: 'Vengeance, Irishmen, vengeance on your oppressors.'

At their trial on 12 July 1798, it took the jury seventeen minutes to find the brothers Sheares guilty of high treason. Beheaded in public outside Newgate Prison, their coffins can be seen in the vaults of St Michan's Church, something which moved Speranza (Lady Wilde) to write her poem, 'The Brothers':

Years have passed since that fatal scene
  of dying,
Yet life-like to this day
In their coffins still those severed heads
  are lying,
Kept by angels from decay.

Hanna Sheehy-Skeffington (1877-1946) 7 Belgrave Road, Rathmines, 6

A Fenian, elected a Parnellite MP in 1886, David Sheehy moved from Kanturk, County Cork, to Dublin, living first at Hollybank Road, Drumcondra and later at 2 Belvedere Place, near Mountjoy Square. Here a remarkable family of four daughters and two sons grew up. The year 1916 saw them particularly stricken. Margaret had just lost her husband, leaving her with four small children; Kathleen, married to Cruise O'Brien, had economic difficulties; Mary, with an infant daughter, had just seen her husband Tom Kettle off to France to be killed at the Battle of the Somme fighting – as he believed – for Irish freedom; Richard, married with a young baby, was soon to die of tuberculosis; and Eugene had joined the British army.

But it was Hanna, the suffragist and the eldest, whose tragedy became part of Irish history. She married Francis Sheehy Skeffington, feminist, pacifist and socialist, who loathed injustice and who, while trying to stop looting during the Rising, was brutally murdered by an insane British officer. Hanna Sheehy Skeffington, with her seven-year-old son Owen, was promptly evicted from their home at 11 (now 21) Grosvenor Place, Rathmines. They found temporary shelter at 43 Moyne Road until Hanna acquired No. 7 Belgrave Road, next door to her friends Dr Kathleen Lynn and Madeleine ffrench-Mullen. The road became known as 'the Rebel Road'.

For all her tragedy, Hanna Sheehy Skeffington pushed aside her grief and mourning. For the rest of her life she suffered insults, imprisonment and privation in her fight for justice and a better deal for Ireland. The life of her son, Owen, reflected all the worthiest attributes of his remarkable parents.

Percy Bysshe Shelley (1792-1822)
7 Sackville (now O'Connell) Street, 1

Shelley hated tyranny. He became a radical in matters political and religious. Indeed, he was a republican, the most radical doctrine of his time. He championed the downtrodden Irish: 'Although an Englishman,' he said, 'I feel for Ireland.' As well as being a poet he was a deep thinker. With his wife he moved to Dublin in 1812, and stayed at 17 Grafton Street. In 1813 he stayed at 35 Cuffe Street with John Lawless, a United Irishman. It was, however, from the windows of 7 Sackville Street that he threw copies of his 'Address to the Irish People', suggesting means of obtaining Catholic Emancipation and repeal of the Act of Union, 'the latter the most successful engine that England has ever wielded over the misery of fallen Ireland'. Despite his youth, his 'Address' reflected wide reading amongst the most advanced thinkers of his time.

With O'Connell he addressed a meeting in the Fishamble Street Theatre, its boxes packed with ladies and gentlemen in evening dress. Shelley was a nine-days' wonder – an Englishman on Ireland's side, and he was received rapturously. He also met and dined with John Philpot Curran, the Irish barrister and orator, and father of Sarah who was betrothed to Robert Emmet. Amelia, another daughter of Curran, painted the only authentic portrait of Shelley, which is now in the National Portrait Gallery in London.

But Shelley was young and eager

and the pace of Irish reform was too slow. He grew discouraged. Afterwards he said: 'We left Dublin because I had done all that I could do; if its effects were beneficial, they were not greatly so. I am dissatisfied with my success, but not with the attempt ...' After Shelley's death Lord Byron wrote to Thomas Moore: 'There is another man gone, about whom the world was ill-naturedly, and ignorantly, and brutally mistaken. It will, perhaps, do him justice *now*, when he can be no better for it.'

Richard Brinsley Sheridan
(1751-1816)
12 Dorset Street, 1

No. 12 Dorset Street was the home of Thomas Sheridan, actor and manager of Smock Alley Theatre, where Peg Woffington became a star. Sheridan's

Richard Brinsley Sheridan

wife was a novelist and dramatist. As parents they exemplified the theory that, mixed properly, the genes will breed genius, for their second son was Richard Brinsley Sheridan, dramatist and politician. At Samuel Whyte's Academy in Grafton Street (the site of Bewley's restaurant, where a plaque records the academy's famous pupils) a term report recorded him as 'a most incorrigible dunce'.

When Smock Alley Theatre was wrecked by rioters, the Sheridans moved to London where Thomas became 'second only to Garrick', and Richard Brinsley was deposited in Harrow School for seven years. At twenty he eloped with a singer. Still without a career, he sat down and wrote his play *The Rivals*. On its first production in 1775 at Covent Garden Theatre, Richard Brinsley Sheridan became a public figure.

With seven successful plays within five years, the most popular being *The School for Scandal* in 1777, Sheridan was written out. He became manager of Drury Lane Theatre, and in 1780 was elected MP for Stafford. In parliament his oratory rivalled that of his fellow countryman, Edmund Burke. In 1809 Drury Lane was burnt out and Sheridan lost his principal livelihood. In 1812 he lost his parliamentary seat. Turning to drink, his debts mounted. Deserted by his friends, he died in poverty. The fame that had abandoned him in life suddenly returned in death. He was buried in Westminster Abbey, his funeral led by two royal dukes, followed by a concourse of mourning celebrities. A pall-bearer, Lord Holland, observed that Sheridan's was a life 'to point a moral or adorn a tale'.

George Sigerson (1836-1925)
3 Clare Street, 2

A professor of zoology, first at Newman's Catholic University and later at University College, Dublin, George Sigerson was a pupil of Dr Jean-Martin Charcot (1825-1893) of Paris, whose book, *Diseases of the Nervous System*, he translated. Sigerson was also a poet and a translator of Irish literature. Douglas Hyde said of him: 'As an Irish scholar he was the last link that connected us with the era of O'Donovan and O'Curry and one of the last that connected us with the men of '48, with Kickham and with Mitchel.' Sigerson was unique in that he became a Free State senator in 1922 whose house was *not* burned down as a reprisal.

Born near Strabane, County Tyrone, Sigerson graduated at Queen's College, Cork, in 1859. When he commenced medical practice in Dublin, he lived in Synge Street, later moving to 17 Richmond Hill, Rathmines. On marriage he finally settled at 3 Clare Street, where his home became a meeting place for literary people. It was there Katherine Tynan watched WB Yeats crystal-gazing and mistaking the window-cleaner at the Medical Hall opposite for some strange symbolic vision. The Medical Hall is still in Clare Street, with its same display of tall coloured bottles.

John O'Leary dined with his physician, Dr Sigerson, every Sunday night until his death. Though he accepted his hospitality, Yeats was unflattering in his opinion of Sigerson: 'learned, artificial, unscholarly, a typical provincial celebrity, but a friendly man'. His appearance was striking – tall-hatted, frock-coated, with flowing white locks and beard, with penetrating eyes that peered through wire spectacles. His daughter, Dora Sigerson Shorter, wrote patriotic poetry. Thousands of Irish students of all ages will remember her poem 'Ireland' in Palgrave's *Golden Treasury*:

Twas the dram of a God
And the mould of His hand
That you shook 'neath His stroke,
That you trembled and broke,
To this beautiful land.

Annie MP Smithson (1873-1948)
42 Claremont Road,
Sandymount, 4

Ireland's most prodigious novelist, as well as being a public health nurse, Annie MP Smithson published twenty-two novels over a period of thirty years. Born at 22 (now No. 42) Claremont Road, Sandymount, the early death of her father and the remarriage of her mother meant an unhappy move to England. With their return to Dublin and to poverty, Annie suffered at the hands of her shiftless mother, a Unionist hater of 'popery', who made no provision for the girl's education. Living first in rooms in Rathmines, they moved to Dargle Road in Bray, then to Barnhill Road, Dalkey, then higher up the hill to Torcaville. Annie's happiest days were spent with her cousins at Orchardstown House in Butterfield Lane in Rathfarnham. She eventually ran away to train as a nurse, first at the Chelsea Hospital, London, and later at the Royal Infirmary, Edinburgh and the Coombe Hospital, Dublin. She became a 'Jubilee Nurse', which meant nursing in patients' homes.

A Protestant herself, on being posted to County Down she was shocked by Protestant bigotry. That, and an unfortunate love affair with a young married doctor turned her attention to another religion. In 1907 she joined the Roman Catholic church. While recovering from tuberculosis (contracted while nursing in the Tuberculosis Dispensary, Charles Street, Dublin), she read the *Jail Journal* and *The Life of Wolfe Tone* and became a confirmed nationalist. In the Civil War she served in Morans' Hotel in Talbot Street and in the Gresham and Hammam hotels in O'Connell Street, and was afterwards imprisoned. As a nurse/novelist, Miss Smithson used her experiences in her books. She later lived in Rathmines, in Harcourt Street and in Upper Pembroke Street.

She is buried in Whitechurch, Rathfarnham, at the foot of her beloved Dublin Mountains.

Edward Smyth (1749-1812)
36 Montgomery (now Foley) St., 1

The son of a stone-cutter in County Meath, Edward Smyth settled in Dublin around 1780 and lived on Essex Quay. He worked with Henry Darnley, a stonemason employed by Gandon on the Custom House in the 1780s. Through Darnley, Gandon met Smyth and asked him to execute some ornamental stone work. Favourably impressed, Gandon employed Smyth to do the stone carving for the external decoration of the Custom House. Gandon lived close to the job, and it was probably for the same reason of convenience that Smyth moved to the North Strand and later to Montgomery Street. His work was so spectacular that Smyth's name has become for ever associated with that of Gandon in creating his Dublin masterpiece.

The four corners of the Custom House are embellished with the arms of the Kingdom of Ireland. For his series of fourteen keystone heads symbolising the rivers of Ireland – and known as the Riverine heads – Edward Smyth became the most celebrated of Irish sculptors. The pediment sculpture on the south front, representing the friendly union of Britannia and Hibernia, was designed by Carlini, and executed by Smyth, who also did the statue of Commerce on the dome. The building was gutted by fire in the Anglo-Irish War in 1921, but was quickly restored. It was lavishly refurbished in the 1980s.

Edward Smyth was also responsible for the statues on the pediment of the Four Courts, and for the ornaments which decorate Lord Charlemont's Casino in Marino. On the foundation of the Royal Dublin Society's Modelling School in 1811, Smyth was appointed its first master.

'Speranza' (Lady Jane Wilde)
(*c* 1826-1896)
34 Lower Leeson Street, 2

Jane Francesca Elgee came of a proud, Protestant family to whom nationalists were dangerous dross. Included in this category would have been the leaders of Young Ireland: Thomas Davis, Gavan Duffy and John Blake Dillon, but then Miss Elgee had never heard of Young Ireland. One day in 1845 her lady-like progress through fashionable Dublin was impeded by an endless funeral. She enquired who commanded such a vast concourse, and was told 'It is the funeral of the poet, Thomas Davis.' Curiosity led her to the *Nation* newspaper which he had edited. She caught the national spirit. Then she discovered she could write poetry. She sent her verses to the *Nation* signing them 'Speranza', and her letters 'John Fanshawe Ellis' instead of Jane Francesca Elgee.

In 1851, 'Speranza' married William Wilde, the brilliant but scruffy-looking little surgeon over whom she physically towered. In due time she mothered Oscar Wilde, and in 1864, with William's knighthood, Lady Wilde conveniently mixed her new Irish nationalism with her new British title, as she opportunely overlooked her husband's randy indiscretions. Her *soirées* at 1 Merrion Square were held in candlelight – to hide her ageing face it was said. Her incautious and snobbish pride brought a libel action by Mary Travers, a personable erstwhile patient of her husband's. All Dublin was titillated by the revelations from Isaac Butt's cross-examination at the Four Courts. Sir William declined to enter the witness box. A jury awarded Miss Travers damages of one farthing.

After William's death 'Speranza' moved to London where money was scarce. Deeply grateful for Oscar's help, she thanked him profusely: 'Best and kindest of sons ... Good and kind and generous you are ...' When tragedy befell him, she was loyal: 'Even if you go to prison, you will always be my son.' 'Speranza' died in 1896. From Reading Jail Oscar wrote: 'She was gentle and good to me here.' She is buried in an unmarked grave in London.

Father John Spratt (1798-1870)
Whitefriar Street Priory, 8

It is not sufficiently well-known that the remains of St Valentine rest in the Carmelite Church in Whitefriar Street, where the casket may be seen behind a grille beneath the altar of a shrine specially built in 1959. The man responsible was John Spratt who was born in Cork Street in 1798. He used to joke that he had been 'in arms'. himself in that year. He became a Carmelite priest, and his boundless energy inspired the teeming Liberties as he did his rounds through Back Lane, Bishop Steeet, Digges Street and Francis Street. He supported every public charity, and founded benevolent houses and philanthropic societies, in which work he was helped by his faithful friends, Lord Cloncurry and Daniel O'Connell. He also founded 'Dublin's Oldest Charity', the Sick and Indigent Roomkeepers' Society. His reputation as a preacher went far beyond the Liberties and when he built, and opened, Whitefriar Street Church in 1825, crowds came to be uplifted.

Invited by the Jesuits in 1835 to give a sermon in Rome, his spiritual magnetism was noted by Pope Gregory XVI, who marked his appreciation: '... we have freely given to the Very Reverend Father Spratt, Master of Sacred Theology of the Order of Calced Carmelites of the convent of that Order at Dublin in Ireland, the blessed body of Saint Valentine ...' On arrival in Dublin the casket was placed in Whitefriar Street Church on 10 November 1836. If Saint Valentine rested in a French, Spanish or Italian church, Irish tourists would be queuing to satisfy their curiosity about the patron saint of lovers.

Father Spratt's political idol was Daniel O'Connell. That regard was reciprocated, O'Connell admiring the other's achievements *before* Catholic Emancipation had been granted. Of John Spratt's funeral, the Rector of St Bride's Church wrote in the *Freeman's Journal*: 'Protestant clergymen and Dissenters stood side by side with the priest and the layman of that church of which the kindly deceased was so revered a minister.' His tomb is beside the steps leading to the O'Connell vault in Glasnevin Cemetery – as near as possible to his idol.

Sir Charles Villiers Stanford
(1852-1924)
2 Herbert Street, 2

A plaque marks this house as the birthplace of a musical prodigy, the distinguished composer and conductor, Charles Stanford. The only child of John Stanford, himself a singer and cellist, at the age of eight the boy composed a march used in a Theatre Royal pantomime. His musical career was carefully planned. He had mastered the violin, piano and organ when, at eighteen, he entered Queen's College, Cambridge. He then studied in London, Leipzig and Berlin, where he learned what couldn't be taught in Dublin – self-discipline. Influenced by Bach, Schumann and Brahms, his own compositions began to attract attention.

On settling in London in 1892, Stanford's musical career really began. A rapid worker, his compositions were voluminous. They were adversely criticised by G B Shaw, then a London music critic – an old spleen carried on from their Dublin days. Stanford produced six operas, the most successful being *Shamus O'Brien*, and many choral works. The main themes in most of his seven symphonies were derived from Irish melodies. His third is known as 'The Irish Symphony'. From the George Petrie manuscript collection, Stanford published over fifteen hundred tunes between 1902 and 1905. He was also a prolific writer of chamber music, and there were eight string quartets.

At the peak of his fame, Stanford

resented the threat of the up-and-coming Edward Elgar, more especially as Shaw invariably poured praise upon the work of the younger composer. From time to time Stanford conducted the Cambridge University Musical Society, the London Bach Choir and the Leeds Festival, where he succeeded Sir Arthur Sullivan of Gilbert and Sullivan fame.

Stanford's ashes are buried in Westminster Abbey.

Grizel Steevens (1654-1747)
Steevens' Lane, 8

Steevens' Lane and Dr Steevens' Hospital take their names from Dr Richard Steevens, a wealthy doctor with a sense of philanthropy. Before his death in 1710 he willed his estate in trust for his sister, Grizel, known generally as Madame Steevens. He stipulated that after her death his fortune should be spent in founding a hospital for the poor of Dublin. Surviving her brother by nearly forty years, and seeing the urgent need, Grizel decided to put his wishes into immediate effect. Accordingly, Dr Steevens' Hospital was built between 1721 and 1733, making it the oldest public hospital in Ireland and one of the oldest in these islands.

The hospital is built around a cloistered quadrangle with lawns bisected by paths at its centre. In the south-east corner once stood the chapel endowed by Stella (Hester Johnson), the friend of Swift. Her will stated that all chaplains must be Irish, must be graduates of Trinity College and must be unmarried. Sadly, in 1909 the chapel was broken up to make an additional ward.

Grizel Steevens wore a veil when visiting the sick, so rumour invented a reason: she had the face of a pig, the result of a beggar woman's curse on her mother. She lived in rooms near the arched main entrance to the hospital where she mostly sat at an open window for all to see. It was her vain effort to dispel the horrible story. But it became a legend, persisting long after her death.

In 1753 Dr Edward Worth, an early trustee, left his library of four and a half thousand books to Dr Steevens' Hospital. When it was closed in the mid-1980s, as part of the Dublin hospital rationalisation plan, the Worth Library passed to Trinity College. When Swift, another early trustee, died the hospital gave the site for nearby Swift's Hospital, now St Patrick's Hospital.

James Stephens (Writer) (1880-1950)
5 Thomas Court,
off Thomas Street, 8

The birth of James Stephens revived the lore of the leprechaun. Like the nightingale in Berkeley Square, Stephens made his appearance, not in Arcadia, so favoured by the little people, but in the shadow of St Catherine's Church in the heart of old Dublin. The family moved to 5 Artigans' Dwellings, off Buckingham Street, where his father died when James was two. His mother moved to 8 St Joseph's Road, off the North Circular Road. She had so little interest in

5 Thomas Court, off Thomas Street, 8

In 1912 he published *The Crock of Gold* and *The Charwoman's Daughter* and moved to Paris. In 1914 he returned to live at 2 Leinster Square, Rathmines. In 1915 he became Registrar of the National Gallery of Ireland and lived at 42 Fitzwilliam Place. A pacifist, Stephens was appalled at the aftermath of the 1916 Rebellion. Some of those executed had been his friends. 'Be green upon their graves,' he prayed. In *The Insurrection in Dublin* he has left the most objective account ever written of that fateful week in Irish history. Disillusioned with the repression of the new Irish Free State, he left Ireland in 1925 to spend the remainder of his life in London.

her son, he was picked up for begging and was committed to the Meath Industrial School in Blackrock. He never again saw his mother. He was befriended by a Mrs Collins who had sons in the school. At sixteen he became a solicitor's clerk at 9 Eustace Street and boarded with Mrs Collins at 30 York Street. Later he lodged in Portobello Road and Essex Street.

In 1907, from 91 Merrion Square, another solicitor's office, Stephens made his first bid for recognition as a writer. He sent a short story to AE (George Russell). Instantly recognising genius, the sage sought out the little clerk in the top-floor office in Merrion Square. Stephens sent another story to Arthur Griffith for *Sinn Féin*. It too was published. AE and Griffith became his friends. He was now living at 17 Great Brunswick Street where he met his 'Cynthia', otherwise Millicent Josephine Kavanagh, whom he married.

James Stephens (Fenian) (1824-1901)
Fairfield House, Sandymount, 4

After the abortive Young Ireland Rising of 1848, James Stephens escaped to Paris and began his first long exile of seven years. Amongst his many intellectual activities in Paris, he translated *Martin Chuzzlewit* into French, thus introducing Charles Dickens to Europe. Despite his dislike of the Irish, Dickens was grateful. Stephens also gave lessons in English 'to scions of the old legitimist stocks and to sprigs of the younger Napoleonic ones'.

Returning to Ireland in 1856, his preparations began for the Fenian Rising, and by 1865 he decided the time had come. An informer, Pierce Nagle, alerted Dublin Castle, and the police swooped on the office of the *Irish People* at 12 Parliament Street, arresting all the leading Fenians. Stephens, the Fenian chief, escaped however, prompting Lord Wodehouse, the Viceroy, to say: 'All our work is undone!' With many Dublin addresses to choose from (Lennox Street, Charlemont Street or Mount Street), Stephens took cover at Fairfield House, at the corner of Newbridge Avenue and Herbert Road in Sandymount where he resided quietly for some months as 'Mr Herbert'. Humiliated, the government offered £1000 for Stephens or £300 for information, while the ballad-makers had fun:

Perhaps you'd like to know,
Says the Shan Van Vocht,
Which way did Stephens go,
Says the Shan Van Vocht.

At six o'clock one morning Fairfield House was besieged by the entire Dublin Castle 'G' Division and Stephens was arrested. While on remand he escaped from Richmond Jail. As a deck-hand on a collier out of Howth, he got back to Paris, where his second exile began, lasting for twenty-five years. Parnell negotiated with the British for Stephens's repatriation. Stephens never regained the Fenian leadership. He lived in retirement in a cottage in Sutton, eventually dying at the home of his brother-in-law, John

Pain, at 82 George's Avenue, Blackrock, County Dublin.

Bram Stoker (1847-1912)
15 Marino Crescent, Clontarf, 3

Bram Stoker is a very little-known author of a very well-known book, *Dracula*. The son of a Dublin Castle civil servant, and one of a family of eight, he was christened Abraham, 'Bram' for short. A sickly child, he yet became a champion athlete at Trinity College where he also became president of the Philosophical Society and auditor of the Historical Society. He entered the civil service but found it boring. He studied law and was called to the Bar. He read the blood-curdling tales of Sheridan le Fanu. As a boy he had absorbed his mother's horror stories. A Sligo woman, Charlotte Thornley had lived through the cholera epidemic of 1832 when coffin-makers knocked on doors touting for business. She had seen whole families die, and she knew some who were buried alive, so great was the fear of the plague.

When he became drama critic for the *Dublin Mail*, Stoker lived at 39 Kildare Street and later at 16 Harcourt Street. While playing *Hamlet* at Dublin's Theatre Royal in 1876, Sir Henry Irving was attracted by young Stoker's critical judgment. He sent for him. An association began which lasted until Irving's death thirty years later. Stoker managed London's Lyceum Theatre throughout the partnership of Irving and Ellen Terry in their golden age of Shakespeare in the eighties and nineties. Before leaving Dublin in 1878

Stoker had married his near neighbour, the beautiful Florence Balcombe of 1 Marino Crescent, who had just jilted the young Oscar Wilde.

The author of eighteen novels, Bram Stoker is remembered only for one, *Dracula*, published in 1897. Based on the fifteenth century Prince Vlad IV of Transylvania, Dracula the vampire retains his universal appeal. After Irving's death in 1905 and the decline of the Lyceum Theatre, Stoker lived out his life in London in comparative poverty. In 1988 in Dublin his memory was revived with the foundation of the Bram Stoker Archives Room in the Graduates Memorial Building in his *alma mater*, Trinity College.

William Stokes (1804-1878)
5 Merrion Square, 2

One of Ireland's greatest doctors, William Stokes was born at 16 Harcourt Street, and grew up at his father's country house in Ballinteer. An indolent youth, he suddenly decided to follow his father into medicine. Educated in Dublin, Glasgow and Edinburgh, he succeeded his father, Whitley Stokes, as physician to the Meath Hospital. There he collaborated with John Cheyne, his one-time teacher, in describing the breathing pattern now known as Cheyne-Stokes respiration. With Robert Adams of Trinity College, Stokes described the fainting attacks associated with a slow pulse, known ever since as the Stokes-Adams Syndrome. Graves' Disease, or exophthalmic goitre, was first de-

scribed by Robert Graves, a contemporary of Stokes at the Meath. This was the golden age of the Dublin school of medicine, and these names are still used every day in every hospital throughout the world.

On his marriage, Stokes moved to York Street and later to 5 Merrion Square, which became a resort of wit and learning. Thomas Carlyle was a guest and Mahaffy regularly dined. Stokes's interests were wide, including archaeology, Shakespeare, and puppet-shows. Mount Malpas, Killiney, was his country house. The publication of several learned works on medicine brought honours showering on Stokes. In 1874 he received the highest academic distinction: he was elected President of the Royal Irish Academy. His statue by John Henry Foley stands in the Great Hall of the Royal College of Physicians. Helped by his distinguished contemporaries, Dominic Corrigan, Abraham Colles and Robert Graves, Stokes launched the Pathological Society of Dublin, which led to the foundation of the Royal Academy of Medicine in Ireland.

His old age was spent at Carraig Breac, his retreat at Howth. From there he was carried to his grave in nearby St Fintan's Churchyard by devoted students of the Meath Hospital. The Stokes family became a medical dynasty, five generations of doctors serving the Meath. I am happy to record that as a medical student and a house surgeon, I was taught by Henry Stokes, a grandson of William, and the last of the dynasty to serve at the Meath.

Barry Sullivan (1821-1891)
Portobello House, 8

Born of humble Cork parents who died young, the orphaned Thomas Barry Sullivan, aged fourteen, became a draper's assistant in Messrs Todds (later Cash and Company). His good looks led to his selection for a charity concert in the old Cork Theatre in George's Street. From there he graduated to the Cook Street Theatre where the costumes floated about when the spring tides came up the sewers. Emigration led to young Sullivan playing 'second heavies' at the Theatre Royal, Edinburgh. Promotion to 'first heavies' eventually made him a Shakespearian actor at London's Haymarket Theatre, where he was the favourite of Queen Victoria and the Prince Consort. At Drury Lane he played all the principal Shakespearian parts, *The Times* calling him 'the leading legitimate actor of the British stage'.

Sullivan's receptions throughout the English-speaking world were wildly enthusiastic. In Melbourne, for instance, he played for a thousand performances to overflowing houses. But it was in Dublin that he always received a special welcome. At the end of his performance at the Queen's Theatre his admirers would tow his carriage back to his lodgings at the Grand Canal Hotel, now Portobello House. There he would address the crowd from the balcony. Somewhere in the crush there would have been a youth called George Bernard Shaw from nearby Synge Street – for Barry Sullivan was the hero of Shaw's young life.

Sullivan died at his home in Brighton. At his request he was buried in Glasnevin Cemetery. Near the O'Connell Tower stands an imposing memorial in marble, sculpted by Sir Thomas Farrell, President of the Royal Hibernian Academy. The great Irish actor stands life-size as Hamlet with the skull of Yorick in his hand. The inscription reads: 'After life's fitful fever he sleeps well.'

Father John Sullivan SJ (1861-1933)
32 Fitzwilliam Place, 2

In the 1890s the best-dressed young man in Ireland was the privileged and handsome John Sullivan. The son of Sir Edward Sullivan, Lord Chancellor of Ireland, socially ambitious Dublin mothers vied to entertain this attractive matrimonial catch. Born at 41 Eccles Street, and baptised at nearby St George's Church, John moved with his family to 32 Fitzwilliam Place (which bears a plaque). Of a mixed marriage, the four Sullivan sons were reared as Protestants and the one daughter as a Catholic. It was said that John's nursemaid had secretly had him baptised a Catholic. The Sullivans had a villa called Undercliffe at Killiney where Gladstone had been a guest and had dandled young John upon his knee.

At Portora Royal School in County Fermanagh John showed brilliance. In 1879 he entered Trinity College Law School. A 'skip' (a college servant) harassed students into going to church on Sundays. Sullivan refused – unless she brought him to her church. Thus as a Protestant he attended Mass. From Trinity he went to Lincolns' Inn and was called to the English Bar.

Aged thirty-five, John Sullivan became a Catholic. Four years later he entered the Society of Jesus. His 'apartness' was soon noticed – humility, all-night prayers, near starvation and threadbare clothes marked a virtuous man. 'Anything that denies self is an act of love,' he said. He was ordained in 1907 and appointed to teach at Clongowes Wood College where he spent most of the rest of his life.

John Sullivan SJ exercised an apostolate amongst the sick and the poor in the countryside around Clongowes. His reputation as a healer spread. People attributed favours to his intercession, and this continued after his death. As a first step towards canonisation his body was exhumed and brought to St Francis Xavier's Church in Gardiner Street, Dublin. Pronounced a 'Servant of God', Father Sullivan's coffin rests in a special chapel which is now a place of pilgrimage for the sick and suffering.

A fellow Jesuit who lived in the same community has recorded his impression of the man: 'the first time I looked on him as "half a Protestant" the second as rather artificial and forced in his spirituality, the third as "a saint" – one who had come in for his full heritage.'

Jonathan Swift (1667-1745)
The Deanery, St Patrick's Close, 8

With justification, all the mysteries and misfortunes of the enigmatic Dean Swift have been attributed to his maladjusted childhood. Seven months after his father's death he was born at the home of his uncle, Godwin Swift, at 7 Hoey's Court, a tall dutch-gabled house which stood in the shadow of

Jonathan Swift

Dublin Castle. Smothered with feminine affection, his loving nurse kidnapped him at the age of three, taking him to Whitehaven in Cumberland. When, at five, he was restored to his mother he could spell – he could even read the bible. Here Uncle Godwin asserted himself, packing the six-year-old off to Kilkenny College where he had to face the shock of readjustment to chilling male authority and the cruel jibes of ordinary boys. Highly intelligent, he was still a bundle of contradictions when he entered Trinity College at the age of fifteen. While he 'felt' English, his sympathy for the downtrodden made him an Irish patriot. He was the first to teach Irish economic self-reliance. Hence Arthur Griffith's admiration in calling him a founder of Irish nationalism. 'Burn everything English except their coal,' the Dean exhorted the weavers of the Dublin Liberties.

After his ambition to become Archbishop of Canterbury was thwarted by the English, Swift made his great compromise – he settled for the Deanship of St Patrick's Cathedral. The greatest mystery he left to posterity concerns his relationship with two ill-fated women who loved him. His affair with Vanessa (Es-ther Vanhomrigh) he relates in *Cadenus and Vanessa*. Aged thirty-six, after she had broken with him, she died. His *Journal to Stella* (Hester Johnson) makes it clear it was she he favoured. Did he marry Stella? And if not, why not? The question remains one of the great mysteries of literary history. If not in life, then at least in death Jonathan and his Stella lie side-by-side beneath well-polished brass plates in the floor of St Patrick's Cathedral.

The Deanery where Swift lived and died was destroyed by fire in 1781. Rebuilt, the original kitchen where Swift prayed with his staff was preserved. With hindsight we now know that from young manhood he suffered from Ménière's Disease, a condition causing giddiness, nausea and deafness. This chronic illness may well explain the quirks and oddities, even the peevish genius, of Jonathan Swift.

2 Newtown Villas, Rathfarnham, 14

John Millington Synge (1871-1909)
2 Newtown Villas, Rathfarnham, 14

'A drift of chosen females standing in their shifts.' It was that word *shift* which precipitated a week of riots at the Abbey Theatre in 1907, when Synge's *The Playboy of the Western World* was first produced, and five hundred police were drafted in to keep order. Six months later London hailed it as a masterpiece, and provincial Dublin was culturally admonished. Five years after that there were even greater riots in Boston, New York and Chicago. In Philadelphia the Abbey Theatre cast were arrested for performing 'immoral or indecent plays'. Irish-Americans were seeing Ireland through a mist of Celtic sentimentality. Some still do.

Born at 2 Newtown Villas, the Synge family moved to 4 Orwell Park, Rathgar. In 1890 they moved to 31 Crosthwaite Park, Dun Laoghaire. Synge, a loner, spent long summer holidays at 'Uplands', near Annamoe in Wicklow. The family seat was Glanmore Castle in the Devil's Glen, designed by Francis Johnston in the 1790s and built around a Norman keep. Wicklow provided the inspiration and the language for *The Well of the Saints* and *In the Shadow of the Glen* – the dialogue that Synge's detractors claimed had never been spoken by God nor man. Yeats despatched him from Paris to the Aran Islands. There he was happiest, escaping 'the nullity of the rich and the squalor of the poor'. And from Aran came his greatest plays: *Riders to the Sea* and *The Playboy*.

In his last illness, Synge was nursed at the Elpis Nursing Home, 130 Lower Mount Street, where his room had a view of the mountains he loved. He was engaged to Molly Allgood (Máire O'Neill), the Abbey Theatre actress, to whom he left an annuity. Perhaps in remorse, his enemies and his feeble friends turned up at his funeral. Grudging obituaries were published calling his work important only in its promise.

Synge is buried in Mount Jerome Cemetery.

Matt Talbot (1856-1925)
18 Upper Rutland Street, 1

With whiskey at threepence a glass and porter at twopence a pint, Matt Talbot, an unskilled labourer, became an inveterate drunkard. At twenty-eight he reformed, adopting a life of mortification in the Christian penitential tradition. In 1952, twenty-seven years after his death, the Holy See established the apostolic process for his canonisation: his body was exhumed and he was declared 'the Servant of God'.

Born at 12 Oldborough, off the North Strand, he lived his life in one room at 18 Upper Rutland Street (since demolished). A bronze slab marks the site beside Matt Talbot Court, a new block of flats.

Matt Talbot knew, and disapproved of, Sean O'Casey. He considered O'Casey's characters to be caricatures of 'dacent Dubliners'. Had he lived to see *The Plough and the Stars* he would have seen his point proved when the name of Fluther Good was introduced to the theatre world in 1926. O'Casey, it was alleged, had over-drawn a real-life character, none other than Matt Talbot's one-time drinking 'buttie', Jack Good, otherwise Fluther Good. Jack mounted an action against O'Casey for 'definition of character' and was awarded damages of fifty pounds.

In his last years Matt Talbot lived on seven shillings and sixpence per week from the National Health Insurance. He died in Granby Lane on his way to Mass. When Jervis Street Hospital reported that rusted chains and knotted ropes were found bound around the body, the Catholic world was suddenly alerted to the saintly mysticism of the unknown labourer. His coffin is on view in a shrine in the Church of Our Lady of Lourdes in Sean MacDermott Street.

Napper Tandy (1737-1803)
67 Bride Street, 8

Were it not for Dion Boucicault's lyric, the name of Napper Tandy might well be forgotten:

I met with Napper Tandy and he took
    me by the hand,
Saying: how is poor old Ireland, and
    how does she stand?
She's the most distressful country
    that ever yet was seen;
They are hanging men and women
    for the wearing of the green.

Born in Dublin, his family was well-off. A radical in politics, and a champion of the Catholic cause, he was hated by the Ascendancy. Secretary of the Society of United Irishmen, in the

years leading up to the 1798 Rebellion, he took refuge by changing his Dublin address often. Some are recorded as follows: 16 Dorset Street (1779); 21 Cornmarket (1780-83); 180 Abbey Street (1785); 67 Bride Street (1786); 97 Bride Street (1787-88) and a return to 67 Bride Street (1789-95).

He fled to the United States and from there to France where, with French assistance, he planned an expedition to Ireland. Admired by Napoleon, he was by then a General in the French Army.

One month after the failure of Humbert's expedition, Napper Tandy landed in Donegal in September 1798. He was captured and sentenced to death by the English. At the intervention of Bonaparte, he was allowed to escape to France. He died in Bordeaux, leaving an estranged wife in Ireland and a mistress in France.

Theobald Wolfe Tone (1763-1798)
44 Stafford (now Wolfe Tone) Street, 1

Wolfe Tone achieved what no other Irishman achieved before or since – a substantial common ground between Protestant, Catholic and Dissenter. He discovered what was to him a great discovery: 'that Ireland would never be either free, prosperous or happy, until she was independent and that independence was unobtainable whilst the connection with England lasted'.

Tone was born at 44 Stafford Street (since demolished). The site is occupied

The former 'Mayro' cinema, corner of Mary and Wolfe Tone streets

by the Private Motorists' Protection Association. The building carries a plaque. He read Law at Trinity College and the Middle Temple in London, but he never concealed his contempt for the legal profession. He really wanted to be a soldier. Always in want of money, particularly during his stay in France where he went to enlist help for a rising against the English in Ireland, Tone wrote of French over-charging: 'A most blistering bill for supper. In great indignation, the more so because I could not scold in French. All my figures of speech were lost on the landlord.'

One brief period of domestic happiness stands out, when his delicate wife was advised to bathe in salt water. 'I hired in consequence a little box of a house on the sea side at Irishtown, where we spent the summer of 1790. I recall with transport the happy days we spent together, the delicious din-

ners in the preparation of which my wife, Russell [Thomas Russell, his greatest friend] and myself were all engaged; the afternoon walks; the discussions we had as we lay stretched on the grass. It was delightful.'

A serious man to the point of suicide, it is hardly implausible to imagine the ghost of Tone wearing what he called a look of 'tender melancholy' as he watches several violently differing republican parties making their strictly separate pilgrimages to his grave at Bodenstown, all on the same day, but at well-spaced hours – each claiming him as the father of their own special form of republicanism. As in life, Tone might well comment: 'Men of genius, to be of use, must not be collected in numbers. Too many wits spoil the discourse.'

Anthony Trollope (1815-1882)
5 Seaview Terrace, Donnybrook, 4

Concerning his arrival in Ireland in 1841, Anthony Trollope, the young English post office clerk, said: 'This was the first good fortune of my life.' And why not? Wasn't it in Ireland he invented that thoroughly English cathedral town of Barchester? And wasn't it in Donnybrook he wrote *Barchester Towers*? Thus adding the county of Barsetshire to the geography of England. Novel-writing began with a walk one evening in 1843 near Drumsna, County Leitrim, where he came on the ruins of a country house. It inspired him. It became Ballycloran House in *The MacDermotts of Bally-cloran. The Kellys and the O'Kellys* followed, and Trollope turned out forty-five novels in the next thirty-nine years.

In Banagher, his first Irish posting, he was popular, and he disappointed a few by returning from leave in 1844 with an English bride. On transfer to Clonmel, his two sons were born in High Street. He then went to Mallow and, in 1853, to Belfast. He expressed certain Irish geographical likes and dislikes: 'I should prefer the South to the North of Ireland, preferring on the whole papistical to presbyterian tendencies ... I hope to be enabled to move to Dublin which is a nice city enough.'

Trollope lived for five years at 5 Seaview Terrace, Donnybrook. Having experienced the Great Famine, his last book before leaving Ireland in 1859 was *Castle Richmond*, a stark account of a nation's distress.

Trollope was happy in Ireland: 'I achieved the respect of all with whom I was concerned, I made for myself a comfortable home, and I enjoyed many pleasures.' For all this partiality, he was never quite able to escape that pompous condescension dispensed by the English to those they consider a lesser race.

Madame Tussaud (1760-1850)
16 Clarendon Street, 2

An orphan, Marie Grosholtz was befriended by a Parisian doctor more interested in modelling in wax than dosing with medicine. From him she learned so well the use of wax that the sixteen-year-old Princess Elizabeth, sister of Louis XVI, invited her, then aged nineteen, to live and work in the Palace of Versailles. A devoted friendship developed between the girls, and for eight years Marie was an intimate of the royal family of France. With the arrest of the King and Queen, Marie Grosholtz became suspect. Imprisoned, she found herself sharing a cell with Josephine de Beauharnais, later Napoleon's Josephine. On the night of Marie Antoinette's execution, Marie Grosholtz was ordered to the Madeleine Prison and forced to make a death-mask of the face she had known so well.

In 1794 Dr Curtius, her benefactor, died leaving her his collection of wax models – and his debts. A year later she married Francois Tussaud who was a no-good. Commissions from Napoleon and Josephine helped to pay her debts. Now the mother of two sons, Madame Tussaud took part of her exhibition to England – unaware that she would never again see Paris. In 1804 she arrived in Ireland where fourteen thousand troops needed entertainment. At fifty guineas per annum she rented the Shakespeare Gallery in Exchequer Street, round the corner from her residence in Clarendon Street. Knowing it pays to introduce a touch of local colour, she made a full-length portrait in wax of Henry Grattan, then the most talked-of man in Dublin. Amongst the 'greats' of the French Revolution the figure of Grattan lent a just-sufficient sense of reality. Despite martial law, Madame Tussaud's drew crowds.

With Dublin as her base she toured the garrison towns. Returning from Waterford through a stormy sea many models were broken. She restored them while still living at 16 Clarendon Street. After a tour of England, while crossing back to Dublin in 1822, her ship was wrecked near Liverpool. She vowed never again to board a ship, not even to see Dublin or Paris.

Amongst the models Madame Tussaud inherited there was one of a reclining figure, a beautiful French girl. She was the young Madame du Barry, the last mistress of Louis XV. That model accompanied Madame Tussaud on all her travels. It survives at Madame Tussaud's in London and is known today as 'The Sleeping Beauty'.

Katherine Tynan (1868-1931)
Whitehall, Clondalkin

One of the most prolific writers of her time, Katherine Tynan published over 125 volumes, including over one hundred novels and three books of autobiography. She began writing at seventeen, and published her first volume of verse in 1885. WB Yeats was twenty and Katherine Tynan twenty-four when they met at John O'Leary's salon on Leinster Road, Rathmines. Yeats regarded her with awe, for she had already been published. For her 'Mr Yeats was as picturesque as one could desire – night-black hair, and beautiful eyes of a southern darkness.' His father, John B Yeats, painted Katherine's portrait in 1886. Hanging in the Hugh Lane Gallery, she wears *pince-nez* to help the weak eyesight her mother attributed to reading too many novels.

Katherine was the daughter of Andrew Tynan, a well-to-do farmer. Whitehall, her childhood home, was a large old-fashioned Irish farmhouse with whitewash and thatch and an extensive orchard. Here on Sunday afternoons there would be a stream of callers with endless talk of poetry, and Willie Yeats would hypnotise the hens. When his family moved to London Yeats was deeply homesick. Through those years his 'dear Katey', through her letters, was his main contact with Ireland, and with all it meant to him. She gave him the understanding he needed, and Clondalkin, like Innisfree, was a symbol of escape from the suffocation of Chiswick.

In 1893 Katherine Tynan married

Henry Hinkson, once Resident Magistrate for County Mayo. They eventually settled in Ealing, and she grew away from the Irish Literary Renaissance, though still protesting her Irishry. She annoyed Yeats by publishing his letters without permission in her *Twenty-five Years*, yet he conceded that the book contained 'a great deal that moves me, for it is a very vivid picture of the Dublin of my youth'.

Arthur Wellesley,
The Duke of Wellington (1769-1852)
24 Upper Merrion Street, 2

A son of the Earl of Mornington, Arthur Wellesley was born at Mornington House, 24 Upper Merrion Street. The dunce of the family, his mother called him 'food for powder and nothing more'. He went to school at Whyte's Academy in Grafton Street (now Bewley's Cafe). At Eton he was considered 'too dull for learning and too quiet for football'. He played the violin and mooned his summers away at the family country seat, Dangan Castle, Summerhill, County Meath. His brother, Richard, got Arthur a commission in the army and had him appointed aide-de-camp to the Lord Lieutenant of Ireland. For five years he idled at Dublin Castle. He fell in love with Catherine (Kitty) Pakenham, daughter of Lord Longford, but because of Arthur's dreary prospects, her father refused to allow the match. Burning his violin, Major the Hon Arthur Wellesley set sail to campaign for ten years in India before returning to

Dublin to marry Kitty in the drawing-room of Lord Longford's house, 11 Rutland Square (now Parnell Square). He lived to regret it. Kitty was tedious and undomesticated, and Arthur ruefully rebuked himself: 'Would you have believed that anyone could have been such a damned fool?'

Wellesley's subsequent career is history. Created a duke in 1814 for his victories in the Peninsular War, his victory over Napoleon at Waterloo in 1815 was the climax of his life. Great monuments went up in his honour, including that at Trim, County Meath,

The Duke of Wellington

and the Wellington obelisk in Dublin's Phoenix Park. His popularity in England was immense. Imitations of a half-boot he favoured became the rage as the 'Wellington boot', the ancestor of today's 'wellies'. As a politician he was less brilliant, though it *was* Wellington who, as Prime Minister of England, granted Catholic Emancipation to Ireland.

Called the Iron Duke, Wellington had an almost feminine sensitivity. He wept like a child when touched by grief. He was a man mistaken for a monolith. In spite of her domestic shortcomings, he stood by his Duchess Kitty to the end. He is buried alongside Nelson in Westminster Abbey.

Oscar Wilde (1854-1900)
21 Westland Row, 2

A plaque proclaims 21 Westland Row as the birthplace of Oscar Fingal O'Flahertie Wills Wilde. One year later his prospering father, Sir William Wilde, an aural surgeon, moved to 1 Merrion Square, the imposing mansion usually associated with the lives of this unique family. Here, with his brother Willie, Oscar was indulged, spoiled and shamelessly exhibited. No matter how distinguished the guests, the boys were allowed to stay up late for dinner. Their dearly-loved ten-year-old sister, Isola, died suddenly at the Glebe, Edgeworthstown, County Longford, while on holiday. Oscar's grief was poignant and private. Aged twelve he wrote:

All her bright golden hair
Tarnished with rust,
She that was young and fair
Fallen to dust.

Having started sluggishly at Portora Royal School at Enniskillen, Oscar left with the Portora Gold Medal for Classics and a scholarship to Trinity College. With Willie, he shared rooms on the first floor of No. 18 in the quadrangle called Botany Bay. Edward Carson, a contemporary, was Oscar's competitor for the Foundation Scholarship in Classics in 1873 and the Berkeley Gold Medal for Greek in 1874. But Oscar was the winner, concluding a brilliant career at Trinity by winning a scholarship to Magdalen College, Oxford.

Powerful academic influences moulded the character of Oscar Wilde. 'Mahaffy and Tyrrell, they were Trinity to me,' he said of his teachers. From John Ruskin at Oxford he learned the necessity of beauty. Attracted by every utterance of Newman, he called him: 'That divine man'. But it was as a disciple of Walter Pater that Wilde learned that physical sensation is an end in itself to which it is

Oscar Wilde

noble to aspire.

It is sadly ironic that at the fateful trial in London, the prosecuting counsel was Edward Carson, Wilde's one-time contemporary and academic inferior at Trinity College, Dublin.

Sir William Wilde (1815-1876)
1 Merrion Square, 2

The genius of Oscar Wilde was inherited. Not one, but both his parents were exceptional personalities in a city noted for its abundance of colourful characters. An accomplished surgeon, and an archaeologist of stature, Sir William Wilde added much to the sum of knowledge in both specialities, earning the distinction of membership of the Royal Irish Academy at the extraordinarily early age of twenty-four. His fame included an historic action for libel against his wife by his erstwhile patient, Mary Travers, a personable young woman in whose defence Isaac Butt's performance in court vastly entertained Dublin society.

The son of Dr Thomas Wilde of Castlerea, County Roscommon, William was apprenticed to Abraham Colles at Dr Steevens' Hospital, where Charles Lever, the nineteenth century's best-selling doctor-novelist, was a fellow student. On qualification Wilde travelled extensively with a wealthy patient, taking every opportunity to extend his post-graduate surgical education. On his return to Dublin in 1838 he set up at 199 Great Brunswick Street (now Pearse Street), later moving to 18 Westland Row. In 1844 he founded St Mark's Hospital at the

1 Merrion Square, 2

rear of 11 Molesworth Street, and in 1851 he married Jane Francesca Elgee, otherwise 'Speranza', the poetess. They moved to 21 Westland Row where their sons Willie and Oscar were born.

Professional progress and social ambition brought them to 1 Merrion Square, then the acme of residential Dublin. It was while they lived at this address that the Wildean family flair both for fame and for notoriety came to its full fruition.

Sir Nevile Wilkinson (1869-1940)
Mount Merrion House,
Mount Merrion

Walking in the woods at Mount Merrion early in this century, Sir Nevile

Wilkinson, a writer of fairy tales, told his little daughters about Titania, the queen of the fairies who, because she had no better home, lived in a crevice in the bole of a tree. Three-year-old Gwendolen, who had seen fairies, begged her father to build a palace so beautiful that Titania would surely choose it instead of a tree. In her honour it would be called Titania's Palace.

After an army career, Major Sir Nevile Wilkinson trained in decorative arts and heraldry at the Royal College of Art in London. In 1907 he resigned from the army to become Ulster King of Arms at Dublin Castle. He commissioned the famous workshop of James Hicks of Pembroke Street to build a palace on a scale of one in twelve, and to furnish it appropriately. It became a sixteen-roomed palace built round a central courtyard, and filled with exquisite pieces and miniature works of art, everything in perfect proportion down to the smallest detail.

Sir Nevile intended that the Palace should be exhibited in aid of childrens' hospital charities. 'If one cripple walks by reason of its making,' he said, 'Ireland's gift to suffering childhood will not have been built in vain.' The Palace was opened by Queen Mary in 1923, and subsequently toured the world many times, raising vast sums of money.

In 1967 Gwendolen Wilkinson sold the Palace at Christies in London in aid of charity. The buyer offered it back to the Irish government, but alas! To our eternal shame, the offer was turned down. This irreplaceable Irish work of art was sold for £350,000. It is now on display at Legoland in Denmark, where it is seen by tens of thousands of tourists who are told that Titania's Palace is an English creation by English artists. The loss to Ireland of this sumptuous treasure is nothing short of a national scandal.

Peg Woffington (c1714-1760)
George's Lane, 7

The rags-to-riches scenario preceded Hollywood. It is as old as time. It was the real-life story of Peg Woffington, the celebrated eighteenth-century actress who was born in poverty in George's Lane, now South Great George's Street. Selling lettuce in College Green, her childish poise and pretty face attracted the Trinity students. More importantly, Madame Violante, a touring actress-manager, spotted the beautiful Peg. Aged twelve, she was cast as Polly Peachum in *The Beggars' Opera*. Woffington never looked back.

At first apprenticed to Smock Alley Theatre, she graduated to the new Theatre Royal built in 1734 at the corner of Aungier Street and Longford Lane, where she became the leading lady. Its first season included Farquhar comedies. Woffington played Sylvia in *The Recruiting Officer*. She showed her versatility in *The Constant Couple*, and set a fashion for actresses by wearing breeches as Sir Harry Wildair, a part she afterwards made her own. A comedienne with a good figure, which enhanced her appeal in parts requiring breeches, Wildair became her most famous role.

In 1740 she took theatrical London by storm, playing Cordelia to David Garrick's Lear at Drury Lane. She became his leading lady and his mistress. In 1742 they played a season at Dublin's Smock Alley Theatre. It was a stormy liaison, yet the inevitable parting was a heartbreak for Woffington. She returned to Smock Alley and lived in Capel Street. A political play provoked a riot and the destruction of the theatre. She left Dublin, never to return.

A charitable woman, Peg Woffington gave her young sister, Polly, an expensive education in French finishing schools. During her last performance she collapsed while playing Rosalind in *As You Like It*. She died at Teddington where she had endowed alms-houses.

William Wordsworth (1770-1850)
Dunsink House, Castleknock

Like the comedian who wants to play Hamlet, Sir William Rowan Hamilton, the greatest mathematician of his time, wanted to be a poet. From childhood he had read and written poetry. In 1827 he visited Wordsworth in England. A family friendship developed, Hamilton acting as godfather to a grandson of Wordsworth. When Wordsworth came to Ireland, Hamilton met him at the boat, entertained him at Dunsink House, and ceaselessly talked poetry, at the risk of boring the great poet.

Hamilton's sister, Eliza Mary, who lived with him, herself a poet, was as undisturbed by great poets as she was by great mathematicians. She noted that Wordsworth wore nankeen trousers, and always spoke with 'an unaffected simplicity, dignity and peacefulness of thought'. He did not talk about poetry until pressed by his hosts.

While Hamilton was Astronomer Royal of Ireland and occupied the Observatory House at Dunsink, the surrounding woods and fields were often explored by poet-guests, like 'Speranza' (Lady Wilde) and Aubrey de Vere. In the rain and under the stars William Wordsworth and Rowan Hamilton wandered through nearby Abbotstown and past the little lake that borders the Connolly Memorial Hospital at Blanchardstown. It may have lacked the beauty of the Lake District, but even little lakes have charms.

By the fireside at Dunsink Wordsworth listened patiently to Hamilton's hexameters, and in turn expressed his veneration for silence 'when legitimately pursued for the elevation of the mind to God' – meaning Hamilton's astronomy no doubt. But for Hamilton, Wordsworth personified his passion – poetry.

Jack B Yeats (1871-1957)
18 Fitzwilliam Square, 2

Born in London, Jack Yeats lived with his Pollexfen grandparents at Merville, Sligo, from his eighth to his sixteenth year. 'Sligo was my school,' he said, 'and the skies above it.' Allowed every freedom, he mixed with the farmers and the sailors and pilots and jockeys, and his special friends were the barefoot boys in knickerbockers and baggy caps, trotting their asses (never donkeys in Sligo) on the dusty roads. He watched the races at Hazelwood and the circuses on the Fairgreen and the funerals at Rosses Point. The magic of Sligo became his ruling passion, so that when he came to paint, he painted it lovingly. 'From the beginning of my painting life,' he said, 'every painting which I have made has somewhere in it a thought of Sligo.'

When he rejoined his family in London, his bereft grandparents moved to Rathedmond in Sligo where they both died in 1892. Sarah Purser, recognising talent, prevailed upon the

61 Marlborough Road, Donnybrook, 4

young Yeats to use it with more industry than his father, John B Yeats, ever did. Married to Mary Cottenham White, they lived in Devon until 1910, when they moved to Greystones, County Wicklow. In 1917 they settled at 61 Marlborough Road, Donnybrook, the house afterwards occupied for nearly sixty years by the family of the author of this book.

Unlike in most things, WB Yeats, with the walk of a king, never forgot that he was a poet of fame. With the swing of a sailor, Jack plodded solidly, as if the footpath were a heaving deck. Their father compared Willie's aloofness with Jack's liking for the commoner; Willie's discourse with Jack's laconic utterance. It is significant that in the Civil War the brothers found their sympathies on opposite sides.

Jack Yeats lived at 18 Fitzwilliam Square until his death. He was an old man before his genius was given the recognition it had long deserved. The avarice with which the money-changers now treat his pictures would have been an obscenity to this most modest man.

William Butler Yeats (1865-1939)
82 Merrion Square, 2

WB Yeats was born at 5 Sandymount Avenue (known also as 1 George's Ville), near the Royal Dublin Society in Ballsbridge. In 1868 when his father abandoned law for painting, the family moved to London where, during the next fourteen years, they lived at three addresses. Meanwhile, WB spent holidays with his grandparents,

5 Sandymount Avenue, 4

the Pollexfens of Sligo, a period he recalls lovingly in *Reveries Over Childhood and Youth*. In 1880 the family returned to Ireland and lived at Island View, overlooking Howth Harbour. From there the boy attended the High School in Harcourt Street (since demolished). In 1883 they moved to 10 Ashfield Terrace (now 142 Harold's Cross Road). Yeats's classics weren't good enough for admittance to Trinity College, so he escaped the dampening influence of academic orthodoxy.

The Yeats family went back to London in 1887 and lived at several addresses until WB struck out on his own, taking rooms at 5 Woburn Buildings (now Woburn Place), which remained his London home for the next twenty-three years. On his marriage in 1918 he rented Maud Gonne's house, 73 St Stephen's Green, while she was in prison. He bought Thoor Ballylee near Gort, County Galway, a Norman tower which he restored. In 1922, as a Senator in the new Free State government, he bought 82 Merrion Square. He was then entering what Gogarty called his 'silk-hat' period. His Monday evenings at Merrion Square were occasions of aristocratic decorum, unlike AE's Sunday evening picnics on the floor in Rathgar Avenue.

In 1928, after leaving the Senate, Yeats lived briefly at 42 Fitzwilliam Square before moving to Riversdale, Ballyboden Road, Rathfarnham, a creeper-covered country house beside a stream. He considered this house far enough out to discourage 'most interviewers and the less determined bores'. Riversdale was his last home.

William Butler Yeats

He died at Cap Martin on the French Riviera. As he had requested, he was buried at Drumcliffe, County Sligo.

'Zozimus' (Michael Moran)
(1794-1846)
14^1/$_2$ Patrick Street, 8

Of all Dublin buskers, few have become a tradition like Michael Moran, the blind bard of the Liberties, otherwise known as 'Zozimus'. 'Me given name is Moran,' he said, 'but they call me Zozimus.' The name arose because of his recitation about the meeting in Egypt of Saint Mary and the holy bishop called Zozimus. Born in Faddle Alley off Black Pitts in the Dublin Liberties, Zozimus remained a Liberty Lad all his life. Shortly after birth he was found to be blind. He explained: 'The pox took away me eyes and left me dark.'

At twenty-two he began his career, dressed appropriately for the role: corduroy trousers, his Francis Street brogues, the entire ensemble topped off with a cape scalloped with age. Guarded by his dog and his blackthorn, he would call: 'Gather round me, boys, will yez, gather round me.'

And when he had an audience he'd recite from his repertoire, or maybe tell of the finding of the baby Moses when after a bathe in the Nile Pharaoh's daughter ran around 'for to dry her royal pelt'. And when she saw the baby in the bulrushes she demanded of her attendant ladies, 'Tare and agers, girls, which of yez owns the child?'

A favourite stand for Zozimus was Carlisle Bridge (now O'Connell Bridge). 'Is there a crowd about me now?' he'd enquire. Yeats called him the last gleeman: 'Free from the interruption of sight, his mind turned every movement of the day and every change of public passion into rhyme or quaint saying. He was the admitted rector of all the ballad mongers of the Liberties.'

Zozimus feared that his body might one day end up on a slab in the Royal College of Surgeons. It didn't. When he died in a top back room at 14½ Patrick Street (since demolished), they buried him in a pauper's grave in Glasnevin. In 1988, Dublin's millennium, justice was done: a group of admirers erected a high limestone memorial over the grave of Dublin's one and only twangman.

INDEX